GUNS AGAINST
THE REICH

The Stackpole Military History Series

GUNS AGAINST THE REICH

Memoirs of a Soviet Artillery Officer
on the Eastern Front

Petr Mikhin

STACKPOLE
BOOKS

Published in paperback in 2011 by
STACKPOLE BOOKS
5067 Ritter Road
Mechanicsburg, PA 17055
www.stackpolebooks.com

Cover design by Tracy Patterson

Printed in the United States of America

10 9 8 7 6 5 4 3 2 1

Library of Congress Cataloging-in-Publication Data

Mikhin, Petr.
  [Voina, kakoi ona byla. English]
  Guns against the Reich : memoirs of a Soviet artillery officer on the Eastern Front
/ Petr Mikhin.
      p. cm.
  "Originally published by Pen & Sword Books in 2010."
  Includes index.
  ISBN 978-0-8117-0908-8
  1. Mikhin, Petr. 2. World War, 1939–1945—Campaigns—Eastern Front. 3. World
War, 1939–1945—Personal narratives, Soviet. I. Title.
  D764.M477 2011
  940.54'1247092—dc22
  [B]
                                    2011005363

Contents

List of Illustrations

PART ONE

The Rzhev Meat-Grinder

Prologue: Training is Hard

The early morning of 22 June 1941 was exceptionally beautiful, quiet and sunny. It was peaceful, except for the airplanes. Their engines roared as they flew back and forth over the city. However, everyone thought that this was just an exercise. People had worried about the possibility of war in early May and June, but one week before, on 14 June, there had been a placating message from TASS, the official Soviet news agency. It stated that we should not be afraid of the concentration of German troops on our borders, as they were only resting there before their final push on England.

We, three students of the Herzen Pedagogical Institute, Aleks Kurchaev, Viktor Iaroshik and I were preparing for our third-year final exam. Our dormitory was located behind the institute, just a short walk away. Suddenly the loud voice of a narrator sounded from a loudspeaker: 'Listen to Molotov's speech at noon.' We decided to linger, as we were interested to hear what the state's second-in-charge would tell us.

Molotov announced the outbreak of the war in a tragic, mournful and entreating voice. His words stunned us. Our hopes, plans, lifestyles and everyday concerns – all were gone. Even our lives no longer belonged to us. Our worst fears had become a menacing reality. But we were all certain that we would swiftly defeat the enemy.

Without watching our steps, we rushed to the third floor of the institute, where about twenty students were standing in the long corridor. I shouted down the corridor: 'Comrades! War with Germany has begun!'

Shocked by the message, students gathered around me and asked where I had heard the news. Before I could say anything more, someone in the crowd sharply tugged my sleeve. I turned around and saw the faculty's Party secretary. 'What sort of provocation is this?! You are making this up!' he roared, firmly holding me by the sleeve. 'Do you know what will happen to you for slander?! Follow me to the Party office now!'

Suddenly at the other end of the corridor, another voice rang out: 'Guys! It's war! War!' The Party secretary ran off towards the new source of commotion, allowing us to step into the classroom where the exam on mathematical methodologies was being held. Our Professor Krogius, an elderly, tall and thin, very strict educator, showed no reaction at all to our announcement about the war. 'Please pick up your exam questions,' he said calmly, as if nothing had happened.

I thought: 'Perhaps this Krogius is a German and he's known about the war for a long time?'

All three of us passed the exam with distinction. We exited the building onto the grounds, which were boiling with activity: crowds of students, discussions, arguments, all sorts of hubbub. Finally, the institute's Party secretary arrived at the scene and everyone fell silent. The secretary briefly repeated Molotov's announcement, called for vigilance and ordered us to wait for further instructions. Students shouted: 'Send us to the front!'

We, students of the Physics and Mathematics faculty, decided to go to the Kuibyshev District *voenkomat* [military commissariat]. Once there, however, an employee of the *voenkomat* emerged to announce that all the students were to gather in the yard the next morning at 8 o'clock, and to bring jackets, spoons, mugs and personal kits. They'd be sending us to the front. We all rejoiced.

The next morning we marched in formation to the Finland Station, where we boarded a train that carried us to Vyborg. There we were accommodated in tents that had already been pitched in a pine forest. A field kitchen supplied us with food. We were shown a prepared trench in the sandy soil and given an order: in the course of the day, each fellow was to cut down twenty pine trees, remove all the branches and cut them into shorter logs. Soldiers would use the logs to reinforce the walls of the trenches, so that they would not collapse. The girls were ordered to dig an anti-tank ditch.

The goal of twenty trees turned out to be very hard to meet, and no one managed to reach it before the onset of darkness. For the next several days, we worked twelve-hour days. We were extremely exhausted, but gradually got used to the work and began to reach the daily norm with daylight remaining. It would have been OK if not for the mosquitoes and flies; we had no place to hide from them.

But where was the promised front?!

We began to demand from the colonel who was overseeing our work to be sent to the front. Two students who traveled to Leningrad to pick up soap told us when they returned that it had been impossible to walk the streets, as every person they encountered had been indignant over the fact that two healthy students were not in the army. We threatened the colonel with a strike, if he didn't send us to the front.

Yet all the same, we had to labor there for almost a month, until our work was finished. A German airplane overhead dropped a bomb on us once. It was frightening, but no one was hurt.

On 23 July we returned to Leningrad and headed off to the local *voenkomat* the next day. There we were formed into four ranks, told to count off, and then were split into two groups and led off in opposite directions. My group marched across the city towards Finland Station, but before we reached it, our column stopped in front of an iron gate. After the gate opened, we were directed inside onto a paved yard and told to take a seat along a fence to rest. No one knew where we were, and there was no one to ask. Only the barbers, who eventually appeared to shave our heads, explained that this was the 3rd LAU – Leningrad Artillery Specialist School. We learned later that our comrades from the second group had been sent to an infantry specialist school.

First, we were taken to a *bania* [bath-house] and issued with cadet uniforms. After we washed and changed into our cadet uniforms, our appearance had changed so dramatically that we could recognize a friend only by looking at him directly in the face. After returning to the paved grounds of the specialist school, we were divided into platoons, shown our barracks and then marched in formation to a mess hall. We liked the meal: it was abundant, tasty and filling. We were all happy in spite of ourselves; thank God, at least we didn't have to worry about our daily bread.

They also issued good uniforms to us. Although they were cotton, not wool uniforms, they were new and durable. Those days not every student could boast of decent clothing. For example, I only had one pair of trousers, which I ironed from time to time, and a felt jacket instead of a proper suit. My friend Viktor Iaroshik from Byelorussia lacked not only a suit, but even proper trousers. He went around in the black cotton training trousers that we were issued with for gym. They looked good while doing gymnastics, because they were tight and emphasized the straightness of the legs when working on the parallel bars or the pommel horse. But when Vitia went to the club for dances in these athletic slacks, they didn't give him a good appearance. Viktor only managed to attract the girls because of his athletic figure and handsome, tawny face.

We also appreciated the canvas-topped boots we received. They were heavy compared to our gym shoes, but they offered good support, and on marches, they seemed to carry us forward all by themselves. But their best feature was that they were waterproof. They were my first waterproof boots; before, my boots had always leaked, especially in the slush and puddles of spring.

The next day was already a full day of training, from reveille at 0500 hours to taps at 2300 hours: morning calisthenics and a jog along the Neva River before breakfast, and then ten hours of classes with only a short break for lunch. In the evening we had two hours of self-study. There was no time for rest. We had to complete the normal three-year course of training in four months. During field exercises, the gun crew of eight had to push around, unlimber and deploy the 12-ton cannon like it was a toy and each shell weighed

43 kilograms. We used a huge mallet to hammer the 100-kilogram steel stakes into the ground to stake down the gun trails. We never got enough sleep. Our entire bodies ached. When at four o'clock in the morning we were marched to the *bania*, we learned to sleep on the move. It turned out to be nothing: you woke up at halts, when bumping into the man in front of you.

On one of the Sundays I got a permission to run to my institute to pick up letters. My brother wrote me from the Moscow area, informing me that he had volunteered for an *opolchenie* (home guard) division. Spirits were high in the *opolchenie*; everyone was very patriotic and eager to get to the front, although they had no training and no weapons. I sensed that my brother was feeling very militant and optimistic, because the political workers were convincing the 17-year-old volunteers that the Germans would soon exhaust their resources and then it would not be hard to defeat them. My brother also wrote that the home guard volunteers were worried that they might arrive too late at the front, and the war would end without them.

Soon these *opolchenie* divisions met a bitter fate. They were used to plug holes in the front and were vainly sacrificed.

Our political workers were also talking to us about the situation at the front. Mainly, they were telling us which towns had been surrendered to the Germans. The fascists' rapid advance unsettled us, angered us and amazed us. We had been raised on triumphant Soviet movies and songs, and we couldn't understand how it could happen that the Germans were already approaching Moscow.

Before the war, we had constantly heard lectures on international affairs at the institute. We knew that the British and the French were dragging out the negotiations and in fact didn't want a treaty with us against Hitler, which forced Stalin into the [Molotov-von Ribbentrop] treaty with the Germans. Of course, the nation didn't believe in friendship with Hitler, and people disapproved of the policy of flirting with Nazis, but they kept this mainly to themselves. For example, my uncle Egor Illarionovich Sakharov, a simple peasant though also a collective farm brigade leader who later was killed at the front, told me the following: 'Stalin is afraid of Hitler, flirts with him and pays him off with grain and coal, just like my son Pet'ka buys off the older boys with apples so that they won't beat him up.'

The Soviet people had lived in the nervous expectation of war. But no one thought that it would start so suddenly.

A month flashed by in diligent training. At the end of August, an order arrived for the evacuation of our artillery school to Kostroma. We transported all the academy's belongings to the Finland Station and loaded them onto trains. On 3 September we set off for Kostroma along the Northern Railway in cargo cars. As soon as we had passed Mga, the Germans captured it and the siege of Leningrad began.

Just like in peacetime, locals along the route were selling berries in paper cups: blackberries, cloudberries, blueberries. They were very exotic for us and we treated ourselves to the berries.

Along the route, just in case, we were issued with old Polish carbines. Although our commanders reminded us about the well-known army saying that even an unloaded rifle can fire once a year, one cadet accidentally killed his neighbor while cleaning his carbine. It was the first death that we saw.

We arrived in Kostroma and found accommodations in the barracks of a reserve regiment that had departed for the front. The schedule of training remained as tough as it had been in Leningrad.

My brother sent me a last letter from a place en route to the battlefield: 'We're on our way to smash the Nazis!' They were without weapons, as I found out later. I received no further letters from him after that.

We diligently studied the artillery sciences all through September, October and November. On 5 December we graduated as lieutenants, and received two little bars of rank for our collar tabs. In all, 480 freshly-commissioned lieutenants were sent to the front, while the top twenty lieutenants in physical strength and political reliability, I among them, remained behind and were sent to Orenburg for a training course as aerial observers. After the training course we would be correcting artillery fire onto enemy positions from airplanes and hot-air balloons.

In the first days of January 1942, we arrived at the 2nd Chkalov Military Aviation School. On the very first night we were robbed. Instead of our fine, long woolen artillery overcoats, we found threadbare little coats with air force insignia hanging on our hangers the next morning. We later had to spend the entire winter in these air force coats.

Training at the Chkalov School was also very intense. In addition to navigation and the rules for directing artillery fire from an airplane, they began to torment us with Morse code training for six hours a day, in the morning, after lunch and in the evening. We had taps of 'ti-ta ti-ta-ta-ta' ringing in our heads and our finger bones hurt from working the key.

Not even a month had passed, when Marshal Voroshilov suddenly arrived at our military aviation school. We were assembled in a hall, about 200 lieutenants from different artillery specialist schools. The Marshal, wearing a simple soldier's overcoat, announced: 'We're bringing you back to earth and returning you to the field artillery.' They didn't want to waste any more officers, as all the previously trained air observers had been killed, because our air force didn't yet have any reliable and maneuverable reconnaissance planes, like the German 'Frame' [the FW 189].

So we were directed to the 25th Reserve Artillery Regiment in Gorkii. Here we got to know the full measure of cold and hunger.

We lived in bunkers, each of which had two rows of bunk beds stretching along both walls, sufficient to accommodate 1,000 men. The bunkers were about 100 meters long, with wide gates at each end. A stove made from an iron barrel stood at each entrance. The stoves were red-hot, but this didn't rescue us from the cold – water would freeze inside the dugout. As we crowded around the stove, our overcoats would start to smoke, but our backsides would be freezing. Only hay covered the bunk beds, which were made from roughly-hewn boards. To try to keep warm, five of us would lie tightly next to each other on our right sides, covered by our five overcoats. Then on command, we would all turn over onto our left sides. This is how we tossed and turned the entire night, almost not sleeping.

Among the lieutenants of our group, there was a young actor from Moscow. He immediately made contact with the Latvian waitresses, who were working in the six officer canteens. The five of us managed to have six breakfasts and five lunches, but we were still hungry – we could get six hundred grams of bread per day in only one of the canteens, while the others served only a watery hot broth.

Most of the officers and men in the training camps longed for the front with only one aim in mind: to get a full stomach. Some of the soldiers could not endure this life, and while standing guard at night with their rifles, shot themselves.

At the end of February, our group was summoned to Moscow, to the personnel department of the Moscow Military District, where we were assigned to military units. Three lieutenants, including me, were sent to Kolomna, into the then-forming 52nd Rifle Division, and there I was given the duty of adjutant to the commander of the 1028th Artillery Regiment.

We arrived in Kolomna at night and were quartered in a hotel. For the first time that winter we laid down in clean beds in a warm room. No one wanted to leave the cozy hotel the next morning.

When we arrived at the regiment, which was stationed in a village just outside of the town, all three of us were placed with a peasant family. It turned out that the adjutant's post was not vacant, so I was appointed deputy commander of a howitzer battery. Our battery commander, Senior Lieutenant Cherniavsky was a *frontovik* [an officer or soldier with front-line experience] and had arrived at Kolomna from a hospital. Thirty-five years old and the former chief engineer of the Murom plywood factory, Cherniavsky was smart, practical and knew his business. Under his leadership, we set about creating a combat battery out of some Gorkii collective farm workers.

The soldiers were getting very little food, we officers a bit more, but we were still all hungry. There was no place to buy extra food, as the locals were also all starving. When the first grass appeared in the fields, my soldiers almost scared me to death. I was marching my platoon down a field path for an exercise, when all of a sudden without my command they all dispersed and began crawling along the ground, like they were under air attack. I was scared – I couldn't understand what was going on. It turned out that the soldiers had spotted some edible grass by the roadside and had all rushed to pick it and have an afternoon snack.

All of us, both officers and men, young and old alike, regarded Cherniavsky like a strict but caring father. He was short, slim, wide in the shoulders and a bit stooped. His swarthy, angular face was always covered with black stubble, even though he shaved daily. The piercing gaze of his dark eyes and his tightly compressed jaws always gave his expression a resolute appearance. We all looked the same in our khaki cotton tunics and trousers; only the three dark green pips of rank and the binoculars hanging around his neck made Cherniavsky stand out among us.

Taciturn, businesslike and demanding – when one looked at Cherniavsky, one also wanted to grit one's teeth and keep working and working. We believed in him and loved him – for his experience, his fatherly care, and for his clear heart. He never lectured us, never swore and never gave us a tongue-lashing. Even when we made serious mistakes, he never rebuked us, but only had to shake his head disapprovingly and a guilty soldier was ready to die from shame. Cherniavsky valued highly resourcefulness and diligence, and everyone tried to display these traits.

At the time our training was more classroom than practical; we had no cannons or almost any other equipment. It was good that I had the thought to borrow four wagons and teams from a nearby collective farm, which our Sergeant Major Khokhlov immediately drove to our encampment. We then attached a meter-long log to each wagon as a gun barrel, and stringers served as the trails. A skilled craftsman carved sights from wood and attached them to the 'gun barrels' – and we had a four-gun 'battery' ready! The training sessions came to life; I conducted all the combat training with these wooden guns. Cherniavsky praised us for our cleverness, and himself began to devise methods of training.

We had to study these and many other subtleties of artillery practice more through lectures and discussions than hands-on experience. But even under these conditions, over three months Cherniavsky managed to form an excellent howitzer battery and to train its personnel well. We conducted marches and maneuvers with these mock guns – soldiers served as horses and were harnessed to the trails, and galloped or turned the 'guns' left and right, and moved the 'guns' into prepared firing positions. The crews rehearsed their routines to increase their speed: the limber gunners, ammo-bearers and fuse-setters all worked with their dummy rounds, depicted by short logs; the gunlayers, breech operators and loaders rehearsed loading the gun, aiming it, and firing on the enemy.

Cherniavsky trained his artillery observers, scouts and signalmen to do all they needed in war without any ceremony. The former collective farm workers worked their 'guns' smoothly, and were physically and psychologically ready to go into their first battle with the Nazis.

We acquired real howitzers, of glistening metal and fresh paint, in Danilov just before our departure for the front. They looked like precious, bejewelled masterpieces to us after the wooden mock guns! We trained on them for two days, but without firing a single round. We fired our first shots at the Germans on 23 July 1942 at Rzhev. Had it not been for our poverty, these shots may well have become our last.

CHAPTER ONE

Rzhev

The ancient Russian city of Rzhev stands 150 kilometers from Moscow. The Germans occupied Rzhev on 14 October 1941. The subsequent German defeat at the gates of Moscow returned the front line closer to Rzhev, and the Rzhev-Viazma strategic offensive that lasted from 8 January to 30 April 1942 left a large salient protruding into our lines, with the still German-controlled Rzhev at its apex. Soviet forces stood poised to the east, west and north of the Rzhev bulge or bridgehead.

We knew nothing about this then. We also did not know that our freshly formed 52nd Rifle Division was to take part in one of the largest battles at Rzhev: the Rzhev-Sychevka strategic offensive operation. With all the enthusiasm of youth we were on our way to the front to win.

We unloaded in the darkness of night on 21 July 1942, in a forest between Staritsa and Rzhev. The battery had not received artillery tractors at its forming, so we rolled the guns straight from the flatbeds into the depths of a pine forest ourselves. We worked hard, but quickly, and after the unloading was done, we stretched out on pine branches next to our guns like dead men. The soft branches still held the warmth of the summer day, and refreshed us with the scent of pine; it was pleasant to lie on them. The pine air, like a balm, quickly restored our flagging strength, and our fatigue seemed to flow slowly from our bodies into the warm, sandy soil...

Suddenly in the inky darkness we could hear the distant echoes of artillery fire. The men sprang to alert. Muffled explosions were also heard on the other side of us and nearer to us. Experienced *frontoviks*, and there were only five in our battery, immediately sensed something familiar and dangerous; for the bravest of them, it was no longer frightening. These men, Cherniavsky among them, already possessed certain combat experience and now they were sensing the rare possibility of a night-time encounter with the enemy. This combat experience was rare, because those tens of thousands of men who had been killed in 1941 and were dying now in 1942 never had a second chance to fight the enemy and to take revenge. Thus the *frontoviks* that had survived were now possessed with that combat fervor, which is so well known to brave men.

The other men in the battery also grew excited. For us, the newcomers to the front, these genuine sounds of artillery, not cinematic, were an omen of something unknown and terrible. We were especially frightened because the fire could be heard from all sides, it wasn't clear where our troops and the Germans were located, and immediately there arose the involuntary apprehension: had we fallen into some sort of trap or encirclement? My heart also pounded: in the battery, I was responsible for the guns, and if something happened, how could we move them without horses or tractors?

'Do the Germans attack here as fiercely as at Stalingrad?' the older loader Trefilov worriedly asked. Then he addressed me: 'Are the Germans close, Comrade Lieutenant?'

'They must be distant, since they unloaded us here.'

Trefilov was still worried: 'You can't really tell. They're shooting from all sides.'

The artillery barrage ended. The exhausted men soon fell fast asleep. I couldn't sleep as I tried to picture my first battle: again and again, I thought of the two trains that had passed us on the way to the front; one was full of wounded, the other was full of destroyed, burnt-out scrap metal. I had been shocked: what happened to the humans if the metal was so mangled and scorched?!

At that time I divided all men into two categories: *frontoviks* and all others. How I envied the wounded sergeant from the hospital train we had met! He didn't seem to be different from us in any way – only his arm was completely bandaged. Happy and talkative, he told us that he had been at the front for just one day, and had been wounded in his very first battle. Just one day – and he was a *frontovik*! He had already crossed over that mystical, frightening barrier that is called the front. I couldn't tell my men that I had been at the front, although they really wanted their commander to be a *frontovik*; then they would have more assurance and poise in the coming battles. Of course, for the common cause it wouldn't have been a sin to tell them that I had combat experience. But I simply couldn't imagine doing something like that; I couldn't even mentally step over that invisible line that separated the rear from the front.

The summer sunrise of July quickly became a bright summer day. The cooks had already made breakfast. As soon as we were seated in front of our mess kits, we heard a low and throbbing rumble that quickly grew, and we realized that airplanes were approaching. The tall pine trees hindered observation, and bombs began to whistle through the air sooner than anyone could imagine. Instead of shouting 'Take cover!' and flattening myself to the ground, I leaped to my feet, and at the same second a powerful explosion erupted in the forest. Millions of hissing and treacherously whispering shell splinters flew all around and the largest fragment cleanly cut a large branch like a razor, which fell heavily at my feet. I just kept standing there, marveling at the never-before witnessed power of an explosion – I was stunned by it!

'Comrade Lieutenant, get down!' Sergeant Major Makukha shouted at me.

'Trefilov has been killed!' gunlayer Osetsky desperately shouted.

The first air raid and first losses shocked everyone, although our losses were lower than those of our neighbors.

We had barely regained our senses and eaten breakfast when Cherniavsky ordered me, the senior officer of the battery, to take an observer, a signalman and four rolls of field cable and follow him. He set off for the front lines in order to find a place for the guns, from where we could fire on the enemy.

At the front, Cherniavsky became noticeably more cheerful and lively. One could see that he was impatient to engage the enemy as quickly as possible, as if he had his own personal score to settle with the Germans. He was seemingly anxious to correct a past mistake and take revenge, and hastening to test his newly-formed, just-unloaded battery and new howitzers on the Germans – which is why he set off at a run across the swamp directly towards the village of Deshevka. There, at the front, he would construct an observation post from where he could observe the enemy and by the next morning his battery, located 2 kilometers behind his post, would be ready for indirect fire and he could finally open fire on the Germans! He seemingly was already imagining the powerful explosions of our rounds and the panic they would sow among the Nazis...

After unloading, our 1028th Artillery Regiment was supposed to have a week to move into positions among the combat units fighting at Rzhev, and to be ready for offensive operations by 30 June. Cherniavsky, however, had obtained permission from the division commander Andreev to engage the Germans immediately! And now, leaping from one dry clump of ground in the swamp to the next, Cherniavksy was literally flying to engage the enemy!

We, his subordinates, signalman Sinitsyn, observer Kalugin and I, were following his every step, also jumping to reach whatever slightly higher ground we could find, barely managing to keep pace with our commander. We were all about half the age of our battery commander, but after 10 kilometers at a run, we were noticeably flagging. But Cherniavsky, like a young man, was in fine form! That is why they had made us run every day in training! We hadn't grumbled then and we weren't going to grumble now. To all of us, who hadn't even shaved yet, the 35-year-old Senior Lieutenant was an old man; he knew everything. We were ready to carry out any order that he would give to us.

A hot summer day was at its peak, the sun was shining brightly, the swampy atmosphere was sultry and smelled of rotting vegetation, and some artillery fire could be heard in the distance to the left and right. It sounded like an approaching thunderstorm, though there wasn't a single cloud in the sky. As we advanced, the explosions became increasingly louder, and sometimes we could clearly hear the staccato chatter of machine-gun bursts. These sounds produced more alarm in our young hearts. But they only stirred Cherniavsky more strongly! He told me once in Kolomna how he had been wounded and miraculously escaped death. Now, it seemed, in his heated brain, iridescent images of the approaching battle alternated with bitter memories of the autumn of 1941 at Smolensk ... A German fighter plane playfully hunting down a solitary, terrified Red Army man in a field ... A German tank assault on Cherniavsky's battery, which had already run out of shells ... Molotov cocktails were of no use: matches wouldn't light in the gusty winds and shaking hands of the men, but the tanks were now among them! With roaring engines and firing on the move, they broke into the battery's positions. The crews nevertheless managed to set two of the tanks on fire! The remaining tanks started to crush the guns mercilessly, savagely spinning on one track, and burying alive the Red Army men hiding in the trenches. Cherniavsky managed to leap from the trench, and a steel track flashed right by his head. At that point the German infantry arrived on the scene, and one of them, stumbling, fired a long burst at Cherniavsky at almost point-blank range. Cherniavsky fell and the Germans rushed past him further into our rear. But Cherniavsky had only caught a round in the left shoulder. He wanted instinctively to cover the wound with his right hand, but he sensed more than saw that a second wave of German infantry was approaching. Cherniavsky froze, closed his eyes and feigned death. A German kicked him between the legs with the toe of his boot to check to see if he was still alive, and then ran on, following the others. After recovering from the kick, Cherniavsky opened his eyes a bit, saw the back of the departing German and happily thought: 'I'm alive!' The next moment the German stopped and doubled back. 'I guess he doubted that I was dead,' Cherniavsky thought, and closed his eyes. A terrifying thought flashed through his mind: 'He's going to finish me off now.' Only a few seconds of life were remaining, as many seconds as it would take the German to run 10 meters back to him. Such a death was terrible, but the worst thing was the hopelessness: the German was returning with an MP-40 machine pistol ready to fire, while Cherniavsky couldn't twitch a muscle. His carbine was buried in the trench, and he only had a useless matchbox in his hand. The Nazi approached him at a run, stomped Cherniavsky's head as hard as he could with his hobnail boot and fired a burst at him just in case. Cherniavsky blacked out. He probably would have died there between the two burning German tanks, if not for a counter-attack by Russian armor...

There were about 5 kilometers left to Deshevka.

'Remember the route,' Cherniavsky told me, 'you'll be going back alone in order to bring up the battery to the position I'm going to show you.'

'Where will I get the tractors?'

'Ask a neighboring unit.'

That was clear. But how could I remember the road, if there was no path? There were just bushes and swamps everywhere, and they all looked the same. There was not even a single tall tree to climb and look around, and the bushes made observation impossible. I had to remember the route by compass and the position of the sun; fortunately, it was a clear day! Two hours later we were on an expansive elevation, densely overgrown with tall grass.

'You will set up the battery here,' my commander ordered. 'But make sure that the guns are on the reverse slope.'

Leaving me there, Cherniavsky moved on towards the front line with his men in order to select a location for an observation post. I headed for the top of the rise in order to get a better view.

It was silent; the sun was shining brightly, and large swathes of beautiful field flowers were now and then blocking my path. I didn't want to crush them, and it was impossible to go around them, so I unwillingly picked a few of the most beautiful blossom clusters, and soon had an amazingly lovely bouquet in my hands. As soon as I had reached the highest point of the field covering the hill, a loud whistle was audible from somewhere above me, which quickly changed into an ominous roar, and a shell exploded with a flash nearby. I was scared and momentarily frozen in place, and only threw myself into the tall grass after the shrapnel had already flown past me with a terrifying sound. Several more rounds exploded nearby, and then the barrage was over. I was still lying in the tall grass with my eyes closed, praying to God that I wouldn't be hit.

I rose to my feet and only then noticed some sacks that were buried deeply in the grass. I gave one of them a tug ... and suddenly realized with horror that these were not sacks, but soldiers' greatcoats. The coats had grayed, but I recognized them as ours, and inside them were human remains, now withered, wrinkled and blackened! I was so shocked and repulsed that without thinking I darted into the nearest bushes. Having calmed down a bit, I caught my breath and then cautiously, remaining concealed in the tall grass, bypassed the exposed clearing.

I reached the reverse slope of the elevation where we would be invisible to the Germans and started to choose positions for the guns. I broke a few bush branches to mark where I wanted the guns, so that later I could place the howitzers in position quickly. After that I immediately returned to the battery.

I had plenty of time, but I ran back across the swamp, with the images of the corpses still in my eyes – the sight had shocked me more than the first air raid and the first artillery bombardment. Those soldiers, whose remains had so frightened me, had tried to capture Rzhev the previous winter – and had remained to lie here forever. Winter had passed, the snow had melted, spring had passed, now the summer grass had grown, and those poor men were still lying there unburied...

My mournful thoughts were soon replaced by an alarming uncertainty: was I on the right track? What if I got lost in these swamps and failed to find my battery? My guns were supposed to be in position by morning, and by then I might only reach their present location! It would be a failure to fulfill an order! I would be court-martialed and lose my rank! I calmed myself down: as we had been running to the front lines with my commander, the sun had been ahead and to the right of us. Two hours had passed, so I simply had to walk in the direction of my shadow. I looked around closely and decided that I was on the right track.

Alternately running and walking, after two hours I made it back to my battery. I ordered the men to prepare for redeployment and ran to look for tractors.

It was growing dark; clouds had gathered and it had started to rain, yet I still hadn't obtained any artillery tractors. Some of the nearby units needed the tractors themselves, while others had the tractors but no fuel. Finally, I found a colonel who ordered a nearby unit to give me tractors. It was already dark when I returned to the battery with four artillery tractors and trailers.

So we drove off. Mud, rain, water and darkness surrounded us. I was showing the way to the tractor driver, but I was extremely worried: would I find the clearing in the night? We drove for about an hour and I stopped the tractors. I jumped down to the ground, and was knee-deep in water and muck. I walked off a little bit in order to check my compass. I was surrounded by my gun crews – former peasants, each of them old enough to be my father. They knew me well, respected me, probably because I was with them all the time, and I'd taught them to 'fire' the mock guns and how to act in battle – and I was not too strict about the little things. They knew from personal experience how hard it was to find your way in a blizzard or in darkness and doubted that I could find my way with a small, hand-held compass in unknown terrain. They couldn't help me in any way, but I overheard their conversations:

'If we had our own tractors, we would have been there already.'

'No way are we going to make it to the clearing by the morning.'

'Has our Lieutenant ever spent any time at the front?'

'It would be nice to have an older lieutenant with some front-line experience...'

When I returned to the tractors, Private Raikov, a loader on one of the crews and a short, stocky soldier about thirty years old, walked up to me: 'Comrade Lieutenant, I'm familiar with that clearing, I used to graze cows there. I'm a local, from the next village. I can show the way.'

I couldn't believe my ears: did I really have a local guide?! I sat him next to me and we followed his directions; he took us more to the left than I thought was correct. But it was as if a heavy burden had fallen from my shoulders, and I was extremely happy; how lucky I must have been, though where had Raikov been earlier?!

The tractors were moving slowly – they were towing trailers loaded with ammo, men, the battery's belongings and also the howitzers. The tracks kept sinking into the mire, the engines, straining, roared and were almost red with heat; the cabins were hot, full of exhaust fumes and it was difficult to breathe. I developed a headache, whether because of the fumes, or more likely because I hadn't slept in two nights, had seen my first air raid and those corpses, and on top of it all I had run 30 kilometers in one day. And now, naively trusting a local man, I relaxed ... and I fell asleep.

I suddenly woke up because of the total silence. I was alone in the cabin. The tractor had stopped. The engine had been shut off. I jumped out in total confusion and saw a group of men off to one side. I approached them, and they were my soldiers discussing which way we needed to go.

'Why did you stop the engines?' I asked.

'Overhead aircraft; we're afraid of an air attack, because the engines are sparking.'

'Let the engines cool down,' the tractor drivers said.

'Where is Raikov?'

'He has a headache. He doesn't have a clue where we should go.'

'We didn't want to wake you up; we thought it would be better for you to sleep while the engines cooled down.'

I ordered the men to get back on the trailers and we drove on. Now, having slept part of the way, I had no clue where we were and which way we should go. What could I do – we had to drive on! Even if I was just guessing, I couldn't show my helplessness to the men. About ten minutes later, I stopped the column, ordered them to keep the engines running, and walked off to one side in the hope of bumping into someone. I was lucky. A sentry stopped me and summoned his lieutenant. We ducked into a brightly illuminated bunker and – what joy! – I saw a classmate from the artillery specialist school who had been assigned to the corps artillery. He had already set up his 'behemoths' in their firing positions. The lieutenant indicated to me their position on a map, and I searched out our clearing, took an azimuth reading, and measured the distance. We had about 3 kilometers to go.

Finally, we made it to the clearing. The men were happy for me; we had found the spot after all! But in the darkness, I couldn't find the branches I had broken to mark the gun positions. I crossed the clearing, trying to sense the elevation's contours with my feet, but had no luck. By now my men were hurrying me: show us where to deploy quickly, so we'll have time to dig in before morning! I had to take a chance and just randomly indicate a position for the Number 1 gun. I showed the spot in the most assured tone of voice. Then I stepped off the distances and indicated the places for the other guns. Heavy work began immediately. We dug the gun emplacements and rolled the howitzers into them. Then we stretched camouflage netting over the positions and threw fresh grass atop the nets.

I ordered all the men to get under the camouflage nets so as not to reveal the positions, but I was beside myself with nervous tension. Had I set the guns up in the proper place? What if we had set up in plain sight of the Germans? Then it would be the end of the battery ... I waited for dawn like a condemned man waits for his execution.

It finally began to grow light; the day was going to be bright and sunny, and visibility was excellent ... and – oh, what horror! – the terrain in front of us was visible for kilometers. In the darkness we had dug in on the forward slope, the one facing the Germans, which meant they would spot us immediately and then...

My men also understood this and started to become restless.

'Why on earth are we here?'

'The Germans can see us!'

'Exactly! We're in plain view, like on the palm of their hands!'

I heard the talk and kept silent, trying not to show my confusion. I pretended we were in the right place. The soldiers didn't dare to question me directly.

In the meantime, Cherniavsky had already passed all the data for the fire mission over the phone. Yesterday, having set up the observation post in Deshevka, he had not wasted any time and had spent the rest of the day observing the enemy. Local scouts pointed out the Germans' weapons emplacements to him, but Cherniavsky was interested in the enemy's command and observation posts. From his vantage point with the help of binoculars, he noticed several light vehicles concealed in a ravine behind the German front lines – evidently a conference was under way at a command post. From the network of phone cables and a bend in the trenches, he also managed to spot a German observation post. Having calculated the fire mission data, Cherniavsky was also waiting for dawn impatiently.

Soon orders from our battery commander came over the phone to the battery. Immediately afterwards, our first rounds were on their way towards the enemy.

It was our first time to fire our brand new howitzers, but we went through the firing routine quickly and skillfully, just like it was a training session. We fired over 100 rounds in several minutes. They were all on target! We struck the Germans at a most sensitive spot – their command post. Our neighbors, observing Cherniavsky's fire mission, were jumping up with joy.

'Well done!' Cherniavsky told us over the phone. 'Your first fire mission was a success. Nice shooting!'

Just as we had completed the fire mission and Cherniavsky, happy at his observation post, had thanked us again for our fine shooting and my crews were grinning with a sense of accomplishment, a shell landed in front of our howitzers with a loud explosion. It was followed by another and then a third one. Then the shells began to land several hundred meters behind our positions and the explosions began to walk back towards us. The surviving Germans had regained their senses and had started searching for the new, irritating Russian battery; not one, but several German batteries were firing at us!

Probably because our clearing was the only dry place in the given direction, the enemy immediately determined where our shells had originated. Back at the artillery specialist school, they had talked to us about counter-battery fire. To an adversary, one's own artillery is the most dangerous and juiciest target. The enemy never spared ammunition to destroy hostile artillery; even when it was strictly rationed they would expend hundreds of rounds to destroy an enemy battery. So I imagined what would happen when several German batteries would start firing for effect. My soldiers also became agitated. Dropping to their knees, they tracked each explosion with a feeling of alarm. 'That's it! We're done for!' they were shouting in panic. 'That's the end of us!'

I didn't duck into the bottom of a trench. I stood by a gun shield, praying to God that my death would come quickly. I didn't want to see the tragic destruction of my battery! Let them kill me – I wouldn't then have to answer to anyone! After all, I was the one who had deployed the battery in plain sight of the Germans!

Only a minute had passed and somewhere in the distance we heard a loud rushing sound, like when a sudden gust of strong wind rustles the treetops in a forest. It was the ominous sound of dozens of incoming shells. The Germans had bracketed us, and now were firing for effect. In an instant the sound grew into a terrible roar, as if a plane at treetop altitude was passing overhead. My men threw themselves to the bottoms of the trenches, pressed their noses into the dirt and covered their heads with their hands. But I kept standing there, frozen in place. I didn't want to live…

But what was this?! Not a single shell hit anywhere near our positions! All the rounds flew overhead and loudly exploded 100 meters behind our battery – *on the reverse slope, exactly where we were supposed to be positioned!* The green meadow there turned into black churned earth, full of shell craters! There, dozens of geysers of earth were shooting into the air in an unending thunder of explosions and everything was instantly disappearing in dust and smoke. But *here* we had only fiercely hissing shell splinters – they couldn't harm us in the trenches and either struck the breastworks or whistled past. [Italics are the author's emphasis.]

As soon as the thunder of the barrage was winding down and only a few individual shells were still exploding, my crews, not yet believing that they had survived, started to lift their heads one after another, smiling broadly and talking to each other:

'It's a miracle!'

'I can't believe my eyes!'

'We've been saved!'

'What a commander we have! Young, yes, but he sure fooled the Germans! It turns out he set up the battery here on purpose!'

'And we'd been cursing him! If we had deployed behind the hill, nothing would have been left of us!'

'Just look, that whole field is ploughed up!'

I heard the talk and was happy. But my thoughts were on other matters. If only my men knew that it was not cunning; I'd mistakenly positioned us here. If they only they knew how I was suffering over this, my blunder! Yet it was a happy mistake that saved our lives and the guns. Of course, our good camouflage had also protected us from this counter-battery fire. The Germans knew this hill well and kept it under constant observation, but they hadn't spotted our battery and had fired by coordinates on our presumed position on the reverse slope. They'd been wrong. They couldn't imagine that the Red Army had such a fool or adventurer, who would set up his battery in the open, and not where the battery was supposed to be by the book.

One more thing saved us from imminent death in this first battle — our equipment shortage, the lack of tractors. If we had possessed all the equipment we were supposed to have, we would have arrived there in daytime, and would have deployed in the 'correct' place, like the book says ... and now we'd all be dead.

This is how our battery started its life at the front.

This experience taught me a lot. Later on in the war, when I was battery and battalion commander, I wouldn't set up my guns by the book (the Germans also knew this book), but off to one side, and the enemy would pound an empty spot.

But now my soldiers thought the world of me, and they seemed ready to toss me in the air like a champion. My personal authority among the men grew immeasurably: whatever the Lieutenant said – that's the law!

CHAPTER TWO

Die, but Don't Retreat!

Kalinin Front, the 30th Army. Events were unfolding rapidly. We had arrived at the front on the night of 21 July 1942 and by the early morning of 23 July we were already firing our howitzers at a German command post. On 29 July we, like all the troops, heard Stalin's tragic Order No. 227. The Rzhev-Sychevka strategic offensive operation began on 30 July.

On the eve of the offensive, Supreme Commander Stalin's notorious Order No. 227, better known as the 'Not one step back!' order, was read to the assembled units of the 52nd Rifle Division. The order sounded terrifying to us. It for the first time revealed the terrible results of the war's first year. It spoke of unimaginable losses and defeats, which were no longer tolerable. The death of our country and people was gaping in front of us like an abyss. The order demanded: Die, but do not retreat! It was necessary to halt the unending retreat of Soviet troops towards Stalingrad and the Caucasus at whatever the cost, while we, the troops standing in front of Rzhev, had to capture the city at the cost of our lives and eliminate the threat to Moscow. Hard measures were necessary, but at the time they were the only ones possible: shoot retreating soldiers on the spot. Moreover, there was the example of Hitler, to which Stalin alluded in his order. A half year before, in January 1942, in order to prevent the flight of his soldiers from in front of Moscow and to avert a collapse of the entire Eastern Front, Hitler had issued a 'stop-order': he deployed detachments behind his troops, which fired with machine guns at fleeing soldiers; those who fled the battlefield were sent to penal companies, in which they had to fight to the death.

Stalin's 'Not a step back!' order saved our country from defeat in the war with Germany. Blocking detachments fired at fleeing troops and hunted down deserters. Penal companies for privates and non-commissioned officers and penal battalions for officers were created, and sent to sectors of the front where they were almost completely destroyed in battles. Only the few lucky wounded survivors, who had redeemed their guilt with their own blood, were rehabilitated and returned to regular units.

In December 1942, two men from our division were executed at the front in a small ravine, according to Order No. 227 in front of a formation. Something unbelievable happened while carrying out the sentence. Just as the command 'At the traitors to the Motherland! Fire!' was ringing out to the firing squad, a stray German plane appeared overhead. It went into a dive and released a bomb. The entire formation immediately threw itself to the ground. One of the condemned men also dropped to the ground, but the other remained motionless and standing. The bomb exploded but didn't harm anyone. The formation reassembled, and the condemned men were executed.

The NKVD [People's Commissariat of Internal Affairs] Special Departments throughout the Red Army zealously and often formally executed Stalin's 'Not a step back!' order, which caused tragedies. I was almost part of one such tragedy, about which I will now tell.

It all happened at the climax of the August fighting. The battery was carrying out harassing fire on concentrations of German infantry. Here and there in an area of four hectares, every ten seconds our shells would powerfully explode, as if warning the Germans: don't try to come, or you'll get a full load! For our own infantry, this was a morale boost. Each of our four howitzers one after the other was to fire four rounds with an interval of ten seconds between rounds. After we had started the second round of firing, something happened with the Number 3 gun; its shot sounded louder than usual. The gun was shrouded in thick black smoke, and the twisted bayonet of a rifle flew spinning from the gun's position towards where I was standing 100 meters away. It angrily twirled past my nose and embedded itself into the ground just a meter away from me. 'Number 3 gun misfire!' shouted the gun leader.

I had no time to investigate what had happened and I continued calling out the numbers of the guns in turn in order to continue the fire. I hurried over to the Number 3 gun only when our fire mission was over.

I ran up to the howitzer and was stunned! My eyes stared at the space beyond the gun's shield, where a 2-meter long, elevated, menacing gun barrel was supposed to be. I was looking at a howitzer without a barrel! It was as if I was looking at a person without a head. The unimaginable loss struck me like a knife in the heart! Then a terrifying thought killed the pain of loss: 'What will happen to me?!' My sorrow over the loss of the howitzer was replaced with fear of responsibility. We had only begun to fight, had not yet lost any equipment, and the loss of a whole howitzer was too much for me.

The members of the gun crew shook me out of my state of shock. They gathered around me and were shouting joyfully: 'We're all alive, Comrade Lieutenant!'

I came back to my senses. My happiness for my men offset the bitterness of the loss and my fear for my own fate. I felt a bit ashamed because I had thought first of the howitzer and myself, forgetting about the crew. But it was really not my fault that I had been trained that way: Die yourself, lose your men, but first of all save your guns!

'How did you escape with your whole skin, boys?' I responded, 'it wasn't just a shell that exploded a meter away from you, but one ton of steel that blew into pieces right in front of you, and the whole barrel sent fragments flying all around!' But I thought to myself, I had been lucky together with them: I didn't lose a single man; perhaps they wouldn't execute me and only send me to a penal battalion. Back then I didn't yet know that a penal battalion was a much worse fate than a quick death.

Why had the shell exploded in the barrel? ... But now I had no time to reach conclusions; I had to report the accident immediately to my battery commander.

'A shell exploded in the gun barrel,' I reported over the phone to the battery commander's command post. 'You are crazy!' Cherniavsky shouted with indignation, secretly hoping that a young lieutenant like me had just made some sort of error. 'Don't you understand what would happen to the barrel?! It would deform! The gun would be out of action!'

'That is exactly what happened. The barrel blew into pieces, all the way down to the gun shield,' I calmly explained, because I had already just gone through an unbelievable event, and was now ready for anything. 'How many dead and wounded?' the battery commander asked in a lowered voice, having calmed down a bit.

'Not a single man; all are safe and sound.'

'That can't be, take a better look!' Cherniavsky demanded in obvious disbelief.

I walked over to the Number 3 gun again and personally checked every member of the crew. No one had a single scratch or a concussion. Loader Birykov had plucked a large fragment out of the back of his rucksack, but he had only been knocked over when the fragment struck, and then sat back up as if nothing had happened.

'The gun shield saved us,' the still shaken crew members explained to me. 'The stacked carbines were blown to pieces, but after all they were standing next to a gun trail, near the breech operator, while we were untouched, as if we were charmed.'

Returning to the phone, I reported: 'No casualties!' The battery commander ended the discussion in a threatening voice: 'You will report to the regiment commander in person!'

What had caused the shell to explode in the barrel? The muzzle cover had been removed from the gun; it was carefully rolled up and was lying in its place next to the howitzer's right wheel. The interior of the barrel had been checked before firing and was perfectly clean. Just before firing, the firing positions had been visited by the deputy division commander Colonel Uriupin. The old professional had taken a look down the gun barrel and had been astounded by its mirror-like sheen. The rifling, like fine lacework, mesmerized the Colonel and he froze in place. Previously he had never had the opportunity to look into the barrel of a field gun; he was well-familiar only with rifle barrels, and had never before seen such beauty. Unable to restrain himself, he cupped his mouth with his hands and yelled into the howitzer's barrel: 'Uriupin, you son of a bitch!' We laughed happily, taking the Colonel's admiration as the highest praise.

The artillerymen of the battery were all anguished over the loss of the gun. The men were disheartened and the crews of the remaining guns gathered closely around their guns, almost caressing them and rejoicing that they were still intact. It was common in our poor society that we suffered less over the death of comrades than the loss of a gun. A beautiful howitzer was an irreplaceable instrument of effective combat against the Nazis. Soldiers literally carried it in their hands, hauled it out of mud, and cleaned and cherished it. Guns were almost like living beings for the men in the gun crews; to some extent they were the embodiment of their wives and mothers in the rear.

A lieutenant from the Special Department arrived at lunchtime on horseback. Together with him, also on horseback, loomed two guards armed with submachine-guns. As they approached the battery, they were talking loudly and laughing. At first I was happy that the person who was going to conduct the investigation was not some grumpy old man, but someone my own age, who was also probably a former student, and possibly also from Leningrad, but from a law school and not a pedagogical institute. But when the guest, without saying hello, carelessly saluted me and quickly introduced himself as Lieutenant Kapitsky, I tensed up.

'Where is the exploded gun?' Kapitsky asked sternly, addressing no one in particular. His black penetrating eyes were looking past me, leaving me no hope for a friendly, confidential conversation, like one between former students. Kapitsky was wearing a freshly-pressed tunic, a crisp new leather belt, and his spick and span trousers were perfectly ironed. The narrow tops of his gleaming leather boots clung tightly to the slender calves of his legs. Even the submachine-gunners that accompanied him looked like they had been plucked out of a candy box, standing in sharp contrast to my artillerymen, like the difference between new shiny nails and old, rusty, bent nails pulled out of a board. One could see that our 'guests' never had to drag heavy howitzers from swamps and had never pressed their chests against the tall, dirty wheels of a howitzer.

The first order of business for the Special Department lieutenant was to scatter the crew of the destroyed gun at 30-meter intervals in different directions from the howitzer and order them to dig a fighting hole in which they were to sit. This was done so that the men could not communicate with each other and so that they would feel as if they were under arrest. While the crews were digging their earthern cells under the watchful eyes of the guards, Kapitsky led me into my dugout and began the interrogation. I was the senior officer of the battery and was thus responsible for everything.

'Show me your weapon,' was the polite request of the *osobist* [a member of the Special Department].

I gave him my submachine-gun. Kapitsky silently laid it at his feet. Then he somehow quietly asked in an everyday tone of voice: 'Why did the barrel of your gun explode?'

'Most likely, the shell had a defective detonator and it triggered the explosion prematurely, when the round was still in the barrel.'

'Or perhaps you forgot to remove the muzzle cover or there was dirt inside?' asked the detective venomously, who then tilted his head to one side and ostentatiously gaped, playing the fool.

'A gun is not a garbage bin for gathering trash; take a look at how well the other howitzers have been treated. Colonel Uriupin can also confirm this. He's just been here. As for the muzzle cover, it is still lying rolled up next to the gun.'

The *osobist* stared fixedly at me in a threatening way: 'You could have done all of this afterwards. Perhaps you deliberately decided to put this gun out of action?!' I had never dealt before with the NKVD and I'd never been under investigation. Thus I couldn't imagine that they would openly ask such offensive questions.

'Today one gun is out of action, tomorrow – another, and soon you'll see to it that the entire battery is out of action,' the Lieutenant continued, paying no attention to my outrage. 'How many dead and wounded from the explosion?'

'No casualties!' I declared with pride.

'How?! You deliberately put the crew under shelter before you blew up the barrel! Which means you spared your men so they wouldn't turn you in!' Kapitsky casually grabbed his belt, shifted the pistol holster around to his front, and then sharply demanded: 'Well, answer me, Lieutenant! For what purpose and on whose orders did you blow up the gun?!'

This question stunned and frightened me. The matter had taken a serious turn.

'Who are your partners?! Perhaps to blow up the gun, you tossed some sand down the barrel?!'

Such a charge was enough to have me executed. But I found a counter-argument: 'And just where in this swamp can you get sand?'

Over and over again I explained what had happened to Kapitsky at his demand. But the *osobist* needed a 'confession': 'The round and the barrel have both been blown to pieces and this is a fact! You have no proof that the barrel was clean. The fact that you had no casualties only aggravates your guilt. Confess, and this will lighten your sentence. Think it over. Meanwhile, I'll interrogate the gun crews.'

The Lieutenant left, taking my submachine-gun with him. A guard began to pace back and forth in front of the entrance to the dugout.

Kapitsky spent a long time questioning the other men of the battery. He was especially thorough with the soldiers of the Number Three gun. When he returned to the dugout, I had nothing new to say.

'Something is becoming clear,' he said vaguely, taking a seat in front of me. 'Confess and tell me who your other accessories to the crime were.'

'I've told you everything. Let's fire the rest of the rounds from this batch to see if there are any defective ones,' I suggested.

'What?! You want me to blow up the other guns together with you?! You want to carry out an enemy order with my help?!' Kapitsky boiled over.

'Why would they explode, if, according to your version, all the detonators are OK, and we'll clean all the other guns in your presence? We have to expend the remaining shells anyway; soon the infantry will be calling for our support.'

'We're going to court-martial you, Lieutenant, for the deliberate destruction of the gun, and you will not get away with this. You're going to accompany me back to the *Smersh*.'

I knew that I wouldn't be coming back from the *Smersh*. There, in the *Smersh*, I had even slimmer chances of proving my innocence, because they had to demonstrate success and show they were doing an effective job. It's a bitter end to die from a Russian bullet as a traitor; it's better to be killed by the Germans.

The investigator, seemingly satisfied that all was clear and that my guilt had been proven, stood up and headed for the exit. At that moment something dawned on me: the fateful shot of the Number Three gun had been its second one! If the barrel had been dirty, it would have blown up with the first shot!

'But it was the second round!' I desperately shouted towards the departing *osobist*.

'Why does that have any significance?' Kapitsky shot back without turning around.

'No, listen, I'll prove to you that you are wrong, Lieutenant!' I shouted at the top of my voice.

My shout and the improper use of the familiar 'you' [Russians still distinguish between a formal 'you' (*vy*) and a familiar 'you' (*ty*); the latter is equivalent to the 'thou' abandoned long ago in English. Using the familiar '*ty*' in certain contexts can be insulting in Russian] upset the detective. He came back to put me in my place. He sat down and looked at me with a smirk.

I began my explanation: 'If the gun barrel had been dirty or still covered, then the first round would have exploded in the barrel. But the first round had a properly functioning detonator and the discharge was normal. Why then did the second round explode prematurely, if the barrel had already been cleaned by the first round and the cover had been torn off by the pressure, as you consider?' Then I triumphantly answered my own question: 'Because it had a faulty detonator!'

Kapitsky became lost in thought. For an agonizingly long time he searched for a rebuttal to my convincing argument, before acknowledging that all his charges were null and void. Then his face brightened up, he smiled and said: 'You're a lucky man, Lieutenant! Two shells were lying in the box: one normal and another with a faulty detonator. Plainly the limber gunner could have grabbed the faulty one first. Then the gun would have exploded with the first shot, and you would have been executed! But here you're right – you are innocent. You should thank your luck.'

There he was right, I thought, and he had figured it out. As for me, if not for my stroke of inspiration, I would have been dead.

That night, the whole lot of suspect rounds was taken away from the firing positions back to the ammo dumps. That was my close call with the Special Department.

On one of these hot August days the rifle battalion, which had only fifty men left out of 200, assaulted German earthworks in front of the village of Polunino on orders of superiors. The entire field, over which the infantrymen charged, was littered with the corpses of our men who had fallen in previous attacks.

Encouraging and also forcing his men to move on, the battalion commander Glyba was running along in the attacking line. I, as a section commander of the artillery battery that was supporting the battalion by fire from its positions well in the rear, ran alongside the battalion commander. Behind me, the signalman with the field telephone – my sole remaining subordinate – was hurrying along with an unwinding reel of field wire on his back. My other four subordinates, forward observers and signalers, had been killed the week before during the repeated attempts to take this same damned trench, and now their bodies were lying among the other corpses. I had a strictly limited number of shells, so I was conserving them for repelling possible German counter-attacks.

When some 200 meters remained to the German trench, mortars joined in with their machine guns. Numerous mortar rounds started to explode all around us. We threw ourselves to the ground. I wedged myself in between two dead bodies, which offered some degree of protection against the shell splinters and bullets. Then one mortar round exploded next to me and threw the corpse on my right onto my head. Maggots spilled down under my collar, and a horrible stench emitted from the corpse's grotesquely distended stomach, which had been lacerated by shrapnel. Although we had already become somewhat accustomed to the nauseating, sweetish stench of decomposing bodies that enveloped the entire field, I almost blacked out from this concentrated dose of putrefying stench coming from the torn stomach of this corpse. But it was a good thing that I didn't pass out! The remaining survivors of the battalion had already started to crawl back to the jumping-off line, and I would have woken up as a prisoner. So I began crawling in pursuit of the battalion commander, who was also falling back while vainly trying to stop the retreat of his men.

Making my way among the countless dead under terrible machine-gun and mortar fire, trying to catch up with the other men, I kept lifting my head and glancing back, to make sure that the Germans hadn't launched a counter-attack. It was a good thing I did! Once I looked back and saw German infantry, under the cover of the mortar barrage, rise from their trenches in a dense line and begin to advance. It would be nothing for them to catch us, while we were still crawling through the mortar fire! Next they would be shooting us in the backs with their submachine-guns, capture our shallow trenches, then break through our thin lines and chase the battalion's remnants away from Rzhev. I had to save the day! No one else could do this except for me!

'On the trench, drop four [a call to reduce the range], battery fire for effect!'

The phone operator immediately transmitted my order to the battery; luckily the phone line was still intact. And then there they were – our shells flying on their way to the target!! They exploded among the attacking German line, right on target. The majority of the Nazis were killed; the rest began quickly crawling back to their trench. The German counter-attack had been repelled!

Meanwhile, our rifle battalion, which had lost fourteen men killed and wounded, crawled safely back into our own shallow earthworks. Sweaty, filthy soldiers exhausted by running and crawling across the corpse-strewn field and worn out by fear, lay sprawled on the bottom of the trench. But the battalion commander, Junior Lieutenant Glyba, the battalion's only surviving officer, was already being summoned to the phone by the regiment commander.

'So, have you captured the trench?' Major Solovev asked curtly.

'We could not. We were pinned down by heavy fire and returned to the jumping-off line.'

'What do you mean "returned"?! Are you nuts?! Resume the assault immediately! I want your battalion in the German trenches today, got it?!'

'Yes, Comrade.'

Of course, the pitiful remnants of Glyba's battalion were in no condition to conduct any sort of attack. The idea was as senseless as it was impossible. However, the next call came an hour later.

'So, how are things?' Solovev asked impatiently. He was in turn being prodded by the division commander.

'Well, we advanced 100 meters,' Glyba answered.

'Push on; I want that trench in our hands by nightfall!'

When the next time the regiment commander called, our battalion commander, convinced of the senselessness of the order, lied again that he had advanced another 50 meters (though may that lie be blessed!). In response, the Major demanded: 'Give the phone to the artilleryman!' Then he asked me, 'Well, is the infantry attacking?'

'Yes, they've advanced some 40 meters,' I replied so as not to betray the Junior Lieutenant, who had already reached his limit. The poor fellow was no longer happy that he'd been promoted from platoon leader to battalion commander in the span of a week. He didn't want to sacrifice his men to no purpose, but the top brass didn't bother to comprehend the situation at the front; they only harped on one thing – attack! – if only to ensure that our worthless offensive kept going.

Meanwhile the Germans started to shell our positions mercilessly, probably to take revenge for the damage done to their company under my barrage. Hundreds of geysers of earth and swampy muck shot into the air. A terrible thunder swelled, the ground trembled beneath us, and it seemed as if the earth itself would vanish and send you falling into an abyss. Clouds of dust and smoke covered our positions, and countless pieces of deadly shrapnel filled the air. Battalion commander Glyba, his orderly, my phone operator and I squeezed ourselves into a small, meter-deep dugout, in order to be safe at least from the shell fragments.

'Just where do they get all those shells? They have no limits,' Glyba said thoughtfully, more to himself than to us. 'When they start a barrage, it seems to have no end.'

The thin layer of soil over our heads seemed to offer us more psychological comfort than any real protection. Hunched over in the dark, we sat in a row on a 'bench' carved from the clay soil. The dugout shook constantly from close explosions, sending showers of dirt onto us from the ceiling. Suddenly a German round smashed the corner of our shelter, and a ray of sunlight cut through the dark dugout, illuminating a dense cloud of swirling dust. Each of us silently prayed to God: Let there not be a direct hit! Then another hit shook the walls of our dugout, and at that moment I felt my phone operator, who was sitting on my right, swiftly but smoothly and decisively push his hand under my armpit. I condescendingly thought the poor boy was just scared. When the palm of his hand emerged from under my armpit next to my chest, I saw with amazement that a small tin can was resting on it. 'But why on earth was he handing me a tin can?' I wondered. I took a closer look and saw that it was not a tin can, but the detonator on the nose of an artillery round! It wasn't the hand of my phone operator, but a 75mm German artillery shell, its aluminium detonator gleaming like a tin can! I froze with horror! Suddenly I understood what had happened: the round had struck the ground next to the dugout, burrowed through the clay soil and had partially emerged from the wall of the dugout – right under my arm! I shouted loudly in fear: 'Get out of the dugout! I have a round under my armpit!'

The other three men spilled out of the dugout like quicksilver. I carefully lifted my right arm, in order not to set off the round, and rushed out of the dugout after them.

Having waited a bit in the trench, I cautiously peered back into the dugout. Two-thirds of the length of the artillery round was jutting from the wall. Apparently, it was a dud.

We'd been extremely lucky! It's a rare case, when a round fails to detonate! It wasn't hard to imagine what would have happened if it had gone off, but it didn't!

For all four of us this was the luckiest event in our lives. But whether the Lord had intended to spare all of us, or just one of us and thereby spared the others – I don't know to this day.

CHAPTER THREE

The Slaughter at Rzhev

I took part in many battles during my three years at the front, but again and again, my thoughts and painful memories return me to the fighting at Rzhev. It is horrifying to think of how many people died there! The Rzhev battle was a meat-grinder and the city of Rzhev was the focal point of this carnage. I never saw anything else like it later in the war. But for me and many of my fellow soldiers, it was also a severe school of warfare.

In August, our army lacked just a little strength and air support in order to take Rzhev. Heavy rains also frustrated us. Yet once the rains had finally stopped, the floodwaters had receded and the ground had dried out, all the means for a breakthrough were removed from our combat positions and sent to other *fronts*: aircraft, hundreds of tanks, and the heavy corps-level artillery with its hundreds of guns. It was around this time that the grand German offensive was rolling into the Caucasus and had reached the gates of Stalingrad, so all of our reserves were sent there. But no one canceled Stalin's strictest order to capture Rzhev at all cost. In the weeks that followed we, the completely exhausted 'local forces' that remained behind within 6 kilometers of Rzhev, were forced without proper artillery, armor or air support to grind against a strongly fortified German line while pouring out our lifeblood.

So a new prolonged, hopeless and doomed offensive began with the remaining worn-out rifle divisions. The result was the same: *fields of corpses, 'Groves of Death', 'Valleys of Death'* [author's emphasis] – across which our men attacked from out of the swamps, storming the Germans' fortified high ground. The Germans also took casualties, as we fought selflessly, but their losses were incomparably smaller than our own...

I was amazed one day when Krasnikov spoke up to go with me to the forward observation post. Of course he was the best forward observer and he would be more useful than anyone else, but it would have been better if he'd been a bit more careful, and didn't always stick his nose into every hot spot. The rest of my men were no less well-trained, but they were too young. Krasnikov and I were both twenty-one, but the rest were at least two years younger. Of course, youth suggests greater lack of concern about danger, but composure and experience were also required here.

Krasnikov never noticed that I tried to protect him a little more than the other guys; after all, he was already married and had a baby son, while the rest of us were still single. When the division had been formed in Kolomna in the spring of 1942, relatives never came to visit anyone else (it was not customary then), but Krasnikov's wife came to see him. She was not alone; she came with a nursing infant. She was younger than her husband and looked quite young. But she looked so beautiful with a baby in her arms! I gave Krasnikov the only separate, small room in the barracks for two days. I dropped by it once to see how they were doing; excusing myself, I left right away. But the idyllic scene I witnessed still lingers in my mind. It was beautiful to see how the plump little tot was nursing hungrily from his mother's breast, clutching it with his tiny little hands, while his small, naked leg jerked with either pleasure or hunger. The young mother, completely occupied with her infant, seemed to have forgotten about her husband, although she had come a long, long way to visit him. How tenderly she looked at her own son! Krasnikov sat across from them and never took his eyes away from his family.

I was happy for Krasnikov, for his son and wife. At the time the only thing I wanted was for Krasnikov to survive the combat that was looming in front of us. We still weren't thinking about our own fates then. It was only at the front that we suddenly realized how badly we wanted to have children. It seemed to us that it was not so scary to die when you had children – they guaranteed that the family would continue, but if we died childless, everything would disappear with us. I always tried to look after the fathers with young children; I didn't want their children to become orphans. Therefore I took along only unmarried men on dangerous missions.

Tall, slender and handsome, Krasnikov was placid in his thoughts and calm in his movements. He did everything in a measured, thoughtful and precise way. He never offended anyone, and was always patient and accommodating. Physically Krasnikov was strong, fast and agile – he was in better physical condition than most of us. Most likely, he volunteered to accompany me under fire out of his respect for me or because he knew he could offer me better support than anyone else. He never thought about his personal safety.

On this occasion, when I refused to take him with me, he told me convincingly, 'Comrade Lieutenant, who can manage this business better than you and me? The other guys are still pups; though they bluster a lot, they can make stupid mistakes.'

Our mission was to cross a minefield unnoticed and to reach a small, grassy rise, which offered a perfect view of the German defenses. There we were to detect and to mark weapon emplacements on a map.

The Germans had planted tripwired 'S' mines [called 'Bouncing Betties' by American G.I.s and 'deboilockers' by the British] in a cabbage field next to the

Zelenkino *sovkhoz* [State Farm]. That autumn the cabbage heads were particularly large and tall, so even in daylight it was fully possible to crawl among them unnoticed.

Before sunrise, Krasnikov and I left our trenches and advanced across no-man's-land towards the cabbage field. When an illumination flare shot into the sky we froze among the corpses, which were lying around in huge numbers. It was rather damp and cold, but quiet. Machine guns spoke up rather rarely, their tracers cutting across no-man's-land towards our trenches from various directions. We stopped in front of the cabbage field and remained prone among the corpses, waiting for the sunrise.

The day dawned and the morning dew sparkled in the sunlight on the cabbage leaves, grass and tripwires like little diamonds. We could clearly see the tripwires, as they were the only straight lines among the intricate patterns of cabbage leaves and grass. We could clearly see which parts of the field had been mined and which were free. Finally, we managed to find a route through the minefield. Crawling carefully through the field, we bypassed the mines and then set up our observation post for the entire day in some tall grass just on the other side of the cabbage field. We would only make our return trip in the evening, when the rays of sunlight would now shine from behind and illuminate the deadly tripwires in the cabbage field.

Having plotted the targets on the map, by evening we safely made it back home. Cherniavsky was delighted to see our 'catch', already picturing how he would smash the German emplacements the next morning.

We hadn't even caught our breath, when Krasnikov walked up to me: 'Comrade Commander, let me and Laptev go pick some cabbage once it gets dark. We're sick of this damned porridge, and our cooks could prepare some nice cabbage dishes. We'll bring back enough cabbage for the whole battery.' 'No way,' I replied strictly, 'I categorically forbid it! You know it's mined; you can't go there at night.' I thought to myself, 'He's even forgotten about his son.' I was certain that the disciplined Krasnikov wouldn't break my order.

It grew completely dark; I was attending a briefing on the next day's mission in battery commander Cherniavsky's dugout. Suddenly the observer Khryapov rushed into the dugout and anxiously reported: 'Mines are exploding in the cabbage field. The Germans have opened a terrible fire.'

I ran out into the trench and began to search for Krasnikov. He and Laptev were nowhere to be seen. Several minutes later Laptev dropped into the trench; hardly catching his breath and extremely agitated, he stammered: 'There, there … Krasnikov is wounded, I've come for a cloak to drag him back …'

My heart sank. My God, I didn't keep him out of danger! 'Grab the cloak and you and Usachev go get Krasnikov quickly! Just be careful, there are more mines there.'

The machine-gun fire sputtered to a stop, and an ominous silence set in. The minutes of waiting seemed to drag on for hours. Finally we heard some shuffling noises and the sound of heavy breathing in the darkness. Staying as low as he could, Laptev crawled to the edge of the trench. We clambered out of the trench to meet him, and all together we gingerly lowered the cloak bearing Krasnikov to the bottom of the trench. We covered the trench with another cloak to maintain light discipline and lit up a *katiusha* (a candle fashioned from an empty cartridge and a wick), and started to examine Krasnikov's body carefully. From his closed eyes and tightly-clenched jaws, it was hard to tell if the observer was still alive.

'Krasnikov,' I asked him, 'can you hear me?'

The answer was only a short, soft moan. The tunic and trousers of our comrade were hanging in dirty, bloody tatters. His chest was bleeding especially profusely. I cut his tunic and undershirt with a pocket knife, and discovered three large wounds torn into his chest. When we were bandaging his wounds and carefully raised the upper part of his body, he again quietly moaned. Finally, we lifted the improvised stretcher on our shoulders in order to evacuate him into the rear. He opened his eyes and in a barely audible voice muttered: 'I did not listen to you, Comrade Lieutenant.'

By the time we had carried Krasnikov to the guns' positions in the rear, he was already dead. We buried him there, on a hillock not far from our guns. All the surrounding villages had been torched by the Germans, and there was nowhere to send a soldier's corpse. We buried all our men like this.

There was no time or way for us at the front to write letters, which is why I suppose we were not meant to inform the deceased man's relatives. That was the task of the artillery battalion staff. We didn't even know each other's addresses, nor did we have any thoughts of living a long life. The chief of staff, or more likely the clerk on the battalion staff, wrote a formal letter, just like to all the families of the fallen, probably similar to the following: 'Your husband gave his life bravely in battle for the Motherland.'

Only now, after the passage of many years, do we bitterly recall our fallen comrades and regret that we still don't know the addresses of their families.

He was still alive...

More than fifty years have passed, but even now I see his face and remember the expression of his eyes. It was the rainy autumn of 1942. At first I thought he was dead. Maybe it was because he was lying motionlessly on his back, with his arms splayed. More likely, it was because no one there could remain alive for very long. Bursts of machine-gun fire riddled that shallow depression from every direction, and so many mortar rounds had fallen there that their blackened craters intermingled. There was no spot left untouched, and that is why almost the entire platoon that had ventured into that low ground, together with their platoon leader, had been killed.

They had thought at dawn to penetrate unnoticed through the tall, dried-out grass in the depression in order to reach the knoll and occupy it, but the plan had failed. The rain and fog hadn't helped either. The knoll was important, because it provided an excellent view of the German positions. It had already changed hands several times, but at the time it was in no-man's-land between the lines.

The division had been so weakened by three months of the offensive, that it not only couldn't capture a village, but even this low mound. One couldn't even call it a hill. Behind us were the 'Grove of Death' and the shattered ruins of the villages of Galakhovo and Polunino; in front of us was the city of Rzhev. To be more precise, in front of us was this knoll, for which so many men on both sides had already fallen. The swollen, decomposing bodies of German soldiers were all around, from which a heavy stench was emanating. Among them were also the corpses of our men, who had fallen there just recently. This wrinkled patch of ground, bristling with dense tussocks of blackened grass, was the lowest place around the knoll and the only place that offered even the slightest cover. Each man had sought shelter in it, looking for anything that provided some concealment from the raking fire.

In order to capture the knoll, the regiment commander had swept the rear area in order to create a reinforced platoon of forty men. Barbers, cobblers, orderlies and other men from the rear, ranging in age from teenagers to forty years old, had been gathered in that platoon. It was twice as frightening for these men to creep towards that hillock; it was frightening for any man to rise from the ground under fire, but these men also lacked any front-line experience. But the men had tried to hide their fears. They didn't want to appear any lesser than those men who in their own times had already bravely faced the enemy fire. A sense of guilt before those who had already fallen inspired an air of affected bravery in them.

'Well,' they were trying to cheer each other up, 'it's our turn now; you can't spend the whole war in the rear...'

My observation post was at the platoon's jumping-off position. When the Germans spotted them and the fire of dozens of machine guns sparkled along their trench line, I opened up with my howitzers. But I had barely managed to knock out several machine-gun positions when two mortar rounds exploded next to our trench in succession. The shell fragments killed one of the spotters and severely wounded my signalman; the blasts hurled me against the rear trench wall and I struck my head with such force that I was knocked out. When I came to and rose from the bottom of the trench, I was shocked by the silence. I could see everything, but my head felt like cast-iron and I couldn't hear anything. But the blood flowing from my nose was slowing, and I was happy that I hadn't been wounded. However, I felt deeply offended by the physical blow to the back of my head that the Germans had delivered, as if they'd struck me with a fist and not a mortar round!

The next day I had recovered from my mild concussion, and Cherniavsky ordered me to reach that knoll. We had to find a German mortar battery, which had been badly tormenting us with its fire. It was its shells that had almost scored a direct hit on our little trench.

No matter how hard I tried, slithering among the tussocks like a grass snake, concealing myself in the wet grass or pressing myself against the bodies of the fallen in order to blend in with them, the Germans still spotted me. All hell broke loose! Two machine guns were joined by a third one. Bullets flew over my head with a terrible sound, clipping the stalks of grass and chewing up the corpses and the ground. Shell explosions deafened me, and their fragments rained down all around me. Each time a bullet or a shell fragment struck one of the motionless bodies of our fallen men, it echoed with a sharp pain in my heart. The dead didn't care any more and no longer felt pain, but by sheltering me, the living, they seemingly continued to fight, so I regarded them as living men.

The German fire continued to rage. I pressed myself into the ground and lay motionless, playing dead for about a half-hour. The fire gradually subsided. I opened my eyes – and that's when I saw him. He was lying on his back, his head resting right next to my own. Rain was falling on his dead face, and small streams of water were trickling down his unshaven cheek. I felt the urge to cover his face from the rain. I gave a tug on his cloak and almost cried out: the eyes of the dead man opened, and he started to look around slowly. Not a single muscle twitched on his unshaven face, the crow's feet by his eyes didn't quiver, and not a single moan or even a sigh emitted from his chest. But his indifferent gaze seemed to have a glimmer of thought behind it. He was conscious, but had lost control over his body and tongue. Apparently, he had been lying here among the dead for forty-eight hours under the unceasing rain and bombardment, drifting in and out of consciousness, and had already reconciled himself to his fate. My appearance neither amazed him nor moved him. But the fact that he was still alive, and especially that he no longer counted himself among the living, shocked me.

'You are alive!' I blurted out. 'I'll get you out of here.'

But he just silently continued to look at me. Then he slowly closed his eyes, as if to say, 'Don't try to comfort me; I no longer fear anything.'

'I'll surely get you out!' I repeated in haste. Then I recalled that I had to make it to the knoll first. I thought: 'I'll get to the knoll, spot the German battery, and then I'll pick up the wounded man on the way back.' 'Only if you survive,' was the next thought that flashed through my mind. I began to argue with myself over whether to evacuate the wounded man immediately, or to continue on my mission. I wanted to get him out of there, while he was still alive. But I couldn't abort my mission, not even in order to save a man. 'Lieutenant, did you get scared?' Cherniavsky would say when I returned; raising his voice, he would add further scorn: 'With an excuse of saving the wounded, you returned with empty hands! What was your mission?! The German battery is slaughtering our men, yet you...'

But no one could save this man except for me, I thought, and he is an older man, most likely he has children waiting for him to come home. Covering the wounded man's face with a cloak, I looked around in order to memorize the location, and then I crawled on towards the knoll. Once I reached the hillock itself, the Germans lost sight of me and only delivered a random fire.

Low, scudding clouds were hurrying quickly to the east, pouring rain on the already saturated ground. The enemy's fire had stopped and suddenly I felt soaked to the skin. Only then did I notice the large drops of water on the supple grass stalks. Maybe, in another situation these wondrous liquid diamonds would have mesmerized me, but now they only made me shiver, as they kept dropping on me all the time.

I could see the German positions clearly from the knoll, but no matter how hard I searched the valleys and hollows, I couldn't spot any signs of the battery. Again and again I strained my eyes looking through the rainy gloom ... and now and then the rain-lashed face of the wounded man appeared before my eyes. It had not been distorted by fear or pain and showed no signs of suffering. There was something detached in his expression, but it was also calm and noble.

Suddenly I saw in the distance to the right a straight row of barely visible puffs of blue smoke popping out of a ravine and then immediately disappearing ... It was the German battery firing, I instantly realized! That's where they were hiding! Mentally noting well the position of the German mortars, I quickly started to crawl back to the hollow, to my wounded man; I was already imagining how I would place him on the cloak and drag him back to our lines, how happy he would be when he came back to his senses and realized he was in a hospital, where he would be treated and he would write letters home ... But no matter how much I crawled around on my belly among the clumps of wet grass, peering into the faces of the bodies lying face up, I couldn't find my soldier; there were only corpses surrounding me. When I rose to my knees in order to get a better look around, the Germans noticed me and opened fire. I crawled around the low area for a long time, but I failed to find the wounded man.

Completely exhausted, soaked to the bones, covered from my head to my feet in mud, and depressed by my failure to find the man, I lay motionless for some time; I no longer cared about the bullets or shells. There was a lump in my throat, and a pinching pain in my heart. My conscience was torturing me, and the doomed look of that wounded man was in my eyes. He was somewhere nearby in those minutes and silently dying.

When I made it back to our lines and reported the results of my mission, Cherniavsky prepared the fire mission data and deluged the German mortar position with howitzer fire. Both we and the infantry sighed with relief; the mortar barrages ceased.

But I felt the pull of that patch of blackened grass; I wanted to find that man. I managed to convince the company commander to give me a medic, and that same night we returned to the hollow. Freezing under the glare of every illumination flare, waiting for bursts of machine-gun fire to subside, we examined dozens of bodies, but didn't find a single living man or a man with his face covered by a cloak.

Two more days passed. The Germans replaced their losses and their mortar battery renewed its work with even greater intensity.

'Sonny,' Cherniavsky tenderly addressed me, 'you will have to go back to the knoll again. Take a signalman along with you and try to take care of this battery yourself.'

It was a scary thought to crawl back there again, but it was sweetened by the opportunity to direct the fire of our howitzers. At the same time, I wanted to take one more look for my wounded man. I was hoping perhaps that he had managed to make it out of the hollow himself.

The signalman and I crawled back into the depression, the field wire unspooling behind us. Again I was among the dead and the tall grass. But the grass seemed significantly shorter than before, as if over these days some giant had hewn it with a scythe. We concealed the reel of field wire in a shell crater and set off at a crawl in different directions, trying to find the wounded man. The Germans opened fire, but we just pressed ourselves in the ground and continued to examine the bodies. When we had approached again to within 20 meters of the shell crater, the signalman tried to talk me out of this venture: 'Why should we look for him, Comrade Lieutenant? So many days have passed, how can a man survive in this hell and in the cold? Look how many of them are lying around here.'

'Protsenko, what if this was your father? Of course, he's just a stranger to you; you haven't seen him.'

'Probably, the infantry carried him off,' he tried to comfort me.

But as it had to happen, I suddenly bumped into my soldier. For some reason his face was exposed again. It had become even paler and shinier, and the stubble on his face had grown a bit longer and darker.

'Over here,' I ordered Protsenko, 'I found him; maybe he's still alive!'

The soldier showed no signs of life. His eyes were closed, his face motionless. 'As I just said, he's dead,' Protsenko said with conviction.

Again I felt uncomfortable, and a new wave of pity washed over me: he hadn't dragged himself off, no one had evacuated him, and he had just died here in the rain. But I still had hope that he was alive.

I began to shake his shoulders and touch his face. Forgetting where I was, I rose too high above him and immediately a long burst of machine-gun fire whipped past me. Protsenko pushed my head down, pressing my cheek against the soldier's wet face. The firing stopped, and I caught the sound of very faint breathing. Was he really alive? I was surprised, and thought it most likely an illusion. To be honest, at that moment I didn't want him to be alive. Just dead, so I couldn't do anything more about it. But if he was still alive ... everything in me resisted that notion: I couldn't comprehend all that suffering, lying in the rain for four days while under fire. The absurd thought that he was still alive had flashed quickly through my mind and disappeared, but the fact that it had existed at all again caused a new wave of guilty feelings: it was all because I hadn't found him before, and hadn't evacuated him. I listened again ... and again I barely heard his breath.

'He is alive! He is alive!' I shouted, as I started to rub his cheeks. The wounded man slowly opened his eyes, looked around, and then his gaze settled on us.

'Hold on just a bit more, please, now we'll get you out,' I told him. Then I ordered Protsenko, 'Wrap the field wire around his foot so we can find him on the way back.' But I thought to myself, 'What a situation: there's no way I can return before I call in fire on the German battery, but while I'm busy with that, the wounded man would die, or the Germans might spot me and kill me...'

Shaken by what had occurred, I crawled to the knoll mechanically, keeping myself pressed to the ground purely by instinct. I kept seeing the wet and pale face of the soldier in my mind, and the same damn question drilled my brain: why, why hadn't I saved him earlier?

I spotted the new German battery rather quickly, positioned in a ravine not far from where the previous battery had been located. I passed on the fire mission data, made a small lateral adjustment to the spotting round, and then called for the howitzers to fire for effect. We fired over fifty rounds. Black clouds of smoke covered the ravine, and I saw some debris flying into the air, and then a huge flame erupted from the target location. The enemy battery had been destroyed. But strangely, I didn't feel the customary joy that I normally experienced while watching an enemy target get pulverized.

'Get a medic to the CP, we have a wounded man with us,' I said over the phone, and we made our way back to the soldier.

Our wounded man was right where we'd left him. When we rolled his body onto the cloak, he gave a moan. Together, Protsenko and I quickly dragged him back to our lines. The medic was already waiting for us in the trench. We anxiously waited for the results of his examination. The medic's voice struck us like a clap of thunder: 'He's already dead.'

A feeling of deep remorse and sorrow over something left undone and lost forever engulfed me. My breath was cut short, and my heart ached. Over the twenty years of my life to that point, I had experienced similar feelings once before, when I woke up one night as a child and touched the cold body of my mother. It seemed I had just called out for her, and she was still alive ... she had passed away while I slept!

On the outskirts of Rzhev

One cannot imagine a more pitiful, uncomfortable and dangerous shelter than the one in which I celebrated the 25th anniversary of the October Revolution. It is also hard to believe that I didn't want to leave it when the order came to do so.

In early November 1942 I was far in front of our trenches, in no-man's-land, just 50 meters from the Germans. Only a low railroad embankment and some swampy undergrowth separated me from the enemy. From these bushes, stooped low to avoid being spotted by the Germans, in the mornings I observed the outskirts of Rzhev. Just beyond the bushes German trenches stretched across some slightly higher ground; beyond them were some scattered small homes on the edge of the city. Concealed from our observers by the buildings, the Germans were living a normal life in the yards and streets – they walked around and drove about in cars and trucks. From the vantage point of my observation post, I could see most of the streets of Rzhev. Somewhere behind the first houses was a German mortar battery that had been troubling us for a long time, firing at anything that moved in our positions. I had to find the battery and destroy it.

The sun was setting; a cold autumn rain was falling. My signalman Riabov and I were lying in a shallow trench behind the low railway embankment. A shelter half covered the trench against the rain, while we had scattered some branches on the bottom of the trench to try to stay dry from the ground water. Due to the high water table, the trench was so shallow that you could only crawl into it on your belly across the branches. Once inside, you couldn't even prop yourself up on your elbows without causing the soaked shelter half to rise and thereby reveal our position behind the embankment to the Germans. The Germans couldn't even imagine that two Russians would spend a day right under their noses, between their minefields and the railroad. Day and night, they were particularly targeting the approaches to the rail line with their mortars in order to prevent our scouts from infiltrating their lines. These mortar rounds always exploded behind us, but we were always afraid a short round would land right on top of us. Machine-gun bullets also tore through branches of the bushes above our shallow trench. It seemed that they were firing right over our heads from less than 50 meters away. To make matters worse, the constant mortar barrages kept cutting our communication line back to our guns, forcing Riabov to crawl through another minefield in order to repair the line.

Over 800 meters of no-man's-land, stuffed with German anti-personnel mines, separated us from our lines. Scouts weren't able to reach our position every night with flasks of porridge and tea; the night before, two of them had been killed while making the attempt. We were ready to go hungry for three nights, so as not to risk the lives of our comrades.

Our schedule was like this. At night, one of us rested while the other was on duty at the field telephone and kept watch against a possible German attack. Every morning before light I would creep over the railway embankment, take cover in some low bushes in water up to my knees, and when it grew light, I would observe the outskirts of Rzhev with the help of a periscope carefully elevated above the bushes. The swamp water was nearly up to the top of my high boots, and I had to stand stooped over: there was nowhere to sit, and I didn't dare straighten up, since the Germans would immediately see my head and shoulders above the bushes. I had to stand in this uncomfortable posture for two hours, while I called in fire on every target I could see in Rzhev. After that, like it or not, I had to chance leaping over the railroad embankment back to my shallow trench in plain view of the Germans.

One day I managed to spot Germans removing the covers from mortars, while other soldiers were unloading boxes of ammunition from trucks. I almost jumped with joy! That's where the bastards were located! They were setting up to open fire. This sight alone was worth all my sufferings and deprivations! In a loud whisper, I passed the fire mission data back to Riabov across the embankment, and he repeated them into the field phone. Soon our rounds were on their way and they landed between the mortars and the trucks. Smoke and dust obscured everything. The mortar battery had been destroyed along with the crews. The battery hadn't been able to fire a single round.

For the next several days I destroyed trucks, panje wagons, and German-occupied buildings on the outskirts of Rzhev. The Germans no longer strolled around openly, but scurried from one place to another like rats.

Approximately on the third day, the Germans realized that someone nearby was directing the fire, and they began to search for my position. They intensified their observation of the railway embankment. I couldn't sit on my haunches all day long in the swamp, and I had to get back to my shelter in daytime. A stone railroad cabin was on the rail line about 200 meters to the right of us – the same stone cabin that had been blocking all of our division's attempts to break into Rzhev. Machine guns blazed from its stone embrasures in every direction, and we hadn't been able to take it or knock it out despite all our attempts. The German machine-gunners defending the cabin were apparently ordered to search for me. The cabin had a great view down the straight ribbon of the rail line, while the embankment itself offered no concealment. Once, as soon as I had leaped across the rails, a machine-gun burst struck the embankment behind me. Bullets rang against the rails, chewed up the wooden sleepers and ricocheted in every direction with an angry buzz. I knew then that the Germans were waiting for me. Each return home was a deadly game of hide-and-seek.

The next time I was sitting under the embankment in the bushes and thinking to myself: the German at the machine gun has been waiting for me since dawn; the poor bastard is probably tired and angry that I haven't appeared yet, so likely he now has his hands off the trigger and is having a smoke ... It's time! Gathering all my strength, I hurled my body over the embankment. A machine gun immediately opened up. Too late; I was already on the other side of the embankment! The German had missed again!

In order to keep the Germans from realizing that we had a lair on the opposite side of the embankment, I tried to give the impression that each day I was making a sortie from the Russian lines. So I made my dash across the railroad line in different places.

Soon I was 'returning home from work' across the embankment for the tenth time. As I crawled into the shelter over the wet branches atop the muck, I was thinking that this game would not have a happy ending for me. They'd either pick me off or ambush me. I was all wet and hungry. Riabov fell asleep immediately. But one of us had to be at the phone all the time, even if today was a holiday, so I attached the receiver to my ear with a hook we had fashioned from some bandaging wrap and listened to what was going on in the battalion on this anniversary of the October Revolution. I heard some happy voices, conversations about parties before the war and about women. The guys were drunk. In their bunkers, it was warm and dry, so they partied. Suddenly in my ear I heard the loud, commanding voice of the artillery battalion commander Gordienko: 'Mikhin,' he addressed me, knowing that I was on the line, 'I congratulate you!'

'I serve the Soviet Union!'

'Do you know why I'm congratulating you?'

'Because of the anniversary of the Revolution, Comrade Major, what else could it be?'

'No-o,' drawled Gordienko in a self-assured tone, while lowering his voice and belching, 'I'm appointing you the commander of the battalion's forward observers! Congratulations on the promotion!'

His words struck me like lightning! He was appointing me in place of the dead lieutenant and of course he'd send me out with the next group to snatch a prisoner! To my certain death! The division hadn't been able to snatch a prisoner for a whole month; specially-trained regimental and divisional scouts hadn't been able to seize a prisoner, though they'd lost many men in the effort. All the attempts had been in vain – it was impossible to penetrate the German defenses, and German scouts at night were prowling in front of our trenches all the time. We had to search painstakingly for some other way to snatch a prisoner and carefully plan an operation. But Gordienko, demonstrating his initiative, volunteered his artillery spotters who were totally untrained for this work, to bring in a captured German. Of course, snatching a prisoner is not the job of an artilleryman, but Gordienko was always being Gordienko: 'Who? I don't have anyone? Of course I will get a prisoner!' he cockily announced to the division staff.

Right, no one else could snatch a prisoner, but he would! With the hands of his subordinates, or, better put, with the lives of his men! Just a week before he had sent six observers into the German lines to take a prisoner, and all but one had been killed. This didn't stop him! A man like him could send a second and then a third group out just to please his superiors and hear their praise! Indeed he did send a second group out, on the same sector of the front and using the same primitive tactics. He wasted in vain two groups of observers one after the other, together with the chief of the battalion's observers! Now he was appointing me, the commander of a battery's fire control platoon, to lead the observers. All these thoughts flashed through my mind in a second, while Gordienko's last words were coming through the receiver: 'So let's go! I'll be waiting for you tonight in my bunker.'

That is why I didn't want to leave my rotten and dangerous lair by the railroad embankment. When I told my signalman about the return, he was happy to hear that we were finally returning to our positions. But for me, this promotion and departure from under the Germans' noses was equivalent to a death sentence. Here, I might be next to the gates of hell, but I was still on the Russian side of the line. But in order to snatch a prisoner, I would have to sneak across the German trenches, and I might not return...

Back at the battalion, I headed over to take charge of the observer platoon, and I was shocked by what I found. The guys hadn't washed or shaved, and they were just lying around on their bunks in complete silence. They'd been so shocked by the deaths of their comrades in the previous week that complete apathy had fallen over them. I thought it best not to inform them that Gordienko had a new mission in store for them. So I held my tongue for the time being.

'Guys,' I addressed them, 'for centuries Russian men have shaved and put on clean underwear, in order to fight and die honorably, but you've even stopped washing. Do you think it's easier to die in such a shabby condition?'

It took me a lot of effort to establish personal connections with the men. As the first order of business, I led them to our bath-house. Our bath-house was simply four posts wrapped with shelter halves, and an empty barrel with some holes punched in the bottom of it suspended above. Some men would pour water into the barrel, while the rest bathed. After bathing, we shaved our faces and cleaned our weapons. I started spending all my time together with them; ate with them, dug gun positions with them, and stood sentry with them. Gradually the men got used to me, and they began to respect me, trust me, and accept me as their commander. We analyzed the mistakes of the previous groups and little by little began to develop our own plan for a new manhunt.

Unexpectedly our training was interrupted. In late August I was accepted as a candidate member of the Communist Party, and all of a sudden I was summoned to the division's political department in order to get my Party candidate membership card.

That night I made it to the rear area of the regiment, and from there moved on to the division's rear. The rear area of the division was some 15 kilometers from us in the area of the village of Deshevka. Germans had put the torch to all the villages around Rzhev, so all the staff and supply personnel lived in dugouts, just like us. The difference was that their dugouts were many kilometers from the front line. There was no enemy fire here and one could walk around openly. The dugouts were also deeper than ours; it was possible to stand up in one, and they were covered by layers of thick logs. They were much better than our kennel, which was covered with a piece of metal from the wing of a shot-down airplane to keep the dirt from raining down on our heads during barrages, and a shelter half covering the entrance instead of a door. Stooping into the dugout from the trench, you had to sit inside bent over – but it was still a paradise! There was no rain, no wind and you were safe from bullets! Only those damn mortar rounds sometimes scored a direct hit, but that was just a rare matter of bad luck.

Naively, I thought that I, a lieutenant from the front, would be welcomed and immediately handed my card, but a sentry said: 'Wait for morning.' It was chilly, I was tired and there was no place to rest, because no one gave me entry into their dugout. It was good that I was at least dry. I sat down on a mound. The sun soon rose, and it became a bit warmer.

Everything in the rear seemed strange to me. The first thing that amazed me was their reveille. The sun was already up, but they were still sleeping. At the front, fire fights erupted at dawn, all the men were already on their feet, and sometimes you had to spend the whole night standing in a wet trench. But here everybody was sleeping until around 0800 hours. So I had to wait until the start of their work day.

A sentry struck up a conversation with me while I was sitting next to him. He was a tall, agile, brown-haired fellow around my own age. I might have accepted him into my observer platoon, but the conversation spoiled the initial impressions: he was dodgy and cunning. He was interested in how things were for us at the front and complained about his own life in the rear. It turned out that things here were always far from fair to them too: it depended on whose orderly you became. One might have access to food and baggage warehouses, another access to tasty buns from a field bakery or else to vintage wines from the medical battalion (which were supposed to be for the wounded, but his officers would drink them); others with more influence were sent after the laundry, to the bathing and laundry team.

'You can also have some fun there,' my new acquaintance told me with a wink, 'because only girls work there.'

Finally, sleepy men in their underwear started to emerge from the bunkers of the military prosecutor's office, the division's newspaper, the political department and of all the other supply and support services. Yawning and rubbing their eyes, they glanced up at the sun and then slowly walked to the well-built outhouses, which were also covered with thick logs just in case. Squinting in the bright sun, they just as slowly returned to their dugouts. One couldn't walk like that at the front! I suddenly recalled how the first time, when we had not yet consolidated a recent gain and still had no continuous trench line, much less an outhouse, as soon as a man got out of his foxhole to relieve himself, well, the German wasn't sleeping – there'd be the crack of a rifle shot, and the man would be dead. It was sad to see how men died in such poses. Of course, there were some jokers who would make a wisecrack even over something like this; not maliciously of course, but more just to try to bolster their own spirits.

The officers in underwear were leisurely washing themselves, plainly enjoying the process, while the orderlies looked after their superiors: some attentively poured the water without stop, others were taking care of the uniforms, picking off the lint, while still more were polishing the boots; the rest carried mess kits holding their officers' breakfasts into the bunkers.

I asked one man in a pair of drawers: 'When can I get my candidate membership card?'

In a dignified manner, he replied, 'Our workday begins at 0900 hours.'

I returned to my perch on the mound. Two more officers, who'd also been summoned to pick up their cards, joined me.

Only around noon did we receive our cards. No one offered us a bite to eat or even bothered to ask how the war was going. The sentry alone was curious, but only because his superior officer had threatened to send him into the infantry. A major from the political department dramatically shook my hand, clasped my shoulder and said: 'Beat the Nazis. Fight like a communist.'

Walking back to the battery I thought they could well have given me the card in the trenches, like they wrote about in the papers, without taking me from my business.

There was a heavy snowfall on 19 November. We donned white camouflage cloaks late in the evening, grabbed our weapons, and moved into the first line of trenches; the time had come to penetrate the German line and to snatch a prisoner.

The commander of the company in that sector, Barkov, greeted us courteously, with sincere compassion and attention, like we'd been sentenced to death. He knew very well that we were heading to certain death – not a single one of the groups that he had seen off ever came back. He promised to stay awake until our return. After a late dinner the infantrymen went to their foxholes to sleep. Our support group stayed in the trench with the machine-gun crews on duty, while we jumped out of the trenches, and started crawling towards the German lines. It felt like jumping into nothingness. I crawled in front, the other five men following behind me. Each man kept constant hold on the felt boot of the man in front, so I could silently pass an order down the file with a move of my foot.

Heavy rain was lashing us. Our white camouflage cloaks quickly turned into dirty rags. Suddenly the Germans stopped sending up illumination flares. The rain and darkness cheered us up. We crawled on. All of a sudden I saw something moving in front of me. There was also movement to the left and right … They were Germans! Crawling towards us! Extended into a line, there were dozens of them, at least a hundred men. An entire German infantry company had decided to sneak up to our trenches and break into them. I gave a signal with my foot and the whole group immediately turned back. We quickly crawled back to our lines and dropped into the trench. The company commander was suspicious: 'Why did you come back so quickly, where is the prisoner?'

'What prisoner?! Swarms of Germans are on the move towards you, rouse your company!'

Within thirty seconds all the men were manning the trench. The Germans were not yet visible. They were crawling carefully, relying on the element of surprise, counting upon the belief that in such terrible weather, the trenches would be empty, and all the Russians would be sleeping in their dugouts.

'Lieutenant,' Barkov asked me, 'take over the right flank, I have too few men there.' Then he ordered his men, 'Don't fire! Let them come right up to the trench.'

The rain kept intensifying. Streams of water poured into the trench, mixing with the foot of snow already on the bottom of the trench and quickly turning it into slush and water. The breastworks and walls of the trench were slippery, and we were standing in the mud, water and slush. While I was positioning my men, the Germans were suddenly right there! The enormous figure of a German suddenly rose up above the breastwork right in front of me. I fired a burst from my submachine-gun, and he fell dead into the trench. But two more Germans appeared above me at the same time. I fired at the one on the left and he fell. The one on my right leaped for my neck with outstretched fingers, but I jerked to the left and he missed my throat. I dropped my shoulder and his right hand slipped on my wet and dirty cloak. He fell to the bottom of the trench, where I struck the back of his head with the butt of my gun, and he disappeared beneath the water. The sounds of firing and struggle quickly subsided. Shocked, I looked around and heard my men yelling: 'We're fine, just two men lightly wounded!'

'You're a lucky man, Lieutenant!' the company commander exclaimed.

'Of course I am. I didn't lose a single man!'

'I'm talking about something else. We have prisoners!'

At that moment I recalled why we were there. Happy about the outcome of the skirmish, I'd completely forgotten about my mission.

Indeed, it was a lucky case! If not for the German raid and the fact that we'd spotted them first, our entire group would now be lying dead in front of the German trenches.

I headed over to Barkov, my men following behind me. The trench was full of dead Germans, but there was so much water that their bodies were completely submerged, with only some hands and feet emerging from the murky water. Barkov's company had also taken casualties, and our dead were also now lying beneath the water. Moving along the trench and stepping on something soft and slippery was very unpleasant, but there was no alternative.

Barkov turned over eight prisoners to us. We led them back to the battalion command post. Gordienko was delighted – he had kept his word to the superiors! I don't know what he wrote in the report about our operation, but the Order of the Red Star was only awarded to Gordienko himself for netting the prisoners. The regiment's chief of intelligence Kopetsky also received the medal 'For Combat Merit', supposedly for organizing the operation.

But we were satisfied that we hadn't lost a single man. For a commander and his soldiers, this is more important than any award.

The Rzhev-Sychevka operation of 30 July–23 August 1942 was the baptism of fire for our 52nd Rifle Division. We had attacked Rzhev from the north, head on. Then together with the 2nd and 16th Guards Rifle Division, we had taken Polunino. In five months of fighting, between August and December

1942, the division lost its entire personnel *three times* over [author's emphasis], suffering casualties of up to 4–5,000 men killed and up to 13,000 wounded. Through superhuman effort, we had managed to advance all of 6 kilometers to the northern outskirts of Rzhev at the cost of staggering losses. Such was the result of a five-month battle of attrition at Rzhev. But we failed to capture the city itself.

Finally, on 2 March 1943, the Germans voluntarily abandoned Rzhev. But we were no longer there. On the eve of New Year 1943 our division was withdrawn from Rzhev.

PART TWO

From Stalingrad to the Western Border

CHAPTER FOUR

From Starobelsk to the Donbas

The German forces surrounded in Stalingrad were still putting up resistance, when in January 1943 our division was transferred by train southward in order to attack towards the west. After two weeks of traveling by rail we had somewhat recovered from the recent terrible fighing around Rzhev, had gotten some rest, and were starting to feel like ourselves again. We were in high spirits: we had gained substantial combat experience and we were on our way to a new offensive. But even after receiving replacements, the division only had 6,000 men instead of its authorized strength of 12,000. On 19 January we were brought to Kalach-Voronezh Station. There we unloaded, and the fighting troops – the infantry and artillery – were placed in tarpaulin-covered trucks and rushed to Starobelsk, on the border with the Ukraine. That's how far the Germans had retreated from Stalingrad! While we rode to Starobelsk, arriving on 27 January, the frigid temperatures and strong winds nearly froze us to the core.

On 29 January 1943, an offensive began under the command of General Vatutin with the objective to liberate the Donets Basin [the Donbas]. The 52nd Rifle Division, as part of General M.M. Popov's Mobile Group of the South-western Front, which included four tank brigades and three rifle divisions, was to advance through Starobelsk and Artemovsk towards Mariupol.

However, just beyond Starobelsk we ran into a well-prepared line of defenses. With heavy losses, we cracked the line and moved on through deep snow. Each village was taken only with fighting. The strong resistance was as unexpected for the command of our Mobile Group as it was for all of us. But inspired by the victory at Stalingrad, we hurled ourselves on the enemy in high spirits, overcoming their bitter resistance without stopping to count our losses. Our desire to win and to continue the triumph at Stalingrad was so strong and irresistible, that in spite of the weather and the enemy resistance we continued to push forward. On the one hand, we had learned to fight, and on the other hand, we no longer feared death. We had already fatefully placed our lives on the altar of Victory, because our experience was telling us that the end of the war was nowhere in sight, yet all the same it was impossible to survive it. You were going to be killed anyway, sooner or later, so what was there to fear?

Our further advance was hindered not only by the Germans, but also the nearly impassable snow. Horses, trucks, guns, men – all bogged down in deep drifts of snow. Only the oxen, provided to us by local residents, saved us. If it had not been for the oxen, it would have been impossible to march along our assigned routes.

The people of the Ukraine greeted us with joy. We would come to their homes out of the snow and cold, often after a battle, and they would offer us a warm place, treat us to everything they had available, and willingly give us their oxen, so we could liberate the Ukraine all the more quickly. After six months of fighting at Rzhev, where all the villages had been wiped from the face of the earth and no civilians remained in the combat areas, our soldiers were deeply missing human dwellings and peaceful inhabitants! With genuine joy they gazed around the peasant huts and chatted with the women and children, while thinking of their own homes, their own parents, and their own wives and children. These encounters were brief, but they lightened our spirits.

We advanced directly, cutting across roads through snow-covered fields, and while the Germans were stuck on the road, we often bypassed them, forcing the enemy to speed up their retreat. But it also happened sometimes that German armor would appear in our rear, catch up with us and unexpectedly attack us from behind, especially because they had more armor and only the Luftwaffe was visible in the air.

Once we were marching across a snow-covered field. The day was calm and sunny, but the bright sun was unable to prevail over the bitter cold, and no one dared sit on the ice-cold gun carriages. The men walked behind the guns or jogged a bit in order to warm up a little. Virgin white snow stretched for miles around us, reflecting the sunlight and almost blinding us with solar glare. The oxen towing the guns made their way across the undisturbed snow like icebreakers, crushing the thin layer of ice atop the snow. The loud crunching of ice and snow was ceaseless as they moved. All were tired but did their job confidently and silently. Using the oxen to tow the guns, we were moving slowly, but we were strictly following our orders to move as fast and as far to the west as possible. There were no Germans around; they could not have slipped past our column undetected in such deep snow.

The black smudge of a village dimly appeared in the distance. Anticipating a good rest, warmth and some food, the tired soldiers cheered up; one could hear small talk and jokes. The oxen also sensed that they would soon get a rest and sped up their pace. The snow-covered houses were mesmerizing to all the men in the column. Now there were only about 500 meters left to reach it, one more push and we could rest. Mounted scouts had already been in the village and had spotted no Germans, so we could enter the village and have an undisturbed rest.

But what was that?! Three tanks rolled out of the village on the single road passing through it – and they had white crosses on them! Where had they come from? They hadn't been there a few minutes ago. They must have just entered the village from the opposite side, driven through it and were now moving in our direction. They were crawling very slowly, hindered by the deep snow, and they hadn't yet spotted us, because we weren't moving directly towards them on the road. But as soon as they spotted us, they'd tear us to pieces! I couldn't lose a second – I had to stop them at whatever the cost! Loudly, in full voice I shouted: 'Tanks on the right! Prepare for combat!'

The drivers halted the oxen, and the gun crews quickly unlimbered the guns and pointed them to the right.

'At the tanks! Fire!'

The rapid fire of all four guns ripped through the air. All three tanks were hit and disappeared in thick black smoke. But before we could catch our breath, two tank shots sounded from the village in quick succession. Our cannons, low to the ground, were almost invisible in the deep snow, so the Germans fired at the oxen. Passing through the bodies of the poor animals, the armor-piercing rounds whistled past with a terrifying sound, without striking either a gun or a person. The soldiers immediately dropped into the snow behind their guns, while I fell prone to the left of the guns with my binoculars. The smoke of their shots still hadn't dissipated, before I managed to spot two tanks that were positioned on either side of the first hut on the edge of the village. While the German tankers were examining the results of their fire, I issued a new order: 'Tanks by the first house! Battery! Fire!'

The tanks managed to fire one more round, before they were hit by shells from our cannons. The right tank immediately burst into bright flames; apparently, its hull was facing away from us, and our rounds had struck the engine compartment. The tank on the left quickly disappeared behind the huts; possibly our rounds had hit the turret and the driver had reacted immediately. We later found this tank abandoned on the other side of the village. But the two return shots fired by the German tanks had done us a lot of damage. The Number 1 gun was destroyed and its gunlayer killed, with two more of the crew wounded.

As soon as the Germans had opened fire on the battery, one young soldier from among the recent replacements had become frightened and started to run off into the field away from the guns. He hadn't even made two steps when a German armor-piercing round flew between his legs. Convulsing with pain, the guy collapsed in the snow with a horrible cry. We ran up to him immediately after the battle ended. The soldier was pale with pain and said that he had been wounded in both legs. But we didn't see any tears in his trousers or any blood. He screamed horribly as we removed his trousers in order to bandage him. We didn't see any wounds on his legs, but saw that they were twisted unnaturally above the knees. We realized then that bones in both of the fellow's legs had been smashed into pieces. We sent him back to the medical battalion with the other two wounded men.

From the area north of Starobelsk, overcoming strong enemy resistance and deep snow, we successfully advanced to the Northern Donets River at the village of Zakotnoe, which lies to the west of Lisichansk, and there we forced a crossing. After an artillery barrage, infantry took Zakotnoe. Beyond Zakotnoe the 431st Rifle Regiment together with our 1st Artillery Battalion and two tanks from Popov's Mobile Group drove the Germans out of Krivaia Luka and entered the village of Voroshilovka. For the first time after a lengthy series of battles and a hard march, the soldiers had enough time to catch up on their sleep and warm themselves up.

At dawn, the infantry set off in the direction of Sol' Station near Artemovsk. Behind it, our oxen and guns formed up into a column of march along the street. As I was running out into the street from the hut where I had spent the night, in order to join the front of the column, I noticed four tanks approaching the village from our rear and rejoiced: Reinforcements had arrived! Suddenly these tanks opened furious fire on our column of guns from their main guns and machine guns at a range of 200 meters! Having realized what sort of reinforcement this was, I loudly shouted 'Tanks!' and rushed to the nearest gun, which was closing up the column. The gun crew members, cut down by bullets and shell fragments, were dropping into the snow, while living and wounded oxen were roaring and thrashing in their harnesses. The air was filled with the crackle of gunfire, the thunder of explosions, and clouds of snow and smoke thrown up by shell explosions! The gun, to which I had rushed, was closer to the tanks than any of the others, but it was still undamaged. However, only one of its crew was left standing, while dead and wounded oxen had fallen onto the trails of the limber. The surviving crew man and I unhitched the gun from its limber, spread its trails and I rushed to the sight, while the soldier started to load the gun. I moved the cross hairs onto the nearest tank, but I couldn't traverse the gun barrel even a bit; we had to turn the entire gun to the left. I grabbed the traversing handspike of the trail but it had been blocked by the axle of the limber when the oxen, crazed by fright, had stepped back. Shell fragments and bullets flying through the air kept us low and we did everything on all fours. We crawled under the axle of the limber in order to free the trail, but couldn't budge it – dead oxen had fallen on the shaft. We started to drag off the oxen – I'd never before given a thought to how heavy they were! Nevertheless, we managed to move them off the shaft, lifted the axle of the limber with our backs and freed the trail. All these operations only took several seconds and at last I could aim the gun again. I put the cross hairs on the tank and fired the gun – the cannon thundered and the shell knocked out the first tank. I aimed at the second tank and was just about to fire, when someone was just a second quicker and his round splashed with fire on the armor of the German tank. Later I found out that this was Cherniavsky. But I also pressed the trigger and the second round penetrated the tank's armor. The steel monster disappeared in black smoke.

The remaining two tanks that were located in the rear and barely visible to us withdrew and disappeared behind a low hill. It had been the forward unit of a German tank column located in our rear at Iama Station. We didn't know about the column then, although we were about to engage them.

Battery commander Cherniavsky was killed in that battle. He had run out of the hut, and crouching behind the gun shield, had managed to fire the howitzer at one of the tanks. But at that moment he was severely wounded, and quickly died from his wounds.

Cherniavsky had fought at Rzhev for six months and had not been wounded once. He died here, on the Ukrainian land. By his personal example he led us into battle, and we fought bravely. Even with songs. Once, back at Rzhev, in a few minutes of silence a frolicsome Russian song affably sounded in the trench at our observation post. The Germans could also hear it as their trench was just 50 meters away. For some time, having fallen silent, they quietly listened to the singing. Then they became disturbed and angered by our happy singing, or, more likely, their officers were outraged. A furious shelling of our positions followed. As soon as the firing stopped, the Russian songs sounded again.

We lost eight men killed and twelve wounded in the battle at Artemovsk. We also lost three cannons and several oxen.

We left the wounded in the village, as our medical platoon had gotten lost somewhere on the snowy steppes. The Ukrainian peasants gave us new oxen and we moved on to catch up with our infantry that was already approaching Sol' Station.

By noon of 2 February, in cooperation with tankers of the 178th Tank Brigade, we had surrounded and had liberated Sol' Station and the village of Sverdlovka. Falling back, the Germans kept the station and village under constant shellfire. Houses were burning, and there were casualties among the civilians as well as our men. We couldn't advance any further, so here in the station and the village we took up defensive positions.

Hero-tankers!

Our 2nd Artillery Battalion had fallen behind us somewhere on the way to Sol' Station. Artillery regiment commander Chubakov who was with our 1st Artillery Battalion ordered me to find out what had happened with them. This was a job for the regiment's scouts, but for some reason he ordered me, the chief of the 1st Artillery Battalion's forward observers, to do the job.

A sunny day was heading towards evening. The Luftwaffe had been bombing our units and villages at will all day long. A nice stroll into the rear to find the missing battalion seemed attractive to me. There were almost no observers left in the battalion and I invited my friend, Lieutenant Georgii 'Grisha' Kurty, who was also a former student, to join me. Together we walked along the road towards the village of Sacco and Vancetti, which was located a little to the west of Voroshilovka.

We were less than a kilometer from the village, when we spotted tanks emerging from it. They were advancing in a deployed attack formation. While we were trying to see if they were Russian or German tanks, the nearest tank fired a long machine-gun burst at us. We threw ourselves on the ground and quickly crawled back behind a hillock. Then we stood up and started to run at a trot. As we ran, we began to discuss what to do if the Germans took us prisoners. Grisha tore the bars from his collar tabs. I looked at him, saw the clear traces of the bars still on his collar tabs, and decided not to remove my own.

The tanks were advancing through the deep snow slowly and very carefully. After ten minutes, we scanned for them while pausing on a low knoll, but they weren't visible. Although we had run about one and a half kilometers, the threat of being captured still hadn't passed. The tanks were fully capable of catching us, and we were still worried. We were no longer afraid of death; we were afraid of captivity.

We ran past a pile of corn stalks. Two tankers were making tea on a campfire next to it. It turned out that it was not a pile of stalks, but a well-camouflaged tank. As we were running to the village, we hadn't noticed it. It turned out that German airplanes had damaged it that morning, and two men from the crew had gone to pick up spare parts for repair.

'Guys, German armor is approaching from the rear,' we warned the tankers as we ran past, but they both just laughed.

I reported the situation to artillery regiment commander Chubakov. He immediately deployed a gun battery on the edge of the village to meet the German tanks. An hour passed. Battalion commander Gordienko called me.

'Well, just where are your tanks? I guess you saw some wagons and got scared,' he angrily mocked me in the presence of Chubakov.

'What wagons?' I was outraged. 'They fired at us. I don't know where they are!'

'Take five men and return to Sacco and Vancetti; find the 2nd Battalion and the German tanks!' Chubakov ordered again.

I only had one observer – Iashka Korennoi, who was about my own age. The rifle regiment provided four more men. But as soon as they heard that they had been selected for a scouting mission, two of the infantrymen demonstrably coughed and a third announced that he had night-blindness. I chambered a round in my gun, and said sternly, 'Whoever is blind, scram. The sick ones too. Quickly!' All three immediately regained their health. Once on our way, the infantrymen warmed up to us, and we made a good team together.

The moon was illuminating the snow-covered road, and the snow crunched loudly under our feet. After we had walked about 3 kilometers and climbed to the top of a rise, we spotted fires below us on the road in front of us. We approached, and saw a closely-packed jumble of burning tanks with white crosses on the turrets. Ten tanks were burning there! The silent, dark hulks of two more tanks stood nearby. Leaving two men with submachine-guns on the road to cover us, with the other two men I crawled up to the side of the non-burning tanks, and then stopped to listen. I heard nothing inside the dark tanks, just the crackle of the flames on the burning tanks. I rapped on one of the knocked-out tanks with my submachine-gun. Not a sound. I climbed up to an open hatch, stuck my submachine-gun into it and fired a burst. Still silence. I clambered into the dark interior of the tank, and my outstretched hands bumped into the corpse of a tanker. One of my hands came across a flashlight hanging on the dead tanker's chest. I switched it on, and it illuminated a sewing-machine inside the tank. Such looting didn't so much outrage me as amaze me: to go into battle with a sewing-machine in the cramped interior of a tank – that's sheer avarice! I collected a pistol, some papers and a note-pad from the dead tanker. Later we read panicky notes in the note-pad about heavy losses, and about the havoc caused by the German tankers in the Russian rear areas, shooting up the supply wagons, and about the tanker's dream: 'I would like to destroy a Russian tank personally!' In the meantime, my companions had pulled a lot of wine, preserves, and dried bread out of the nearby tank, and had managed to stuff their pockets so fully that they could barely move. I ordered them to empty their pockets and to hide all of it in the snow until our return. 'If we do return,' I thought to myself.

Who had knocked out all these tanks? Walking several hundred meters further along the road, we saw scattered clumps of corn stalks, a quantity of empty shell casings, and deep imprints of tank tracks in the snow. Just then I recalled the two tankers from the 178th Tank Brigade, who had been brewing tea when Kurty and I were fleeing from the German tanks. This meant that they had heeded our warning after all and had managed to man their concealed tank before the German tanks emerged from behind the hill. The Germans had not paid any attention to the stack of corn stalks, and had driven past it. Our tanker-heroes had allowed the Germans to pass by, and then had fired at the German tanks' lightly-armored rears: they first knocked out the lead and last tanks in the column, and then destroyed the rest of the tanks one by one as they had struggled to escape the trap through the deep off-road snow.

We were struck not only by the outcome of the battle between a lone, damaged Russian tank and a whole German tank company. We were amazed by the courage and stoicism of the two Russian tankers! What was it like to sit in a tank, when a dozen enemy tanks are slowly rolling past you? What would have happened if it had occurred to just one of the German tankers to fire at the suspicious heap of corn stalks by the side of the road 'just in case'? But it had all turned out well. The entire German column had been destroyed in just a few minutes. Apparently, the rest of the Russian tank crew had returned with the spare parts later. They had made the repairs to their tank, and then had turned around and driven off.

We found the village of Sacco and Vancetti almost entirely in flames. Destroyed wagons, dead oxen and dead Red Army men were lying on the road at the village entrance. Cautiously probing more deeply into the village, we found knocked-out guns, apparently those of our regiment's 2nd Artillery Battalion, and two knocked-out German tanks. We understood that the 2nd Battalion had experienced the same thing that we had endured the day before in Voroshilovka. But they had been destroyed by the very German tank company that had fired on Kurty and me, which had then found its end at the hands of the heroic tankers.

I wanted to find at least one man alive in the burning village from the 2nd Battalion, even if a wounded one. On the right side of the road there were two huts still untouched by the flames. I cautiously entered one of them. The hut was empty, but my hungry men immediately ran over to the Russian stove. There were pots in it containing hot cabbage soup and potatoes. We quickly gobbled down the food. As we were leaving, one of the soldiers took a glance behind the stove and spotted someone. In the light of my flashlight, I saw it was a sleeping Russian soldier. I was happy; now he could tell me what had happened in the village. But the soldier, once awake, was amazed to see that the neighboring buildings were burning. He turned out to be a driver from the 2nd Battalion, who had delivered the food with the sergeant major; chilled, after eating a bite of lunch, he had laid down behind the stove to rest. We returned to Sol' late that night, stopping to recover the German food found in one of the tanks on the way.

The staff house was stuffed with sleeping soldiers. I reported on the results of our reconnaissance, and together with the regiment commander we made ourselves comfortable and passed around some German wine and preserves. It wasn't possible to squeeze between the sleeping men on the floor, so I fell asleep propped up against a windowsill.

I woke up when someone strongly yanked me by the legs from the windowsill. 'What kind of stupid prank is this?!' I shouted angrily, falling to the floor, before I could even open my eyes.

My exclamation was silenced by a machine-gun burst that shattered the window above me, raining pieces of wood and glass splinters all over me. When I opened my eyes I found the room completely empty, except for my orderly Iasha Korennoi sitting on the floor. It was he who had jerked me from the windowsill just a second before it had been hit. It was already light in the room and I could see a dense cluster of bullet holes on the wall opposite the window. Iasha silently pointed at the next window. I carefully peeped out of it. A solid wall of German armor was standing on the Iama–Artemovsk road just 200 meters distant, blazing away at the village with their main guns and machine guns.

Korennoi and I scrambled out of the door in a low crawl, and all of a sudden we saw an abandoned German gun standing next to the walls of the neighboring hut with its barrel pointed directly at the road, and a neatly arranged stack of shells next to it. I couldn't restrain myself and crawled over to the gun. Iasha rushed to the breech. I aimed at the nearest tank, and an armor-piercing shell was soon loaded. A shot! The tank burst into flames. But as soon as we ducked behind the hut, a long machine-gun burst chattered. Staying concealed behind buildings, we headed towards the opposite side of the village. There was an explosion behind us. I looked back and saw the German gun we had fired flying into the air.

We did not manage to hold on to Sol'. The Germans had brought up to forty tanks to hurl at the station. In contrast, we had no tanks, and many of our guns had been knocked out. After three days of exhausting combat against superior forces, we received the order to pull out of Sol' and Sverdlovka. On the night of 5 February, we had to withdraw about 10 kilometers to Fedorovka village. Here we spent a week to take on replacements and re-equip, before being sent around Artemovsk through Slaviansk to liberate Barvenkovo, which was located south of Kharkov on the Krasnyi Liman–Slaviansk–Barvenkovo–Lozovaia rail line.

CHAPTER FIVE

Encircled!

We entered Barvenkovo on 25 February against very light resistance; the Germans had pulled out of the town before we arrived. But soon thereafter enemy armor began attacking the town from all sides. The Luftwaffe was bombing us mercilessly and going unpunished in return; we had no anti-aircraft guns. We had almost nothing left in general. In constant fighting along the 1,000-kilometer path from Stalingrad, we had lost a lot of men and equipment, while our supply units were stuck in the deep snow somewhere in the rear. Two exhausted rifle regiments and a dozen guns – that was all that we had in the town.

I, the observation platoon leader of the 1st Artillery Battalion, received an order to report to regiment headquarters: I was to pick up a dispatch and take it to the city of Izium, to army headquarters. The order arrived early on the morning of 27 February and I left the front before dawn, happy to get out from under enemy fire for a couple of days for what I thought would be an easy trip to the rear.

In Barvenkovo, the regiments' headquarters were in buildings on the far edge, away from the front lines. Staff officers composed the dispatch in my presence, while I waited. I sat with unaccustomed nonchalance on a chair in the room; with nothing to do, I idly studied the intricate patterns of frost on the window, taking an occasional glance around. This was my second time at regiment headquarters; I had visited the rear of the division once before six months earlier when I had to pick up my Party candidate's card. It was again interesting for me to observe the life of people far removed from the front line, where one didn't have to duck for cover and crawl on the ground under enemy fire. In high spirits, I shifted impatiently on the chair while waiting for the packet with the dispatch, studiously trying to avoid overhearing the staff comments as they worked on the message, and I didn't notice the anxiety on the face and in the movements of the regiment chief of staff. But all of a sudden I caught the words: 'Barvenkovo is encircled by strong enemy armor and infantry forces. We are holding the town, with no contact with higher command, and all of our attempts to establish contact with our superiors have failed ...'

I jumped up as if someone had dumped boiling water on me! My complacency instantly vanished. Encirclement and captivity were always the most frightening things to me. I now faced a suicidal attempt to break out of the encirclement in broad daylight, not a nice stroll to the rear!

'How can I make it?!' I blurted out spontaneously. The major encouraged me: 'That's why we're sending you, Lieutenant, as it is a very hard mission, but we believe in you.' I tucked the packet into my overcoat pocket and set off at a run back to my battalion to take an observer along with me.

But as I made my way back through Barvenkovo, there was an air raid! Bombers began to bomb this part of Barvenkovo mercilessly. I dived into a ditch. Something horrible was happening all around me. Forty Stukas, approaching from the rear, were diving in two columns on both sides of the street, targeting each building in turn. Roaring engines, howling sirens, chattering machine guns, whistling bombs! The ground quaked beneath me. Trees were toppling, and large bomb fragments were striking the ground with unimaginable force. The Stukas' yellow bellies flashed as they pulled out of their dives. Against the backdrop of the silvery-white snow under the rays of the sun, colorful clouds of smoke rose high into the sky – black from the explosions of bombs, red from shattered brick, and yellow from adobe and clay. Building fragments were being hurled into the sky faster than the rising dust and smoke, and burying civilians alive under the debris. Suddenly this entire red, yellow, black and white, smoking and exploding, flying and crashing, howling and roaring scene was cut like a knife by the high, piercing, soul-shaking cry of a woman. This almost inhuman wail lifted me from the roadside ditch where I had sought shelter, and caused me to look around. I could barely make out through the thick clouds of smoke the figure of a slender woman, standing upright in the chaos. Clenching her head with her hands, she stood there in a light dress, with her long hair let down. Pointing at a collapsed small house, she kept yelling the same words: 'There are children there! Children! Children!'

Her entire appearance filled me with alarm and pity, and her cry called for immediate help. I jumped up and, ignoring the dangers, threw myself at the collapsed house. I grabbed one beam that was sticking out of the rubble, and removed it with great effort. I took hold of another one, but immediately realized that in this fashion I'd never reach the children before they suffocated; there was no one around to help, because everyone was still taking cover from the air raid. I furiously went back to work, peering into the rubble again and again with hope, but finding no one. The woman had also disappeared somewhere (later I learned that she was a relative of these two children buried in the ruins; she had miraculously escaped from the collapsing building, losing an eye in the process).

Suddenly I saw a man nearby moving around in short rushes. I called to him; he stood up and I saw an unfamiliar sergeant major. With a calculating eye, he glanced up at the diving Stukas and over at the ruins, and with a dismissive wave he gestured that there was nothing to be done, and then started to dart off on his own apparently more urgent business.

'Come here!' I yelled furiously, grabbing for the holster of my pistol to sound more convincing.

The sergeant major reluctantly obeyed. He seemed about twice as old as me and with his entire demeanor, he was indicating that he was being forced to obey a teenage know-nothing lieutenant who was pursuing a completely useless venture. Together, flinging the debris to the right and left, we quickly dug through to the center of the home and found the corpses of an old man and a young woman, who was holding a dead baby in her arms.

'Had enough, Lieutenant?' the sergeant major mockingly asked.

There was nothing left for me to do but to apologize to the decent sergeant major for forcing him to risk his life for nothing. In despair, I yanked at the backboard of a bed we had uncovered in the rubble, and through the crack between it and the mattress, I suddenly saw a pair of frightened human eyes under the bed. I heard a high-pitched young boy's voice: 'Uncle [a respectful form of address to an older man], don't leave us! Save us! I'll grow up and also help you!'

My Lord! How many feelings were in this pleading cry for help and promise of future assistance! Fear and anxiety! Hope and fear of being unheard, misunderstood, or unheeded! This crying boy had been waiting to coax a potential savior. After the terrifying explosion and quaking, the tomb-like darkness and the constricted space, suddenly there had appeared a light and with it, the hope of salvation! Probably, not even the finest actor could express such a range of emotions, sufferings and hope in his voice that this dying child had uttered so quickly.

The sergeant major, realizing that there was someone alive under the bed, also dropped his recalcitrance and rushed back to help me. Together we slightly lifted the side of the debris-covered bed. We saw a child's tear-covered face emerge; he took a deep breath and then began to try to widen the gap, clearing debris as quickly as he could in his frantic urge to get out. The sergeant major and I could barely support the bed – we couldn't drop it on the boy's head, nor could we raise it any higher. But we strained not only because the bed was heavy. Under the other end of the bed, we heard the cries of other children.

'Quickly, get the plaster off the bed!' I ordered, with all my might supporting the heavy load alone.

Having finally turned the bed over, we discovered five children and a dead woman who had shielded the children with her body. On the faces of the children, distorted with fear and suffering, widely-opened eyes glittered with life. With their little fists, they hurriedly wiped the tears from their eyes, smearing tears, blood and dust over their cheeks. In the filtered light of the winter sun, the joy of resurrection immediately transformed their suffering faces from tears to smiles. But the bombing was continuing; thunderous explosions and shrieks were assaulting our eardrums, and the dust clouds were obscuring the sun and choking us. We quickly started to evacuate the children from the ruins, carefully lifting their warm, soft, and oh so fragile bodies into our arms. During the months of war, dealing with cold rough metal, our hands had become so coarse, that this delicately tender work was more stressful to us than had been the clearing of the debris.

'Uncle, there were also children under the table,' said the boy that we had rescued first. We removed four more children from under the flattened table. While I was setting the children into a crater, the sergeant major quietly slipped away; I didn't even get to know his last name. The children, dressed only in long undershirts, were sitting in a close circle, shivering with cold, shock and fear, and pulling their shirts down over their knees. As the only adult around, I was responsible for their lives and couldn't leave them. I looked around, but the street was empty. I still had a dispatch in my pocket to deliver, and I'd been delayed quite a bit. Luckily, I spotted the head of an elderly man poking up from a cellar. 'Grandpa,' I begged, 'please take the children, I don't have the time.'

I didn't know what became of the children. Almost twenty years after the war, I managed to locate eight of them. In 1963 on my way to a vacation in the south, I learned I would be passing through Barvenkovo, but I didn't really give a thought to stopping; the train would be arriving in Barvenkovo at 6:00 AM, and I didn't want to disturb anyone at such an early hour. But I decided to inform the town of my transit anyway. The morning we reached Barvenkovo, I stepped up to the door. There was already a man there, preparing to get off, and he commented, 'They're welcoming someone here. There's a band playing and a crowd of people.'

I peered over his back out at the platform and said, 'Yes, someone's being welcomed.' The stop in Barvenkovo was only for two minutes. The man exited the train, while I kept standing in the door. I saw people running towards my car from every direction, shouting 'Petr Alekseevich! Petr Alekseevich!'

My name?! Then I understood this was all for me. They delayed the train, and without any discussions I was pulled off the train together with my things. Unfamiliar men and women ran up to me from different directions with tears in their eyes in order to embrace me – they were my godchildren!

But let's return to the past. I, a 20-year-old lieutenant, had been handed a dispatch and instructed to make my way out of the encirclement and to take it to army headquarters. After the air raid, which delayed me about forty minutes, I finally made it back to my unit on the front lines. But there the penny-pinching battalion commander Major Gordienko refused to give me either an observer or a horse.

'You have to understand,' the Major explained, 'you're going to a likely death, and you have no choice; this is an order. Clearly, you yourself may die, but why waste horses? I would also hate to waste a scout; they're needed here as well. Take the driver Ahmet. All of his horses have been killed, so we can do without him.' The Major pointed at an old driver, who was temporarily serving as his orderly. Then he concluded, 'You can't prance around on horses all the time. This time, you'll walk.'

So Ahmet and I set off along our lines to search for a place where it might be possible to slip past the Germans in our rear. The sun was blinding, and pristine snow stretched from our trenches to some German tanks that were slowly prowling about a kilometer outside the town, firing at our positions and buildings from time to time.

'Why aren't our guns firing at them?' the puzzled Ahmet asked me as he crawled up to my position. 'What are we supposed to hit them with? We're cut off, and our crews are conserving ammunition in case of a German attack. We'll also have to break out,' I explained.

But what could we do now? We couldn't wait for nightfall. It would be suicidal even to crawl, much less run, without white camouflage cloaks – the Germans would spot us and cut us down immediately. There was only just one place, where there was a gap of about 800 meters in the line of German tanks, because of a frozen lake that was shining like a mirror in the bright sunlight. We decided to dash across this patch of ice into the deep snow beyond it, as this seemed our only possibility to get past the tanks.

Hiding in the snow, we crawled on our bellies to the lake. The Germans didn't spot us. We now only had the lake to cross.

'Ahmet,' I told the driver strictly, 'you'll stick with me, and don't fall behind. When I get down, you get down. When I get up, you get up.' I was lying there thinking that we could probably cross the frozen lake in three rushes, but somehow we had to be clever and deceive the German tankers.

Overcoming our anxiety, just as if we were about to plunge into cold water, we jumped up and started to run across the ice as fast as we could. The Germans spotted us immediately and the tanks on the right and left opened fire from their main guns. The angry reports of shots rang out, and their loud echo struck our ears, and pushed our hearts into our throats. The rounds exploded quite nearby, deafening us and sending out thousands of splinters. The shell craters destroyed the virgin beauty of the ice. We dropped, and covered with ice dust, we lay there like saints – not a single splinter struck us. Only our ears were ringing and our hearts were pumping like crazy.

For some time the Germans scrutinized us, trying to decide whether or not they had killed us. But we lay there motionlessly, in order to convince them that we were dead. Once they became convinced of this, we would only have to wait a little longer. When they got tired of looking at us and became distracted by something else, we would jump up and make another rush.

Some fifteen minutes later we sprang up and ran forward again, until the tanks managed to point their main guns at us again. As an artilleryman, I knew exactly what the German gunlayers were doing – and we dropped to the ice at just the right moment. As soon as we hit the ground, shots rang out again. This was the scariest time! Explosions, the hiss of splinters, clouds of smoke and ice dust enveloped us … And again we were safe and sound. The Germans' aim had led us by a bit too much; dropping when we did, the rounds exploded 7 meters in front of us, and all the fragments had flown over us.

After raging for some time, the Germans calmed down. We had one last rush to reach the saving snow. But this time the Germans wouldn't take their eyes from us, and in order to convince them that we were dead we would have to lie motionless for even longer. All sorts of things were running through my mind, all sorts of scenarios … then a sudden thought struck me, shaking me out of my state of relative calm: what if they thought to come and search us, the 'dead'?! We'd have no choice but to fight, and then no one would deliver the dispatch to the army headquarters.

The Germans, however, were apparently too lazy or didn't want to take any chances, and we lay motionless there until we were frozen to the bones. And now the last rush! But what's this?! We're running and the Germans aren't firing! Did they not see us or did they forget about us? I was praying on the run to either the Germans or to God, 'But wait just a minute longer, until we reach the snow!' Then suddenly another terrible thought: they wanted to take us alive! Likely they were already out there somewhere in the snow, crawling to intercept us and to take us prisoner!

I scanned the snowy field in front of us, but I didn't see anything suspicious. I raised my eyes a little higher and saw a German aircraft flying towards us. It was approaching quickly, and I could already see the ominous black crosses on its wings. Would it really bomb us?! No, the pilot wouldn't waste a bomb on two men. But we were trying to break through the encirclement, so we had to be messengers. However, it was flying from our rear area; it must have already dropped all of its bombs … It's already too close to us, too late to drop its bombs. The bomb would fall far behind us. As soon as these calming thoughts flashed through my mind, I saw what looked like a log detach from the aircraft. It was a bomb! I grabbed Ahmet's hand and we ran forward as fast as our feet could carry us, in order to put as much distance as possible between us and where the bomb would land. But then my good Ahmet slipped and fell, grabbing me by the overcoat, and together we tumbled onto the wind-polished ice. The bomb was now close; its whistling sound had passed and it was no longer visible. At some moment, with bitter anger I thought of my executioner – the battalion commander. He hadn't given me horses and, what's worse, he didn't let my trusted observer Iasha Korennoi accompany me – Korennoi wouldn't have slipped and we would have outrun our death! While the clumsy Ahmet and I tried to disentangle from each other and stand up to run, the bomb exploded! But not behind us, as I had assumed, thinking that the German was late in releasing his bomb – but 10 meters in front of us! The earth shook and countless splinters hummed over our heads. We were so close to the bomb that we were in the dead angle of the explosion. Not a single fragment hit us. I was amazed by the marksmanship of the German pilot: he had accurately accounted for his own speed and our speed at a run. If we had not fallen, we would have been hit.

Ahmet slipped at just the right moment! So we were saved from death by the stingy and cold-hearted Gordienko, who didn't give me a good escort. If the commander had not been so miserly, Iasha and I would have run straight into the bomb explosion, and we would have both been killed. I suppose evil can also be good sometimes.

Not wasting a second, we again sprang up, bypassed the bomb crater that was still filled with smoke and threw ourselves into deep snow. We did it!

The most dangerous part of our journey was behind us. Fortune had smiled on us and we had survived. But we had to move on as quickly as possible. We crawled through deep snow to a nearby pile of hay. After resting there, we walked on upright. We bypassed villages in order to avoid meeting Germans.

That evening, completely exhausted, we entered a small village. There we found the division's field bakery, which supplied all the units and elements of the division with bread. Famished, we were delighted that we could get hold of a loaf of bread and quench our hunger. But the fat Lieutenant Bukreev, chief of the field bakery, checked our papers and demanded to see our food ration cards. But how could he find one on us? We weren't on a business trip, but were running with a dispatch from the front lines! Despite all our entreaties, and our efforts to convince him that German tanks would soon appear in the village, he refused to give us any bread. Angered, we prayed to God that this fat supply officer would end up in the paws of the Germans together with his bread.

After the war at a veterans' gathering, Captain Bukreev, who had become quite obese since the war, approached me to give me a friendly embrace as an old fellow soldier. I recalled that incident with the bread (which was the only time we met in the war, as he was always far in the rear, while I was at the front), and I could barely restrain myself from slugging him in the face. Especially after a few of the former staff officers had told me that over the three years of the war, Bukreev had been baking pastries for the top brass and had impregnated four of the bakery's girls, promising to marry each one of them after the war.

After the blunt refusal in the bakery of our own division, we walked on to the next village. We entered a hut and tearfully requested something to eat. A merciful old lady shared all she had with us, boiled us potatoes and together we had dinner.

For the rest of the night, we walked. The next morning, having walked over 20 kilometers, we entered a village on the right bank of the Donets, almost directly across the river from Izium. There we found the artillery headquarters of our division. The commander of the division's artillery, Colonel Chubakov, was happy at our arrival, immediately passed along the dispatch to the army headquarters, and allowed me to stay together with his staff.

That was the end of my much-desired 'easy walk' to the rear. I had managed to make it out of the encirclement in broad daylight with a message and to deliver it according to my orders. Our regiments, surrounded in Barvenkovo, received an order to break out. They did so the next night, fighting their way through the ring of Germans. Not without losses, of course, but that's war.

From Barvenkovo we retreated to Izium, and then fell back to the Donets River. Here, we constructed defensive positions and held this line from March to July 1943, until the battle of Kursk.

CHAPTER SIX

Kursk

In June 1943, I was the commander of a howitzer battery, supporting a rifle battalion with our fire. My observation post on the edge of a small grove was next to the battalion's command post. In front, 20 meters below my post, ran our first line of trenches; further on was no-man's-land, the Donets River, and on a high forested hill on the river's opposite bank – the Germans.

Captain Kochelaba, the assistant chief of staff of our artillery regiment, arrived to check whether I was indeed positioned where I had said I was. Such lack of trust from the regimental staff was offensive to me, but such checks were necessary. To our shame, some cowardly regular officers set up their observation posts somewhere in the rear for the sake of their own safety. Sometimes they set up in the backyards of houses, where they would be out of sight of the Germans, or sometimes even in cellars. But they were reporting that they were in the front line itself. It was just these dapper liars who exaggerated German strength in order to get more reinforcements. It was they who exaggerated their victories. The headquarters staff didn't believe them even before receiving the reports and made necessary corrections to them, because staff members themselves were guilty of similar sins in the reports to their superiors, especially in recommendations for decorations. But it was the honest officers who suffered from this old army disease. The honest officers were mostly the reserve officers, former students from universities and high schools, who hadn't passed through the harmful school of eyewashing. Mainly it was the honest officers who suffered from all this chicanery.

In addition to checking on our location, Kochelaba brought an order from battalion commander Gordienko to snatch a prisoner. I knew well that the division's headquarters had been trying vainly for two months to obtain a prisoner, in order to reveal the strength of the enemy in front of us. Scouts had been passing through my observation post every night. Our section of the front drew the scouts because a meadow with intervals of thick scrub brush stretched between our position and the river, while just barren expanses of sand stretched out towards the river from neighboring sectors. The bushes were of no help either, though, as the Germans used them to set up perfect ambush positions. Twenty-two groups of scouts, each ten to twelve men strong, had passed through my observation post in the past two months, with the same result: virtual destruction of the entire group. Germans were lying in wait for them in the bushes, and then shooting them down and taking them prisoners. Only rarely would a group of two or three survivors return, bringing back a severely wounded comrade on a rain cape.

It was not our job to snatch prisoners; we had other tasks, and we lacked the necessary training for such work. But our battalion commander Major Gordienko had recalled how successful we were in our prisoner snatch mission at Rzhev, while forgetting of course that the two groups that had gone out before us back then had been wiped out to a man. Placing hopes on our success on this occasion as well, he decided to distinguish himself again and called for another snatch operation. Of course, I was ordered to execute the mission, since I had previously been the chief of the battalion's observers. After a year of fighting, only three of the participants of that operation at Rzhev remained: two observers and I, their commander. It was the three of us that Gordienko was counting upon.

When I announced to my observers that we had been ordered to snatch a prisoner, the guys blanched. We all regarded this order as a death sentence, but no one uttered a word against it. Everyone knew that it was impossible to snatch a prisoner and it was also not possible to make it back alive. But each one of us understood: a talking prisoner was vitally important.

We started to look for a place to launch our manhunt. On the right flank of our division at the village of Khotomlia, the Donets made a wide loop and swung deeply into a German-controlled forest. At nearly the same point, a tributary flowed into the Donets from the east, from our side of the river. Between the mouth of the tributary and the bend in the river, a large swamp had been formed, about 2 kilometers wide, which was split in half by a slough. At the top of the loop in the river, the currents had created a wide island. An idea struck us: What if we tried to make our way across the swamp, the slough and the island, and there, deep in the German rear, swam across the Donets right under the noses of the Germans? Far from the front lines, the Germans were probably less vigilant.

I ordered the sergeant to find a boat and prepare a group of ten men for the mission. Together with Korennoi, who had been with me on that snatch mission back at Rzhev, I decided once the sun set to make our way across to that precious island and from its banks monitor the Germans on the other side of the river.

Once it grew dark, we picked up an infantry lieutenant and several infantrymen for escort and moved out. We crossed our barbed-wire fence and minefield, advanced about another couple hundred meters through no-man's-land in the direction of the swamp, and reached an outpost: here, in tall grass, a machine-gun nest with a phone line had been concealed. The infantry lieutenant and his men remained here, while Iasha and I eased our way further into the unknown, towards the swamp, dropping at every sudden flare of an illumination round. We had to determine if the swamp was passable, whether or not Germans were on the island, and assess the river channel. It turned out that the swamp was completely overgrown with thick grass, split only by the shallow water and reeds of the slough. The dense grass, deep mud and clumps of duckweed slowed us down. When a flare burst into light, we ducked under the water. The water was first knee-deep, then waist-deep and in some places up to our chins. In order not to leave a trail behind us – the Germans would have noticed it immediately the next morning among the undisturbed grass – we zigzagged sharply to the left and right. Although this lengthened our path, it also ensured that the grass and reeds obscured the trace we were leaving behind as we moved.

Finally we stepped onto the firm ground of the island. We camouflaged ourselves on our bank of the river channel, now 2 kilometers from our own lines and in the German rear. We listened closely and peered into the darkness of the opposite bank. There was dead silence. No hum of activity, no sounds, and no flickers of campfires. It had to mean that the opposite bank was unguarded. At dawn we saw the opposite bank: it was steep and forested. Parallel to the river bank and about 50 meters away from it stretched a barbed-wire fence. Through binoculars, I could spot tripwires in the area between the barbed wire and the river, which meant it was mined. The emptiness of the far bank made me both happy and anxious: where were the Germans? We waited. Just after sunrise, in the bushes among the trees we caught the flash of two white hats. The German cooks, with submachine-guns dangling from their necks and buckets in their hands, made their way through passages in the barbed wire and minefield and noisily ran down to the water. They cautiously and diligently took a look around, and examined our bank with particular thoroughness to make sure there were no Russians there. Once satisfied, they tossed several hand grenades into the water, gathered up the stunned fish, filled their buckets with water and headed back. These were the little dears we'd be pinching tomorrow, Korennoi and I happily thought.

Not a single soul appeared on the far shore for the rest of the day. Only from time to time did some muffled voices carry to us from the depths of the woods beyond the river. As darkness fell, we set off on our journey back. When we got back to our trenches, we found ten men ready with a boat and full gear. We hoisted the boat onto our shoulders and, without wasting a second, we traced our path back to the island.

Again, water, grass, and zigzagging. We barely managed to drag the boat up to the slough, as we no longer had any strength to carry it on our shoulders.

Korennoi got into the boat and started to row it down the slough to the main channel of the river, telling us to meet him with the boat at the spot where we'd been sitting that day to observe the German side of the river. I led the rest of the team to the location on the island – but Iasha and the boat weren't there! Had the Germans caught him? Terrible anxiety seized my heart. We felt sorry for Iasha, but also knew that the operation was over without the boat. But a moment later, we calmed down when Korennoi's boat slid into the grass along the bank.

I quickly reviewed the actions that the men should take in different possible situations. I left a support group on our bank, ordering them immediately to dig a trench in the bushes, and then with the capture group I crossed the river to the other bank. Beforehand we had tied a long German steel cable to the stern of the boat, and when we reached the German bank, I attached another long cable to the bow. At my signal, the support group pulled the boat back to the island using the cable attached to the stern, while I played out the cable attached to the bow. I then placed the end of the cable under the water to conceal it. Once on the other shore, the support group hid the boat in the tall grass. The German bank was sandy and completely barren, so there was no place to hide a boat.

We settled into the bushes close to the water, next to the path that the cooks had taken. With the sunrise, we waited for the cooks to appear. We waited and waited. The morning passed and was closing on lunch-time, but there was no sign of the Germans. Upset, chewed up by mosquitoes, hungry, and in foul spirits, we lost hope. Were they really not going to show at all? In this case with the coming of darkness, we would have to crawl through the German minefield and over the barbed wire, search for a dugout and seal it off – and this would be a very risky proposition, from which we might not return and never even reach a German to capture.

Our entire plan of operations had been based exclusively on the appearance of the Germans on the river bank and that they would enter the water. Our roles had been distributed accordingly: my mate and I were to kill the German on the left, the powerful Zakharenko and another scout were to capture the German on the right, the fifth man would cover the path down to the river with his submachine-gun, while the sixth man would locate the cable and haul the boat back to our bank.

We had completely given up on the appearance of the German cooks, when suddenly above us we heard the clink of empty jerrycans. What a joy – they were coming! Then worry: how would everything turn out? We had planned to capture them at dawn, when everyone was still asleep, but here we were now in the afternoon and all the Germans were up and about, while our guys on the opposite bank likely weren't waiting for us, expecting that we had postponed the operation until nightfall. We looked up: two Germans were standing by the barbed wire. They were young blond men in black uniforms without helmets, with submachine-guns hanging from their necks and jerrycans in their hands. These were no cooks – they were tankers! They seemed struck by the beauty of the verdant meadow across the river, illuminated by the setting sun. But time was passing! The Germans were lost in admiration, while we were tense with anticipation, and I almost wanted to cry out: 'What are you standing around for, get down to the river!' Finally, the Germans ran past us at a trot. They waded into the river, leaned over, and lowered the empty jerrycans into the river, before lifting their heads and examining our bank of the river carefully. Bubbling and splashing, the jerrycans slowly began to fill. I silently lifted and then sharply dropped my right hand – the signal to spring into action. In two bounds I was at the left-hand German and had already raised my knife to strike him, when the German abruptly stepped away from the bank, tossed aside the canisters, grabbed for his submachine-gun and started to turn to face me. Our rapid approach across the sand had been silent; the German could hardly have heard it, but more likely some instinct or intuition had kicked into gear. Using my momentum, I piled onto his back and grabbed his weapon with my left hand, while my right hand began to stab repeatedly at his chest. Shifting his submachine-gun around to his front, the German parried my blows, while trying to turn his weapon on me at the same time. Finally I delivered the decisive strike and the German went limp. At that moment the German on the right began to howl as if he'd been sliced, and indeed he had been. I handed my German over to my partner, who to this point had been doing nothing behind my back, and told him to finish the German off and to search his pockets, while I rushed over to Zakharenko to keep him from killing the intended prisoner! I rolled up my side cap and stuck it into the Nazi's mouth, and he fell silent. It turned out that Zakharenko, having pounced on the prisoner, had wanted to shove a piece of cloth into his mouth, but couldn't get it out of his pocket. So he had instead grabbed a handful of sand and stones and had tried to shove that into the German's mouth. The German had practically bitten off Zakharenko's thumb in the process and had violently kicked Zakharenko with his boot. Just a piece of bone was left of Zakharenko's thumb. Wild with the intense pain, the scout had planted his knife into the German's side, which is when the German started to howl.

We heard cries of alarm from above us. Firing on the move, Germans were already running through the forest in our direction. Our man responsible for the boat couldn't find the end of the cable in the water, panicked, and swam across the river to our side, although later he told us that he had gone to get the boat. We made so many mistakes due to our lack of professional training! I ran a little deeper into the water, located the cable and hauled the boat back to our bank. We tossed the wounded German on his back into the boat, I jumped on top of him and the guys on the other bank started to pull us through the water. Five of the scouts, already in the river, grabbed onto the sides of the boat. The cable was as tight as a string! It seemed about to snap! The five men hanging onto the sides of the boat increased its resistance many times over. I watched the vibrating cable with unimaginable fear, expecting it to break at any second, and already picturing how the current would sweep us under the fire from German bunkers ... but the cable held. As soon as the scouts could stand up in the water, they started pushing the boat towards the bank. Finally, hustling our prisoner along, we ran over to the prepared trench. I was calming the guys, bandaging the German, but thinking to myself with alarm: now the Germans would grab the boat that we had left, cross the river with some reinforcements, engage us in combat and we would remain on this island forever together with the prisoner.

The Germans opened fire at our bank with every available weapon. We waited out this furious barrage in the trench. Artillery shells and mortar rounds exploded nearby, but we were unharmed, sheltered by the deep trench. After some minutes the Germans slowly shifted their wall of fire into the swamp, assuming we were now crawling through the tall grass of the swamp towards our lines. We sat a bit longer in the trench, and then moved out at a crawl through the tall grass at a respectful distance behind the walking barrage. Again we zigzagged in our movement and it was a long, hard journey through the swamp until we reached our lines.

We dropped into our trench barely alive; it was already dark. The entire division quickly learned about our success through the phone network and celebrated, knowing how costly the previous attempts to snatch a prisoner had been. Finally, we had one in our trench! All the top brass, right up to the army headquarters, were also happy. An interpreter, sent to us by the division commander beforehand, was waiting for us in the dugout. He immediately began to interrogate the prisoner; everyone was afraid that the wounded man might die. The Nazi, in the hope of medical assistance and that his life would be spared, quickly spilled the truth: he was part of the *Grossdeutschland* Panzer Division, just arrived from France.

By morning we, together with the German, were at division headquarters. Division commander Colonel Fadeev embraced each one of us and promised to decorate us. We were happy like little children – let's paint the town red, fellows! We made camp in a clearing next to the division commander's dugout; we warmed ourselves with a little jogging, while all our wet uniforms were drying on bushes. All of a sudden the Colonel called for me again. Well, I thought, I was going to receive a bit more praise. Happy, clad only in my underwear, I ran back into the division commander's dugout. I immediately became alert to the worried expression on the Colonel's face.

'The prisoner didn't have any papers on him,' Fadeev said sadly; 'army headquarters is demanding another prisoner to verify what this one's saying. No one can do this except for you, so I want a new prisoner in my dugout within forty-eight hours.'

I was dumbfounded! Where could I get a second prisoner?! I couldn't use the old route, and there were no other suitable approaches! How could I break this news to the guys?! It was a death sentence! But there was nothing to be done about it, and I headed back to the scouts.

They also received the shocking news with great sorrow. At first all my guys couldn't say anything, and a deathly silence descended on us. But we couldn't do anything. This was our destiny.

'Let's not arrange our funeral prematurely,' I addressed my friends. 'Let's think how we can carry this order out.'

'The second German, the one that we killed, did he not have a single piece of paper in his pockets?' Korennoi asked my partner. Everyone knew that I had given him the job to search the pockets of our victim after finishing him off.

At first the scout swore that there had been nothing in the German's pockets, but when his friends pressed him, he confessed: 'There was one little paper, but I'm afraid it washed out of my pocket when we were crossing the swamp.'

'Perhaps it fell out instead when you were shaking your clothes to dry them?' his comrades continued to press.

We lined up, dropped to our knees and began to search the grass in the clearing, looking for the paper. We studied every single blade of grass – and found nothing. Then one of us noticed a wrinkled piece of paper beneath the bushes where we were drying our camouflage cloaks. The paper had already dried out in the sun. The guys carefully laid it into my open hands, and holding my breath, as if I was approaching a great saint, I carefully took the paper to the Colonel.

The translator carefully pressed out the piece of paper and began to study it carefully. It seemed to me that he was studying it for a whole eternity. I wasn't looking at the piece of paper, but at the translator's face: what would it reveal now, ten deaths or ten lives? Then suddenly the face of the translator began slowly to brighten. His eyes opened wide, and he slowly said: 'This is a postal receipt. The German was sending a parcel home. I think I still can see the field post number on it.'

'Decipher it!' we shouted in almost one voice together with the Colonel.

Finally, the translator announced the field post number. It was immediately reported to army headquarters. Now I began to wait for the return call from the headquarters with a palpitating heart.

Finally a call came. The division commander picked up the receiver.

'The field post of *Grossdeutschland*?' he asked; the face of the Colonel relaxed into a smile, and the translator and we understood that our prisoner had yielded accurate information about his unit.

When the Colonel told me that a second prisoner wouldn't be necessary, I almost jumped up to the ceiling and scurried back to my men. Likely, I gave them the happiest piece of news that each one of them had ever heard in his life. We felt as if we'd been born again, and we thanked God for the scrap of paper that saved our lives.

We'd been extremely lucky! A piece of paper saved at least ten lives.

With the start of the Kursk offensive, the Germans tried to attack our sector as well. But we firmly held our lines.

On 9 August we forced a crossing of the Donets and seized a bridgehead on the German-held bank. But the German fortifications were so strong, and their resistance so stubborn, that we only overcame them with unbelievable difficulties. The intensity of the fighting was like it had been at Rzhev. We suffered enormous losses. In the first week of savage fighting alone, the division lost up to 70 per cent of its men – about 2,000 killed and over 4,000 wounded. German armor with air support constantly counter-attacked us. While advancing, we constantly had to stop and repel enemy attacks.

Somewhere about halfway to Kharkov, the battery and the entire division took on replacements and refitted. We ground slowly forward, and then there it was, the city of Kharkov. We finally captured it on 23 August. The Battle of Kursk was over and the Germans had been beaten. Orel, Belgorod and Kharkov were liberated. But our division received orders to press on to the south.

CHAPTER SEVEN

On the Heels of the Enemy

Bled white after the battle for Kharkov, our division fought its way into the Ukraine. Our task was not to allow the enemy to dig in, and to shove the enemy as far as possible to the south. The Germans fell back from village to village, from one forested belt to the next, and every time we had to take each village and each strip of woods with fighting! They were hunkered down with their machine guns in well-built trenches, firing at the attackers, while we were running into their machine guns across flat stubble fields. But our main problem was the lack of shells. And how could I pry the Germans out of their next position without ammunition? My howitzer battery was supporting Captain Abaev's rifle battalion, which meant that I was in the attacking line all the time, and in step as we advanced, the guns of my battery had to be brought up in turn by section to new firing positions behind the infantry.

One day I was running with my signalman next to the battalion commander in the attacking line of infantry as we pursued retreating Germans through a field of harvested hay. It was in the last days of August 1943, the fields were sunny and it was warm; wherever you looked, golden stubble fields stretched into the distance, with tall, fresh haystacks scattered here and there. The infantry were running around the stacks, while Abaev and I climbed each one of them to have a better view of the battlefield. We watched, as the German infantry entered a forest belt. Hardly had our soldiers (and only around fifty of them remained in the battalion) approached to within about 200 meters of this strip of woods, when suddenly a dense black line of Germans – about 200 men – emerged from the woods to meet them! The enemy was counter-attacking with fresh forces! Our men were stunned and flopped to the ground. The Germans, firing on the move, advanced quickly, as enemy machine guns opened up on us from the flanks.

Our infantrymen were rattled by the advancing horde of Germans. At first, we could see men crawling away one by one to escape the Germans, but then all of our infantry rose to their feet and fled in retreat. I called in fire from my battery on the attacking German line, and pinned it down. Abaev jumped off the haystack and ran towards his fleeing men with a drawn pistol, cursing and firing over their heads. But he couldn't halt his fleeing battalion. Just at that critical moment of the battle, I suddenly lost connection with my battery! Apparently the field wire had been severed, and I sent my only signalman to find the break and repair it. I remained helplessly on the pile of hay with the phone receiver pressed to my ear, and watched what was going on with a quaking heart. The Germans, seeing that my artillery fire had ceased, rose from the ground and resumed the pursuit of our small battalion. Then soon not only our retreating infantrymen were running past my perch on the haystack, but Germans as well – and now I was in the German rear with still no communications! I was helpless. Soon, the line of German infantry was at least 500 meters behind me! What could I do?! There was supposed to be another signalman running from the firing positions to meet my signalman to splice the line, and judging by the elapsed time, they should have encountered each other a long time ago! What had happened?! Why was there no connection?! Not only could I end up as a German prisoner, but the German infantry might also storm our battery and capture the guns!

I turned around and continued to watch as the dense line of damned German infantry receded into our rear. I needed a connection so badly, in order to stop the Germans with my fire! All of a sudden there was a crackling sound in my ear, and I caught the deep bass voice of Mineev: '"Kolomna", can you hear me?'

'Sight setting two–zero, battery, fire!' I shouted in response.

I dropped several rounds in front of the German line and brought it to a halt. Then I opened rapid fire on their position. First they started to come back slowly, but then the Germans began to flee back towards the forested belt. I waited as they ran past my haystack onto the open stubble field – and then I really let them have it proper! My rounds were exploding in the very midst of the fleeing Germans! Fewer and fewer men were left standing. As I was finishing off the last groups of retreating Fritzes, an exhausted Abaev climbed up on my haystack. His battalion had resumed pursuit of the retreating Germans. He was squealing with joy as he watched the slaughter of the Nazis.

Soon there were no more targets. Once I had calmed myself down, I wanted to find out why the phone line had failed us in the battle.

'Why did we lose the connection?' I asked over the telephone in an unusually demanding voice of Sergeant Mineev, who was the signals squad leader of my battery. The Sergeant was with the guns behind a hill about 2 kilometers in my rear, while I was at the forward observation post.

'A shell exploded beneath me,' the Sergeant complained without explaining. 'That's why there'd been no connection, Comrade Senior Lieutenant.'

To any other sergeant I would have said angrily, 'You're lying, Sergeant!' The ten-minute gap in communications at the most critical point in the battle had cost us dearly up at the front; I couldn't fire upon the Germans with my battery, our infantry had taken casualties as they had retreated under the pressure of superior enemy forces, and I had almost ended up as a German prisoner! But I kept my cool with Sergeant Mineev and replied, 'Are you out of your mind, Kapitonych (Mineev's middle name, which I often used to address him)?! How could a shell explode beneath you, and yet you're talking with me now?'

'Just so, Comrade Senior Lieutenant, a round blew up beneath me. If you don't believe me, come take a look for yourself.' There was so much injury, bitterness and disappointment in the Sergeant's voice over the fact that a close friend for some reason didn't believe him, that I felt sorry for the Sergeant.

I had developed very warm and friendly relations with Sergeant Mineev almost two years ago, when our division had been forming up in Kolomna. Mineev was about forty-five years old – old enough to be my father. He was of average height, strongly-built and agile; his hair, eyes and the stubble on his face were black as pitch, while his voice was calm and deep. He was a stable, older man with plenty of life experience, caring and businesslike, a man upon whom one could rely. He immediately attracted my attention. He was also a good signals squad leader; communications under his command ran like clockwork: any second of the day and night I could call in battery fire just where I needed it.

I tried my best to protect this good man in battles, because he had four children in Penza. So I constantly kept him with the guns, far behind the front lines, where at least he wouldn't be exposed to small-arms fire. I only brought younger men along with me to the front. I addressed him only as Ivan Kapitonych, or simply Kapitonych. He treated me like a father would. Sometimes I would return to the battery from the front for an hour or two, wet, hungry and tired, and he would attentively dry my uniforms and boots, treat me to some tea, and be happy to see me safe and sound out from under the bullets, shellfire and foul weather.

But what he had just told me was beyond comprehension. My bewilderment only grew. 'Absolutely, I'll come have a look,' was my dry and formal reply to the Sergeant.

In the meantime, our infantry had reached the belt of woods and had started digging in on the far side of it, as the enemy had set up defenses in the next wooded strip and had opened a heavy fire.

Seeing that another attack by our guys or the Germans seemed unlikely for the rest of the day, I decided to run back to the battery and see what had happened there. I left the signalman Shtansky in the woods next to Abaev. If the Germans made another move, Abaev would summon me over the telephone. The gun crews happily greeted me, as usual: 'The Senior Lieutenant is here!'

'Safe and sound...!'

I walked over to the Number 1 gun, behind which Mineev would normally be located. Happy to see me, he rose to his feet and started to smile, but as he recalled my demanding tone over the phone, he lowered his head.

'So, show me where the round exploded,' I sternly asked the guilty Sergeant without even a greeting.

'I'm standing on the very spot where it threw me. Come over here, and I'll show you where I was sitting when the shell blew up underneath me.'

I saw in the grass a virtually vertical hole about the diameter of a bucket. Splinters from the shell were sticking out all around the perimeter of the hole.

'Right here, above this very hole, I was sitting, passing your orders on to the senior battery officer...'

He continued to explain, but I already understood everything. A round had burrowed deeply into the ground 1 meter away from him and then exploded directly underneath him. The layer of earth had saved him from death, but the blast had thrown him some 6 meters away. But Ivan Kapitonych [Mineev] continued his story:

> I listened as the sight setting kept decreasing, so I understood that the Germans were attacking. Suddenly I felt a heavy impact quite nearby, the ground quaked, and before I knew what was happening, I was flying through the air. I sensed a sharp pain in my head and back. When I regained my senses, I saw the receiver in my hand with a piece of cable dangling from it. I crawled back here, to the crater, where I found the phone set with the severed cable. What could I do? The spare sets had not yet been brought up from our prior position. I knew that there was a battle going on, and I had to splice the cable quickly, but instead of colored wires inside the cable, there were only white wires! I didn't know which wires to connect! While I tested all the combinations, my head was spinning and I hadn't yet recovered from the blast, while time kept running...

It was well that Kapitonych survived; even better that he had also managed to re-establish communications, so we could drive the Germans back to their start line. Otherwise I would have stayed in the German rear – as a prisoner or dead.

'You're an educated young man, with experience at the front, and even you didn't believe me,' the Sergeant sadly said. 'Who'll believe me at home, if I ever get back there alive?'

Ivan Kapitonych did survive the war. Neither the Germans nor the Japanese managed to kill him. I handed him his discharge papers in Mongolia in

November 1945, and saw him off to Penza.

I recalled Mineev and his artillery round adventure as late as in 1960. I wrote to the Penza *Pravda* newspaper and wanted to find the old Sergeant. Some soulless bureaucrat only replied: 'There must have been many cases like that in the war.' What could I say?

A half-second saves two lives

The division continued to attack to the south. We captured Borki Station after heavy fighting. The small village of Sidory lay in front of us – with just a small cluster of ten houses, we thought it would be a piece of cake. But it turned out to be a well-fortified German strongpoint! It fell to us after incredible difficulties. The three days of bloody fighting here placed the village on the same level with Rzhev, Sol', the Dnestr River, Belgrade, Vienna and Prague – other places where our division took especially heavy casualties.

My battery was continuing to support Abaev's battalion. The howitzers were 2 kilometers in the rear behind a grove, while my observation post was just to the right of the village, on the sandy edge of a pine grove, next to Abaev's command post. His infantry companies were dug in some 100 meters in front of us. The 1st Rifle Company was led by Lieutenant Spartak Beglov. In the 1980s, he would become a famous television narrator, but on that day, 5 September 1943, he was badly wounded.

The Nazis not only stubbornly defended their positions, but also often counter-attacked with tanks and infantry, so each sunrise I was already sitting at my stereoscope, looking for any changes in the Germans' positions that had occurred overnight. In the sandy soil, we only dug our trench waist-deep, like the infantry. There was a small pine tree about a half meter in front of our trench, and we had bolted the stereoscope to it. Next to me on the breastwork of our trench with a phone set was the battery's youngest signalman, Volodia Shtansky. We were well camouflaged with pine tree branches; only the tip of my scope barely rose above the foliage. The stereoscope had a tenfold magnification, so the German positions 500 meters away looked as if they were just 50 meters away. The sun was rising on my left; its bright rays were getting under the glare shields of the stereoscope's lenses, frustrating my observation. Suddenly I saw the turrets of German tanks emerging from behind a knoll in the rear of the German trench. They quickly grew in size, revealing more and more details of the steel monsters. The gun barrels were now visible, and I could see they had muzzle brakes – they were medium or heavy tanks!

'To your positions!' My order flew to the battery over the phone. 'At the enemy tanks, sight setting ... battery-y-y, ten rounds, rapid fire. Fire!'

The tanks were moving quickly and were approaching their infantry's trench line. I had accurately calculated the speed of German tanks and the amount of time my rounds would be in the air. The signalman reported: 'Shot!' which meant that the rounds were already on the way. There were over twenty tanks. As soon as they reached the trench, my rounds rained down on them. The steel armada disappeared in the smoke of explosions and clouds of fine sand particles. The tanks were blinded. They couldn't see anything in front, where to go or where to fire. So they turned back. When the smoke and dust cleared, the empty field was full of craters and two tanks were burning brightly. The heavy 25kg howitzer shells had done their work.

But the German tankers didn't give up. They had an order to bury our infantry alive in the sand. So having regrouped behind the hill, they headed towards us again through a ravine on the right. But our fire could reach them there as well! Tall fountains of earth shot into the sky among the tanks, again covering the whole formation with dust and smoke. The tanks again retreated behind the hill. This time they were lucky – we hadn't hit a single tank. We were delivering indirect fire, after all.

As the tanks were pulling back for the second time, I watched as one of them separated from the formation and headed far to my left. A malingerer, I thought with disgust; the rest of his comrades were fighting and he was running away. For a third time I called in fire on the tanks as they emerged from behind the knoll, and again I chased them back behind it. But just in case, from time to time I glanced over at the 'malingerer'. One time when I sharply turned the stereoscope to the left and focused on the 'malingerer', I saw the turret and gun barrel quickly sweeping our trench line back and forth, pausing here and there as if searching for something. 'What was he looking for?' I thought. Then I immediately realized that this was no malingerer, but an ace hunter, whose task it was in the heat of battle stealthily to seek out the enemy observation posts, guns and tanks, in order to hit them unexpectedly from the flank.

The German tanks, fearing my fire, were compelled to maneuver far to the right in order to try their luck in battle with our neighbors. But even this time fortune did not favor them: a gun battery, which had been secretly deployed there the night before, smashed the German attack with direct fire. The Germans were unaware of this battery, and with sudden rapid fire from close range, the anti-tank battery destroyed over ten of the German tanks. The rest managed to escape. This time I didn't have to fire, and with satisfaction I observed the burning German tanks.

Then suddenly it was as if someone was whispering into my ear: 'Take a look to the left, and see what that "malingerer" is doing.' I quickly swiveled the stereoscope to the left, took a look – and was stunned: through the scope I saw that the tank was pointing its main gun straight at me; the long barrel was no longer visible, and instead I could only see the black maw of the gun's muzzle. Still I was confident that he couldn't see me because we were well-camouflaged, and I thought spitefully: 'If the German gunner only knew that the forward observer who was responsible for the destruction of two of his comrades' tanks was right in his sights, he might have blown me to pieces!' But since he didn't know we were here and couldn't possibly see us, I could look right down the barrel of his gun without a bit of fear.

However, before my happy smile had left my face and while I was still feeling smug with the euphoria of victory, I clearly saw the tank and its main gun recoil in a puff of blue smoke. I instantly realized that the tank had fired at me! Mortal fear dissolved my state of bliss into a split-second instinctive survival reaction. I grabbed Shtansky, who was still completely unaware of the tank, threw him to the bottom of the trench and fell on top of him. At almost the same instant, the explosion of the tank shell thundered above us. The shell struck the base of the pine tree, blowing the tree and the stereoscope to pieces and covering us with sand. The blast wave didn't strike us, but partially collapsed our trench, filling it with sand up to our knees when we finally stood back up. The trench was filled with smoke, and the disgusting stench of TNT filled our nostrils. There was no time to waste! While the German tanker was examining the results of his shot, we quickly slipped out of the trench under the cover of the smoke and hid in some nearby bushes. The German was happy with the result of his fire and probably jotted down in his combat diary that he had destroyed a Russian observation post. But I didn't waste a moment, and gave an order to the battery to fire on this new target; fortunately, the phone set had fallen to the bottom of the trench together with Shtansky and was still intact. As the happy German was writing his victorious note, my rounds were already in mid-flight. Sixteen rounds, fired rapidly and targeting the tank, raised hell around the tank with their powerful explosions, and probably the Germans inside it were deafened. Then one round struck the engine compartment and the tank exploded in flames – I don't know if any of the crew managed to escape, as I no longer had my stereoscope, and with my binoculars it was hard to see anything through the smoke.

Later after the battle, when I had calmed down, I calculated how much time had elapsed from the moment when I saw the muzzle flash until the explosion above our heads. The distance to the Panther, and that's exactly what it was, was 600 meters. The muzzle velocity of its round was 1,200 meters per second. So the shell was in the air for all of a half-second. But this half-second gave me just enough time to save two lives. It was very good that I had glanced over at the tank at just that moment, and the main thing, spotted when it fired. Of course, my instant reaction was also important. If I hadn't seen the moment the tank's main gun had fired, the shell would have blown me and Shtansky into pieces. But how on earth had the German spotted our observation post?! After all, we were so well-concealed! He might have overlooked us, if not for the sun.

The rising sun betrayed our position, as the German commander or gunner had caught a glint of sunlight reflecting off the lenses of the stereoscope. I can imagine the flash that the German saw when he looked in our direction! Even a small piece of glass brightly reflects the sun's rays, and there were two huge optical lenses in the stereoscope.

I still recall that incident whenever I see a piece of glass on the road reflect the sunlight, or whenever I see a timer on a televised sports broadcast counting down the hundredths of a second. Half a second flashes by before you can say a word. Somehow in that half-second, I managed not only to dive for cover, but also to shove my signalman into the trench ahead of me. It was fortunate that I had seen the muzzle flash! It must have been my guardian angel that whispered in my ear to take a look at the 'malingerer'.

There were many such cases in the war. One day a signalman and I were walking down a communication trench that ran perpendicular to an anti-tank ditch and fed into it. I had just turned the corner of the trench's clay wall into the ditch, while my signalman was just two paces behind me, still in the trench. A mortar round struck him, while I was left unharmed. If the round had fallen just a meter short, it would have hit me, and the signalman around the corner would have survived. There are a host of reasons for why a round could fall short: a gram less gunpowder in the charge, or a barely noticeable puff of headwind. If we had walked a bit faster, we both would have survived. If we had walked a bit slower – we both would have been killed.

Such incidents were just a confluence of random chance. Favorable or unfavorable chance, luck or misfortune, but their price was a human life.

How rarely did the desired guest Lady Fortune appear at the front! Amidst the thousands of deaths, fate would smile upon only one lucky man at a time, if that. Why it was precisely this soldier that was lucky was quite a question. Was it fortune obliging the man or the man obliging fortune? No one knows. But I can firmly state that every veteran of the front lines can recall many occasions when death seemed unavoidable, but due to some happy chance he remained alive. Perhaps the Lord intervened? Who knows?

From childhood, we had all been raised as atheists in the Soviet state, and most of us didn't believe in God. But when in a tough spot, when pinned down by a machine gun, or when a bomb, shell or mortar round exploded nearby and you were ready to burrow into the earth with your bare hands, if only to remain intact – where was our atheism? We all prayed to God: 'Lord, help me! Lord, help me!' He did help a few men, but not often.

By their manifestation, lucky cases in the war were amazingly different, rare, unpredictable, unique, unexpected and capricious. They happened not because of prayer or compassion, not even for the sake of justice or retribution. At the front, we knew that there was luck; in secret, we even hoped for it ourselves, but we spoke about it with trepidation, with superstitious delicacy, reluctantly, quietly, in order not to scare our luck away. But many superstitious men – and in war, almost everyone is superstitious – sought not to talk about this topic at all. They were afraid.

Death often punished not only cowardice or clumsiness, but also excessive caution or inspiring examples of foolhardy heroism. On the contrary, it more often spared bravery, courage, self-sacrifice and prudence. Death often bypassed a battle-seasoned, experienced warrior, heading out on a dangerous mission as if it was a regular job. A different man would be sent out on a suicide mission, but having completed it, he would return safe and sound. Here, unquestionably, experience also played its own role. But chance played an even greater role. There were cases when plain stupidity, petty tyranny, or else even the greediness of superiors saved men from death.

I, like a few other men, was lucky in the war. In three years at the front under constant enemy fire, bombings and attacks, and with occasional forays into the German rear, I was only wounded three times. I was shellshocked many times, though. But they didn't kill me. Yet there were cases when without question I alone, or together with my men, should have been killed. But because of some strange, sometimes unnatural combination of circumstances I remained alive.

Our battalion commander Gordienko, an old professional officer, was a petty tyrant and fond of drill. He demanded that we in the trenches have our recently introduced shoulder-boards be straight like the wings of archangels, not wrinkled or worn. My scouts inserted pieces of plywood into their shoulder-boards, while I used steel plating from a downed German aircraft in mine. This annoyed us quite a bit in combat. But a little later we were hit by an air-burst barrage: the rounds exploded above us and there was no place to hide from the rain of steel. We sat down on the ground and hugged our knees against our stomachs in order to decrease our body's surface area. A shell fragment struck my left shoulder and knocked me to the ground. I thought my arm had been torn off. They removed my tunic – my entire shoulder was badly bruised and swollen. It turned out that a small fragment had expended its energy while penetrating the steel plate and had become trapped in the 'tongue' of the shoulder-board. If not for the steel plate, it would have pierced my shoulder and heart. So the stupidity of my superior saved my life.

Yet another example, when the only signalman I had with me at the moment was shot and killed, and I alone had to lay out the cable and carry the field phone. I didn't want to leave the carbine of the dead signalman behind, so I slung it over my back. It was hard to carry all this gear under the cold autumn rain and the German fire. However, the carbine saved my life. An artillery shell exploded nearby and one of the fragments hit me in the back. If not for the carbine, it would have penetrated my heart. But it struck the carbine, and not the round gun barrel, which would have simply deflected the fragment into my back, but the flat side of the cartridge chamber. The velocity of the splinter was so high that it buried 1 centimeter deep into the steel chamber. I was left with a long, carbine-shaped bruise on my back. Again, it was a lucky coincidence.

It is amazing that such fortunate and unfortunate coincidences sometimes repeated themselves in every detail with other people. A carbine later saved the life of my signalman Shtansky in exactly the same way: a splinter struck the cartridge chamber.

On the other hand, thousands of shell fragments in thousands of other cases bypassed the potentially life-saving cigarette cases or pocket knives and killed people. Others were rescued by a metal medal on their chest or the star insignia on their side cap.

I once counted that I had twenty-nine lucky coincidences in the war. I guess the Lord recalled me in those moments and spared the life of this sinner.

CHAPTER EIGHT

On Defense along the Ingulets River

Continuing our pursuit of the enemy after the battle of Kursk, our division for more than a month advanced with fighting to the south. We liberated Krasnograd and entered the oblast of Dnepropetrovsk. However, in the constant fighting the division had become so worn out that only one reduced battalion remained of the three rifle regiments, and only one or two men in each gun crew. We were withdrawn to receive replacements at the end of September, and spent until 26 October 1943 resting and refitting in the city of Merefa near Kharkov. We gave the new replacements the most elementary training and then set off on foot again to catch up with the *front*, which had continued the offensive through Krasnograd and Poltava and over the Dnepr River.

We crossed the Dnepr on a pontoon bridge on 3 November 1943 and finally reached the front in the vicinity of Kirovograd oblast's Petrovo on the Ingulets River, a tributary of the Ingul River that flows into the Black Sea at the city of Nikolaev. Our replenished 52nd Rifle Division was to replace the completely exhausted 80th Rifle Division in the line, as its remnants could no longer attack and were barely able to contain the usual German counter-attacks.

A familiar routine resumed: again our attacks, tenacious German resistance, combat and losses. But we nevertheless took and occupied the next village, Grafit. However, when we approached the upper course of the Ingulets, we were unable to take the small village of Bairak on the opposite bank after a week of fighting. The armor that arrived to assist was of no use either. We had run into a previously prepared, strongly fortified German line of defense.

So we and the entire 2nd Ukrainian Front, having completed the expansion of the Kremenchug-Dnepropetrovsk bridgehead over the Dnepr, remained for the whole winter on the Ingulets River. We occupied and constructed our own defensive positions. At night we dug trenches, dugouts, and latrines, and built observation posts, machine-gun nests and ammunition storage bunkers.

Life on the defense follows its own pattern: keeping an eye on the enemy, patrolling, security, artillery barrages, and short spells in the dugouts. Casualties from mortar rounds and artillery shells, machine-gun fire and sniper fire are much lower than when on the attack. Our main task was to know what the Germans were doing and permit them no rest either day or night. At any moment you had to be ready to rush out of the dugouts into the trench to engage the enemy. Therefore, at night, the greatest luxury we could take was to loosen our belts and remove our felt boots.

Machine guns were manned around the clock, the gunners jumping up and down in place to try to keep themselves warm. A stereoscope for the artillerymen had been set up next to the breastwork, through which the forward observers could monitor the enemy's defenses, keeping watch for the appearance of any possible target. If they spotted a group of soldiers, a cart or a vehicle, they called in fire immediately. Shells flew overhead and exploded on the Germans' positions.

Our trench was laid out in zigzags, so that a bullet or shell splinter couldn't fly down the length of the trench line, and so one could take advantage of dead angles. The trench was 1.5 meters deep, plus the breastwork of the excavated earth. Standing, one could see the enemy and fire from the breastwork. But one had to move around in the trench at a stoop. A lid from an ammo box in the wall of the trench – a door – marked the entry into a dugout. In summertime, a combat cape hanging at the entry would serve as the door. The roof of the dugout was made of sticks, branches, and scraps of metal from a downed plane, covered with several inches of earth. It was crucial that the roof of a dugout merged with the surrounding terrain, or else the Germans would spot it immediately and plaster it with mortar rounds.

Dugouts were normally 4 meters square and 1.3 meters high, though in swampy terrain they could be as low as a half-meter. Boots were removed and left in a depression by the entrance, and hay or straw covered by capes served as the bedding on the floor. Rucksacks served as our pillows. There was enough room for six or seven men to lay down side by side, covered by their overcoats. Or they could sit in a crouch with their heads against the ceiling. In the rear, at the headquarters and political departments, dugouts were built deep enough for a person to stand up in, and they were covered with three layers of logs so they could withstand a direct hit by an artillery shell – even though they were normally well out of artillery range.

To the right in a wall would be a niche for a lamp fashioned from a small-caliber shell casing, flattened at the top. A wick made from a strip of wool from an overcoat would be inserted into it. Petrol and salt would be poured into a drilled hole in the casing – the salt prevented the petrol from detonating. There was also a larger niche in the dugout for a small stove, with a small hole carved into the ceiling above it. At night-time, when it was possible to build a small fire in the stove from scraps of ammo boxes, a tin pipe would be inserted in the hole to vent the stove. A stove like this provided heat to the dugout, and enabled us to warm water from melted snow in a canteen. On the left in the corner there were two Thermoses: one with porridge and one with sweet black tea. In the same corner would be five loaves of bread and a bottle of vodka, which contained our 'front-line' ration of 100 grams of vodka each. Personal belongings – canteens, towels, tobacco – would be in our rucksacks; spoons and razors – strapped behind our bootlegs. Rations were delivered to artillerymen by couriers, while the infantry's rations were delivered on sleds.

In daylight hours, forward observers took turns at the observation post, while the signalmen also took turns at the field telephone. We placed a sentry outside our dugout at night. We stayed in constant communication with the battery over the phone. Both here at the front and back at the battery, signalmen manned the phone, tying the receiver up to their ear with a strip of bandaging. To keep awake, they would chat with each other or with the signalmen of other batteries. But from time to time they had to call each other: '"Orel", can you hear me?'

'"Sula", I hear you well.'

I, the battery commander, could order at any second: 'To your posts!'

The signalman at the battery would repeat the command and the fire section leader would yell to the artillerymen: 'Take your positions!'

The gun crew members would spill out of all the dugouts at a run to their guns. Once they reached their positions, not a spare motion or moment was wasted! A shell would be exploding on target in less than fifteen seconds.

If a phone line was cut – a wagon, a vehicle or a shellburst could sever the cable – a signalman would set out immediately from each end of the line, and run along it with the line in their hands. If one of them reached the break in the line, he would have to find the other end and splice them together again. Enemy patrols sometimes cut the line on purpose and would lay an ambush to snatch the signalman who appeared to repair the line. Communication for an artilleryman is more important than oxygen! Without communications, the guns remain silent.

Such was the life of an artilleryman on the defense.

The same life went on over on the German side. Their dugouts were more comfortable, though, normally with wooden walls, wooden beds, pig-iron stoves and also pillows and blankets that they had looted from the civilians.

Our men were less sensitive and more stoic. We were better adapted to hunger, cold, dirt, and physical and psychological stress. The Germans on defense had lice and boils on their bodies. If you would, our skin was a bit thicker. If we picked up lice from a visit to a German dugout, a sergeant major and a medic would place a barrel above a campfire at the battery position, pour a bucket of water into it, lay about five logs across the rim of the barrel, and drape all our uniforms and underwear across the logs. The steam processing lasted for over an hour and it would take care of all lice. We took turns going to a *bania* in the rear. When it was your turn to wash, you had to do it quickly, in order not to freeze in the frigid weather.

If a German soldier wasn't in a bunker and had to sleep in a trench, he would lay his head on a knapsack, just like we used our rucksacks. But our rucksacks were no match to a German knapsack, which was sewn together from soft calfskin. The contents of their knapsacks were also richer than those of our bags. If we had any of the so-called 'untouchable rations', it was dry bread, rarely a tin can of American Spam. Soldiers would often eat the untouchable rations just to make sure the food was not wasted if they were killed. But what didn't the Germans have in their knapsacks! Portable stoves and dry spirit tablets to warm up food, small lamps with paraffin and wicks, a combination fork and spoon, a knife, preserves, Portuguese sardines, French wines, crackers, artificial honey, chocolate, cheese, smoked sausage, and personal hygiene items. Letters and photos were always present. Quite often they also carried a harmonica.

On the attack, when circumstances permitted it, our soldiers often stopped to hunt for German knapsacks. Once my signalman was chasing a fleeing German with a knapsack on his back; the German was running like a jack-rabbit. My soldier shouted at him, but the German didn't stop. He shot the German in the back, but below the knapsack so he didn't damage the contents! The German fell flat on his stomach. The signalman tore the knapsack from the German's back and impatiently opened it to see what goodies might be inside. But the German wasn't dead, only wounded, and as my man was investigating the contents of the knapsack, the German turned over and pointed his submachine-gun at him. It was a good thing that another of my men was nearby and fired first. Otherwise, the inquisitive signalman would have paid for his curiosity with his life.

We spent all winter in our little shelter. We didn't build larger dugouts, because it would only increase the chance of a direct hit by an artillery or mortar round, and it was also warmer in a small space. We talked about all sorts of things in those three winter months, but mainly about the things we missed the most – home, women, pre-war parties and holiday gatherings. Every inhabitant of a dugout knew all about each other – about his family, friends, even neighbors. We also liked to listen to all sorts of tales and unusual stories. I spoke a lot about Leningrad, its palaces, museums and theaters, and the books that I had read. Not a single political officer visited us during the entire winter. They were afraid of the front line, even when we were on the defense, when casualties were low. So I had to keep my men's morale up and and give them combat training.

Such was the slow-paced life of a battery commander's observation post at the front. My four howitzers were in a valley 2 kilometers behind me and my gun crews, situated in their bunkers and invisible to the enemy, were always ready to open fire.

Throughout that winter on the defense on the Ingulets River, there were no special events. However, we lost one man, and it was a damn German cannon that was to blame!

In February 1944, blizzards and strong winds set in. If one could have stood at full height on the battlefield and taken a look around, he would have only seen a broad, snow-covered field and the raging blizzard. Only an experienced soldier would have noticed stretching along both sides of the Ingulets River the rows of trenches and subtle mounds of the dugouts under the snow – the German ones on the higher bank of the river, and ours on the lower. It was the retreating Germans that had the choice of defensive ground, so their position was always superior to our own.

Hundreds of men, Russian and German, were sitting underground in the dugouts beneath the snow. Just a few thoroughly chilled sentries were standing in the trenches at the stereoscopes and machine guns. Now and then they would take a careful look at the enemy's positions. Not a single movement, not a single wisp of smoke could be seen. Everyone was hiding and motionless. Bored and frozen, the sentries jumped, slapped their hands together and jogged in place.

The machine guns were normally silent during the day, in order not to reveal their positions and get plastered by mortar rounds. During the night, on the contrary, the machine guns chattered all the time, beating out a fanciful rhythm, depending on the whims and musical skills of their owners.

The heavy guns were also silent. There were no targets and our ammunition was strictly limited on the defense. Occasionally, one could hear the whistle of two or three mortar rounds in the blizzard, followed by abrupt explosions. The blizzard would quickly cover the blackened blast stains in the snow. These mortar rounds did little harm, but they severed the phone cables often and the signalmen had to clamber out of the dugouts and run through the deep snow to find the break and repair it.

I was in my small dugout with two pairs of forward observers and signalmen in the front line next to battalion commander Abaev's command post. Two of the five of us were always on duty day and night. One would be in the dugout at the phone, the other in the trench at the stereoscope. If anything happened, my battery was ready the same minute to cover the battalion's 3-kilometer sector of the front. I had studied the German defenses well, and I knew the location of all their bunkers, machine guns, trenches and lines of communication. I was 'looking after' the Germans, not allowing them to emerge from their trenches or to open fire from machine guns. As soon as they tried to disobey, I would 'flick them on the nose' with a single round.

But about a week before the death of our comrade, the Germans had deployed an artillery piece set up to fire over open sights from a low ridge behind their line of trenches. The gun was so well-camouflaged that we could not locate it at all. The Germans had been terrorizing the entire division's 10-kilometer front to a depth of 8 kilometers with that one gun. Whatever might appear in our sector, the gun would destroy with a single direct-fire shot! A sudden shot – and then silence again! Try to find such a gun! At every observation post of the entire division, observers were searching for this damned gun's position and couldn't find it.

Their gun had a superb field of fire from that ridge – nothing on our side could seem to hide from it. Meanwhile, we were looking up at the German lines; it was like trying to spot something on a shelf in a room while peering under its door! To make things worse, the blowing snow was in our eyes, blinding our optical equipment and making it impossible to see anything through it but white snow. But we couldn't stand up in our trench to take a good look without immediately becoming a target, and a machine gun or that same damn gun would kill you.

I spent days and days standing at the stereoscope and watching the German hill intensively, waiting for the gun to fire. I studied each snow-covered hillock on the German side, but never saw anything suspicious. The stinging blowing snow was in my face, getting in my eyes and rubbing my cheeks raw like sandpaper. Frozen to the bone, with swollen eyes and a wet, reddened face I would crawl inside for a half-hour to warm up a bit in the cold dugout – we couldn't heat it during the day - and immediately I had to listen to battalion commander Gordienko's angry voice in the receiver: 'Damn you! Have you spotted it?!...' – and the curses went on and on. The bitterness of the unjustified losses, the audacity of the Nazis, my injured pride and some malevolent frenzy of the hunt gave me no rest.

On the day before the fatal episode, I spent all the hours of daylight in the trench: frozen, my cap completely covered with ice, my cheeks and eyes stinging from the blowing snow ... and once again I failed to spot the damn gun. It grew dark, I crawled into the dugout, unfastened my cap, and the guys lit up the stove and heated up some tea. As soon as I started my cup of tea, Gordienko was calling again and howling into the receiver: 'God damn you! You can't find some lousy gun! What a former forward observer! The best officer of the battery! Do you think their damn bitch will hold us in fear the whole winter?! It killed three signalmen yesterday and destroyed two supply wagons today! I will rip off your legs if you don't find it and destroy it!' And that was the end of another scolding by Gordienko.

That night in the dugout, when the stove was hot, our only topic of conversation was the damn gun – whom had it killed today, where it could be, why it was invisible … The reminiscences of girls and pre-war parties had vanished. The only common opinion that we had was that the gun was changing its position each night, as the sound of its shot seemed to originate in a different location every day.

'How much would you give, Khlyzov, to find the gun?' asked Shtansky with concern and a hint of tart Ukrainian humor.

'I would pay a thousand rubles,' Khlyzov answered sincerely, not noticing the sarcasm. As Khlyzov had told us before, he had never had more than thirty rubles in his life.

'I'd pay any amount!' echoed Iasha Korennoi.

'The damn bitch already got twelve men!' the signalman Drachev mourned.

'The signalman that was killed yesterday was a friend of mine from the rifle battalion,' Shtansky sadly said.

Only I remained glumly silent. I got to know all my men much better during that winter in the dugout. There was one in particular I affectionately envied: Drachev. Although he was my own age, he was already married and had a son. If I were killed, I'd leave no descendants after me. I tried to protect Drachev as much as possible at the front.

The next morning, when I re-entered the dugout to warm up again, two mortar rounds exploded one after the other nearby.

'The line is down,' Shtansky said with worry.

'I'll fix it,' Drachev said quickly and ran out of the dugout.

'Put on the snow camouflage!' I shouted as he left.

He just waved his hand: 'I'll be back in a second.' With that he disappeared.

The German gun barked almost the same second, and I heard an explosion close by. I grew worried: 'Was that Drachev? Have a look, guys.'

The dying Drachev was brought into the dugout a few seconds later. He passed away as we were bandaging him. It is hard to describe our feelings in the dugout. Drachev's death shocked us all.

After another fruitless session at the stereoscope, I returned to the dugout in the evening, and Gordienko called again. With no greeting, he said: 'Take a map! Do you see square 10-17?'

'I do.'

'I want you in that square with a radio operator the next morning. You will find and destroy that gun with your battery! Understood?!'

I took a closer look at the map and blanched: the square was behind the German front line; in order to reach it, I would have to cross minefields, a barbed-wire fence and trenches full of Germans.

'I see-e...' I said slowly, continuing to study the map, 'but it will be very hard to get there.'

'Do you know what's easy to do?' Gordienko spat out angrily and sarcastically.

'What?' I asked automatically, in a naive manner, still thinking about the horrible order I'd just received.

'To piss in a *bania*!' clarified Major Gordienko and rang off.

'What did he say, Comrade Senior Lieutenant?' the questions came as my men gathered around me.

'We are ordered to get behind the German lines and to find that gun,' I answered, having recovered from the initial shock.

'How on earth can we reach it?!' the men murmured.

I looked at all of them attentively and said: 'I only need one man. Who will come with me?'

Three men volunteered.

'Volodia Shtansky will go, I need a radio operator,' I summed up shortly. Then I addressed Korennoi: 'Iasha, prepare two snow overalls and a white cover for the radio set. We also need some dry bread and preserves. You, Volodia, wrap the submachine-guns with white bandaging and bring along five grenades. When they bring up dinner, send Drachev's body away with them; let them bury him in the village.'

Shtansky informed me, 'There is a letter for you, Comrade Senior Lieutenant. The cooks will bring it with dinner. I got the message over the phone.'

'Volodia, we won't wait for dinner,' I said, but then thought to myself: 'That letter will never be read.'

Thirty minutes later Shtansky and I were standing in the trench in white snow suits ready to go. My men and battalion commander Abaev were there to see us off. We said our farewells. I put my hands on the breastwork in order to jump out, but lingered a moment. I was realizing that as soon as I left this last trench, I would be leaving behind everything Soviet and everything native. Never before had I stopped to think about how difficult and frightening it was to tear away from the last thread connecting me with the Motherland. Here, at the very edge of my country, in the last cold and wet trench before no-man's-land, under enemy fire – I was still at home.

Sinking in deep snow, we slowly made our way across no-man's-land towards the German trenches. In front of us some 300 meters, machine guns were firing short bursts. Here and there along their line, illumination flares soared into the night sky. We had to crawl forward, freezing under the light of every flare. Soon there should be a minefield; I had to warn Shtansky and started to crawl more slowly. A flare shot up into the sky just to our right and very close to us, and I had a chance to look around in its light. Right in front of my eyes there were coils of barbed wire, clearly visible in the sputtering white light of the flare. With horror, I recognized that we were already in the minefield.

'Careful, we are in a minefield,' I whispered to Shtansky.

The concertina wire was half-buried in snow. The intricate entanglements of the wire gave us no chance to crawl through the middle of it, although we hoped that our felt boots, padded jackets and pants would keep us safe from its razor-sharp tines and let us climb over the prickly spirals. But as soon as we put our guns on top of the wire, using a moment of darkness, empty tin cans that were tied up to the wire rattled and a burst from a machine gun lashed at us from the left, spraying snow powder into our faces. We burrowed into the snow. Shtansky was behind me. Illumination flares shot into the sky one after another. Two more machine guns joined in. They were firing tracer bullets. Three bright red snakes reached towards us from the enemy trench. The deep snow rescued us. The noise of bullets flying over my head was terrifying: it turned out that when a machine gun fired at you from a distance of 50 meters, the bullets don't whistle but produce an evil hum. We were motionless in the snow for a whole hour under intense machine-gun fire, waiting for the crews to lose interest. Luckily, not a single bullet hit us. We waited thirty more minutes for things to settle down, and then started crossing the wire carefully and very slowly.

With slashed and bleeding hands and stomachs, we stealthily approached the first German trench line through the snow, heading towards a point between two blazing machine guns. Melting snow soaked our wounds and they burned like fire. But we ignored the pain. Having waited for a good moment, we leaped over the breastwork and quickly started to move into the German rear. We wanted to get higher on the hill, so that the gun for which we were searching would be behind and below us. From the hilltop we would have a better view of the German defenses from the rear and have a better chance to locate the damned gun, because it was concealed somewhere nearby, on this long ridge. The cuts from the barbed wire on our stomachs and hands were stinging unpleasantly, especially those on our wrists. But the danger of this undertaking and the importance of the mission dulled the pain. Finally, finding our bearings from the light of illumination flares, we decided that we had reached the planned location.

Dawn found us in a deep snow hole. The overnight snowfall had securely covered our tracks, and our white hoods blended into the mounds of snow. We were sitting in the hole back to back, so that Shtansky faced the German rear and I was looking towards our defenses. Shtansky set up the radio. I was impatient to determine our exact location, but it was still too dark. When it gradually lightened, I looked through my binoculars and was amazed: 'Volodia! Take a look at the view of our positions! They can cover dozens of kilometers from here with fire!'

I examined our own defensive line with interest, lowered my binoculars, and shuddered: through the six-fold magnification of the binoculars, I had seen the back of the head of a German machine-gunner looming right in front of me, as well as the rag-wrapped heads of other Nazis, bobbing up and down in rhythm above the trench as they hopped to warm themselves.

'They're freezing, the devils, trying to warm up,' I grinned. Then I reminded Shtansky, 'Keep a sharp look to the rear – anything could happen.'

For two hours, I thoroughly studied the German line on the slope below us; I had a splendid view, but the gun was nowhere to be seen. 'Where on earth is it hiding, where is the damn thing?!' I thought, getting more and more nervous. We were freezing to our bones, but I was more anxious about failing to find the gun. Suddenly Shtansky jostled me in the back: 'Look!' he said in a scared voice, pointing towards the German rear.

I turned my head and was horrified: coming over the hill, a group of Nazis in white snow suits were walking straight towards us. They were looking into the distance over our heads, in the direction of our defenses. I thought bitterly about why of all places we had set up on a German path.

'Prepare for battle!' I ordered Shtansky, turning my gun towards the Nazis.

The Germans were approaching; I could hear the lively, guttural sounds of their discussion. 'This is the end,' I thought, 'of course they'll see us, we'll have to engage them and no one will be left to find the damn gun.'

'Let's cut them all down now, Comrade Senior Lieutenant, before they spot us.'

'You can't kill them all at once, and you'll surely give away our position. Perhaps they won't notice us,' I said as I tried to calm my radio operator; but I thought to myself: 'The main thing is not to be taken prisoner.'

Suddenly the Nazis stopped; with their hands shielding their eyes, they were scrutinizing our distant positions: something had caught their attention and they were excitedly exchanging opinions. Then they bent low, turned sharply, and ran off to one side. They dropped into the snow about 200 meters away and quickly started to crawl down the slope towards their trench.

'Why the fright, why are they zigzagging and hiding?' my radio operator asked.

'They're definitely not frightened by us. They haven't spotted us. Maybe they're hiding from our forward observers. But we're very lucky this time – they missed us.'

The Nazis were lying in the snow motionlessly, but with raised heads; they were again carefully examining our defenses. All of a sudden they noticed something and pointed at it with their hands, shouting to each other. I could not restrain myself and looked in the same direction. Deep in our rear there was a supply wagon drawn by two horses rolling down a road. Two of the Germans quickly rose to their knees and moved something in the snow. All of a sudden two white sheets opened up … and I saw the dark green breech of a 75mm gun! I almost died with joy and amazement! I finally found what I wanted, the gun we were risking our lives for here!

'To your posts!' I said to Shtansky in order for him to transmit the order to the battery. But I kept wondering how I had failed to notice the white sheets for two hours!

'Target – bunker, right zero thirty, up eight-zero,' the message flew to the battery.

The German crew failed to fire a single shot that would have doomed our wagon – my first round landed in front of their gun! They crouched down, hiding behind the gun. It was funny to see the Fritzes hiding from observers in our line, with no inkling that the observers were behind them.

The second round exploded behind the gun and forced the crew to lie down under the gun, but shrapnel from this round generously showered down on our hole as well.

'Comrade Senior Lieutenant, won't we hit ourselves here?' the radio operator asked worriedly.

'I am not afraid of my own rounds! Transmit the message: "Back the target up towards the first round and lay down a sheaf of fire! As a battery, four rounds, rapid fire, fire!"'

Sixteen powerful rounds rained down on the target. One shell exploded between the gun trails, and flinging the crew like rag dolls, capsized the gun.

'Urah!' we could hear in the earphones. It was the voices of our forward observers, who were viewing the death of the gun from their observation posts.

Finally! The job was done! The damned gun had been destroyed! Deeply satisfied, my radio operator and I fell back into our snow hole.

About thirty minutes later, another group of soldiers in white snow suits approached from the rear with stretchers. As they searched for any survivors among the bodies of their comrades in the snow around the shattered gun, I ordered over the phone: 'Fire!'

Another batch of sixteen rounds landed on the destroyed gun thirty seconds later. The whole group of German soldiers was wiped out. No one tried to approach the gun after this.

We spent the rest of the day calling in fire on enemy weapons emplacements, clearly visible to us from our vantage point in the German rear. We were no longer afraid: whatever might happen, we had completed our main mission and had destroyed the damned gun.

Once it grew dark, we headed home. The difficult way back went well at first. But when we reached the minefield, I was worried that the heavy radio set on Shtansky's back would sink him into the snow and cause him to detonate a mine, so I ordered him to take the radio off his back and drag it by its antenna.

But, as we all know, the path to hell is paved with good intentions! The heavy radio ploughed into the snow and struck a mine. The explosion blew the radio to pieces and raised the alarm among the Germans. Illumination flares shot into the sky, and machine guns quickly opened up one by one ... Bullets flailed the snow in the minefield frighteningly close by. But the Germans were firing at the location of the mine's blast – and we had already managed to roll to one side and dig into the snow.

The fusillade lasted for over an hour, the bullets blanketing our previous location. If we hadn't rolled away, we would have been shot to pieces.

How many 'what ifs' had we overcome in the past twenty-four hours? What if the nearby flare hadn't illuminated the concertina wire right in front of my face and shown that we were in the minefield? ... What if I hadn't been in deep snow when the tracer bullets streaked towards my head? ... What if the German gun crew hadn't veered off, when we were in the snow hole? ... What if our gun crews had overshot the gun by a few meters? ... What if we hadn't rolled to the side after the mine went off? ... But fate spared us this time as well.

Once more we had to wait for a long time for the Germans to settle down so that we could make a move again.

How happy was the battalion, when we came back to our battery safe and sound! Not only the 1st Artillery Battalion was happy, but all the units at the front line, as they had been watching the duel between the Germans and our artillerymen.

Battalion commander Abaev's miscalculation

Life at the front began to gather pace as we started to prepare for the new 1944 spring offensive. Local engagements to adjust the lines began to flare up here and there. My battery was continuing to support Abaev's rifle battalion. Captain Abaev was a smart and brave officer, but also a bit stubborn and too self-confident, which proved disastrous for us.

One night in March, when thick fog was blanketing the ground and consuming the dwindling remnants of snow, Abaev's battalion received an order to capture the German trench in front of us. The under-strength battalion spread out in a line 300 meters long, clambered quietly out of our trenches and moved towards the German lines in short rushes. When about 200 meters remained to the enemy's positions, the battalion dropped to the ground on Abaev's command and began slowly crawling on their bellies towards the German trenches. The battalion commander was on the left, while company commanders led the troops in the center and on the right. The platoon leaders had all been long since killed or were out of action with wounds.

I was next to Abaev on the left flank of the battalion. I was being escorted by signalman Prokushev, who was always ready to connect the phone to the line in order to call in the battery's fire.

'Listen, we're moving parallel to the German trench line,' I whispered to Abaev anxiously.

'Our direction is correct!' replied the battalion commander stubbornly, disregarding my worries.

We crawled another 200 meters through the thick fog.

I became worried again: 'We have pivoted and the entire line has turned to the right! We're crawling along the German trenches! That's why we haven't run into them yet!'

'The direction is correct!' Abaev angrily snapped in reply.

Abaev was my good front-line friend, but he was eight years older than me and didn't want to listen to a former college student. Well, it was his business and his battalion; my battery was only supporting him with its fire. I wasn't his subordinate, but I couldn't just leave him and head back: I would be treated as a coward who had left his comrade behind without artillery support in battle. So I followed Abaev's battalion with my signalman.

'Forward! Forward!' Abaev's tough order was constantly being passed along the line.

Extended in line, under the cover of darkness and a fog so thick that no illumination flare could penetrate it, the battalion quietly but rapidly continued to crawl, so it seemed, towards the Germans – in order to attack them suddenly while they were asleep.

All of a sudden rain began to pour down. The fog quickly dissipated, and through the dawning light the attackers – to their dismay! – saw the German trenches 40 meters to the left. The Germans also spotted us and one machine gun immediately opened fire at point-blank range. A second machine gun joined in with a long burst, and then several other light machine guns opened up; the whole field became swallowed in a cacophony of machine-gun and submachine-gun fire.

Everything happened so suddenly that many of our men didn't even have time to turn their weapons towards the enemy. The terrible flanking fire immediately pinned down all the survivors – no one could turn around or even move. Only a few scattered brave men, under the storm of German fire, tried to return it, but they were almost immediately cut down by bursts of machine-gun fire. The Germans were feasting! Soldiers were spilling out of dugouts and running to add their fire to that of the machine-gun crews. The battle was lopsided: the Germans were in their trench and we could see only the tops of their helmets, while they knew every inch of the terrain in front of them by heart and could see us lying on the frozen ground, pinned down under the deluge of machine-gun and small-arms fire.

I was on the extreme left; to my right were my signalman Prokushev, then

Abaev and the rest of the battalion in a ragged line, some seventy men. The very first burst hit us from my left-front. The first bullets flew over my head with a terrible sound. Just as I buried my head into a depression, the German machine-gunner slightly lowered the barrel of his gun and a bullet sliced open the left shoulder of my sheepskin coat.

'Drop, don't move!' Abaev's order passed down the line, while the battalion commander himself froze in place.

Signalman Prokushev was hit immediately as he tried to connect the field phone to the line. The battalion, frozen with fear, was being mercilessly cut to pieces by German automatic weapons fire.

Although the rain continued, the visibility gradually improved and the Germans, having annihilated the battalion, were hunting through binoculars for any survivors. As soon as someone moved, tried to shift the position of their stiffened body, or even just opened his eyes, there would immediately follow a well-aimed machine-gun burst, and it would be joined by the fire of soldiers who hadn't yet found a different target on their own. They would fire at a man until they spotted the next victim.

Clenching my teeth with anger, I was lying on my right side, facing the Germans. My right cheek was firmly pressed against the frozen ground. Opening my right eye next to the ground in a shadow, from time to time I looked at the Germans. They were craning their necks, carefully studying the bodies of our men and trying to discern the slightest sign of life among them. Suddenly, the tallest of the German soldiers sticking up above the trench line quickly and with effort waved his right arm above the breastwork. Before I realized what the motion meant, a grenade landed just some 5 meters in front of me. It bounced off the frozen ground a couple of times, before it skittered right by my head. I closed my eyes in terror, waiting for the explosion. Luckily, the grenade slid down into a small shell crater behind me and exploded there. The dull, brief blow of the blast wave squeezed my head from every direction, and numerous splinters whizzed past me.

The rain intensified. Our sheepskin coats and overcoats were saturated with water and covered by an icy crust. In addition to the sound of bullet impacts, each drop of rain echoed in my ears. The day seemed endless. I was completely frozen and lapsed into unconsciousness from time to time, and then a sequence of visions slowly rolled through my brain: Germans … gunshots … rain … moans … cold … pain … sleep … awakening … and then again rain, gunshots, unconsciousness … We, the survivors, waited endlessly for the salvation of nightfall.

When it finally grew dark, our medics crawled up. They started to search for the wounded, and struggled to detach frozen bodies that had become stuck to the ground and to evacuate them back to our lines. Several men, including

Abaev, were luckily unharmed. It took us a long time to set our stiffened bodies back into motion towards our empty trenches. The Germans started sending up illumination flares and opened a sporadic fire in the direction of the dead battalion.

Some ten wounded survivors who had been rescued by the medics were sent back to the medical battalion. The seven unharmed men that returned to their old dugouts were massaged with vodka and given a lot of vodka to drink. Compassionate men of a brother battalion that had witnessed the tragedy took off whatever they could to give to the survivors to wear. They dressed us in dry uniforms, gave us dinner, and then put us to bed. The large quantity of vodka was the best medicine. The next day, we returned to action without even catching a cold.

I was among the lucky seven who were by some miracle untouched by German bullets. But for the rest of my life I recalled how difficult it had been to stretch my stiffened arms and legs after a day of no movement, and to make my way independently out of that meat-grinder. I also remember how tenderly we were treated when we staggered back into our trench.

I woke up late the next morning and saw that I was again lying in water, and I could see light steam rising from my body. The depression in the clay soil that had served as my bed was now filled to the brim by rainwater, pouring from the ceiling of the bunker. I didn't tarry for long, crawled out of my pitiful shelter, squirmed over the hill behind our trench on my belly, and then ran as fast as my feet would take me to my battery. My dear gun crews treated me to the same procedures I had received in the trench the evening before. I had a good sleep in a warm, dry place, and the next day I was ready for action once again at my observation post.

CHAPTER NINE

The Spring Offensive

The Ukrainian spring arrived early, in March. The thaw revealed the defenses of the opposing sides clearly. There they were, just across from us: the German trenches, dugouts, the coils of concertina wire and the round metal cans on the ground – anti-personnel mines.

On 8 March 1944, now as part of the 64th Rifle Corps in the 3rd Ukrainian Front's 57th Army, we launched the spring offensive. The objective was to liberate the rest of the Ukraine beyond the Dnepr River. The operation unfolded like this: we attacked and the Germans, having engaged us from a well-prepared delaying position, quickly fell back to the next one. The Germans had more mobility than our units and often counter-attacked with infantry and armor. Sometimes we lost contact with them – they had vehicles, and we advanced on foot.

One day, we were again lagging behind the retreating Germans, who had broken contact with us. Our artillery regiment had already arrived at a small village called Voroshilovka, while the infantry was still somewhere behind. Division commander Major General Miliaev ordered all eight batteries of the artillery regiment to set up in front of the village, prepared to fire over open sights in case of a German tank attack prior to the infantry's arrival.

Our 1st Artillery Battalion had already deployed its 1st Battery before receiving the division commander's order. Its location was 3 kilometers to the right of a road leading into the village from the west, because the dried-out steppe allowed for the enemy tanks to maneuver freely. Gordienko took the commander of the 2nd Battery, and me, the commander of the 3rd Battery, into some fields on the left of the road in order to find tactically favorable positions for our batteries. Leaving our guns and gun crews in the village, we walked almost 5 kilometers before we found suitable locations to deploy them.

The sun in the Ukraine in March is very warm, especially when one is wearing a sheepskin coat, a fur cap with earflaps, and heavy boots with seemingly dozens of kilograms of mud stuck to them. Before returning, we decided to have a little rest on a dry hillock. I couldn't restrain myself, and lay down on the previous summer's grass. I stretched out my tired arms and legs.

We were so tired that I thought: 'This is it; I won't go anywhere else. Gordienko can shoot me on the spot, but I need the rest.' The fatigue hadn't come from just one day of walking. We, the men at the front, had been living in conditions of constant stress. Those of us still around were extremely tired of the war, although no one dared say this aloud. They'd immediately come for you and haul you off to the Special Department for 'defeatist attitudes'. This was the real tragedy for us, the 'untouchables' who had not yet been killed or wounded.

My body had been used up in the ceaseless, day-to-day fighting. But really was it just my body? I was ready to die on that sunlit hill and end it all. But after a few minutes of rest, I'd recovered, recalling a poem by Lermontov: 'But not with the cold sleep of the tomb ...' – yes, indeed, 'I do not wish to fall asleep forever in that cold sleep of the tomb; I want the life force to slumber in my breast and to breathe silently in my sleep ...' I opened my eyes and the sky was very blue and endless; there were still no larks singing in it and in fact no birds were visible at all, but all the same it was beautiful. I don't know what my comrades were thinking about during those few blissful moments on that sunny hillock. They were both silent, but I, continuing to gaze up into the sky with widely-opened eyes, started to sing to myself: 'I'm looking into the heavens, and I'm pondering that puzzle: Why am I not a falcon? Why can't I fly?' But apparently the time for verse and lyrics was over, and it was as if someone had nudged me in the ribs: *Look to the west* [author's emphasis]! I sat up, looked to the west, scanned the horizon – and saw tall clouds of dust far off in the distance, about 7 kilometers away.

'Comrade Major,' I addressed the regiment commander, 'it looks like tanks are raising dust, look over there.'

Gordienko stood up and took a close look, then said: 'Those look like tanks. Get up, boys, and let's get back to our guns in the village.'

Oh, how I didn't want to stand up! I hadn't managed to rest up a bit from the daily marches or this damn stroll. But I had to get up. We quickly set off back to Voroshilovka. At first we walked quickly, constantly glancing around to look for the approaching tanks, and then we started to jog. When we saw several tanks split from the main group and head in our direction, we started to run as fast as we could. But my strength had already given out a long time ago. Breathing heavily, the tall, slightly cowardly Gordienko ran in front. He was followed by Kovalev, and I brought up the tail. Constantly glancing back, I saw that the tanks were racing forward in two groups: the larger group was heading towards our 1st Battery's positions, while the smaller group was closing in on us. We had already forgotten about our brief sojourn on the hillock and kept running, breathing not with our second wind, but likely our fifth or seventh. Our throats were dry, our lungs were burning, and our hearts seemed ready to jump out of our chests. The lead tank fired several bursts, the bullets flying low over our heads, and bullets whistled to our left and right. The tank chased us, firing machine-gun bursts over our heads, as we were fleeing across the open field. It wouldn't be anything to finish us off from a machine gun or the main gun, we were only about 800 meters away, but the Germans didn't do that. We realized with horror that they wanted to take us alive! They had to find out where our troops were: had they already gone on ahead, or were they only now approaching? In order to find this out, they wanted to catch us, and I was carrying a topographical map with all our units' locations. The German tank crew kept firing over our heads, warning us and demanding that we stop! But we kept running as fast as we could: let them kill us; just don't let them take us prisoner! We feared captivity more than death itself!

Gordienko didn't look back and picked up his pace, while Kovalev and I began to lag behind. The lead tank was gaining on us, getting closer and closer, and there was still a kilometer left to the village! To our luck, we suddenly happened upon the dry course of a small, winding creek which quickly became deeper – stooping, we ran into it, hoping for salvation from the bends in its twisting course. But soon the course of the creek ran out, and we were again on open ground, having lost our only shelter, no matter how imaginary it might have been.

Shallow gullies ran into the creek bed from both sides, scoured into the steppe by melting snow each spring. The gullies held vegetation and tall, dry grass from the previous summer. I realized that this was the only place on the steppe where I could hide my map case. On the move, I bent over and stuck it under a small bush in one of the gullies. A machine-gun burst ripped through the air, fired from such short range that the sound of the shots forcefully hammered my ears. The bullets flew over my shoulder with a menacing noise. I turned and saw the tank just 50 meters away, approaching us at high speed! At a loss, we stopped and began to dart back and forth, not knowing what to do. We were like mice trapped by a cat in the corner of a room. Simultaneously, without a word, we drew our pistols. Not to fire at the tank, but in order to shoot ourselves. There was nowhere to hide, nothing to use against the tank, and we couldn't just sink into the earth. We didn't know what was going to happen next – would they execute us with its machine gun, fire at us with the main gun, or just grind our bodies into the ground with its tracks, because we hadn't surrendered? The tank stopped and fired another burst between us, forcing us to lie down. A steel hatch opened, and a German emerged and shouted: '*Rus*'! Drop your weapons!'

The hatch closed immediately, and the tank started to roll towards us. Other tanks of the group closely encircled us, aiming their main guns and machine guns at us. The situation was hopeless. I put the barrel of my pistol against my head. I only had to pull the trigger. But I couldn't bring myself to do it immediately. If you have never been in that situation of total despair, when there was no way to avoid captivity, and you only had a few moments to muster your will and pull the trigger, I guess you could calmly and only ask fifty years later: 'Why didn't you just shoot yourself?' Yet this was the very question asked of our men who had been prisoners-of-war upon their return from captivity. So, were all 6,000,000 men who had been taken prisoner supposed to commit suicide?

We were afraid to shoot ourselves, even when the German tank was rolling towards us to crush us. I think it would have taken me a couple more seconds to muster the courage to kill myself, yet those two seconds of indecision saved our lives. The tank suddenly stopped, and in the twinkle of an eye it spun around on one track and drove away at full speed. The other tanks followed it. Stunned, we looked back over our shoulders ... and saw the beautiful sight of dozens of Red Army tanks emerging from the village! Fearing them, our tormentors forgot about us immediately. It was an unimaginable event, just like in a film. We already had our pistols to our heads, yet our salvation came just in the nick of time! Just one second later, and we probably would have pulled the triggers.

While our personal drama was unfolding, our 1st Battery was already engaging the main group of German tanks, knocking out several of the enemy machines...

A chase

The German was fleeing from me as fast as he could run. Two Germans had run out from under the bridge, but when I started in pursuit, one of them turned around and fired a burst at me. I returned fire and he dropped dead on the ground. The second German was trying to escape across a field, following the Nazis that had just abandoned the village. About 50 meters separated us.

It was good that I had decided not to wait for our infantry to catch up, and had set off after the fleeing Nazis with three of my men. Otherwise the little bridge would have been blown sky-high! It was also fortunate that I had thought to glance under the bridge, when two men in gray, mouse-colored overcoats emerged from under it at a run. Indeed, they had prepared the bridge for demolition and had already lit the fuse! Of course, the bridge was a small one, but if the Germans had destroyed it, my howitzers, which had already been pulled out of their concealment, wouldn't have been able to cross the swampy creek and would have been left behind for a long time. I pulled out the burning fuse, threw it aside, and took off in pursuit of the fleeing demolition team.

Battalion commander Morozov had been delayed in front of the village because he couldn't force his exhausted men to leave the German trench they had just taken. They had tumbled into the trench almost as soon as the Germans had left it, and then just continued to lie on the bottom of the trench. Morozov shouted hysterically, roundly cursed them, kicked men with his boots, threatened them with a gun, and even fired into the air – but they didn't budge. The battalion had orders to capture not only the trench, but also the village beyond it. The job had to be done quickly before the Germans recovered and consolidated in it. But the men wouldn't move. Their physical and inner strength had been all but spent in the five previous assaults on this damned trench. The men that had survived the five assaults were no longer afraid of anything. The entire slope in front of this trench was littered with our dead and wounded. So the survivors didn't care that their battalion commander had a pistol – he couldn't shoot all of them.

Morozov somehow finally grasped all of this, spat on the ground and sat down on the breastwork. This tall, slim, energetic and handsome man also seemed to break down. He sat hunched over, with his elbows propped on his knees and his hands covering his eyes. He looked like the most miserable man on the earth. He had exerted himself since dawn as much as any of his men. As usual, the political officer, the Party secretary and the *Komsomol* secretary were nowhere to be seen once the fighting started. His company commanders, not to mention the platoon leaders, had all been out of the game long ago. The final company commander had been killed in one of the five assaults that very day. The whole battalion had only about thirty men left after the fifth assault. But Morozov still heard the hysterical cry of the regiment commander over the phone ringing in his ears: 'I will execute you, damn it, if you do not capture that village!' How could he capture it?! Germans were occupying a deep trench in front of it. Our rounds were exploding around it, striking the breastwork and collapsing the trench's walls, but the Germans were waiting out the barrage, safe and sound on the bottom of the trench! As soon as we ceased fire in order not to hit our own infantry, the Germans jumped up, set their machine guns up on the breastwork and slaughtered our men! Yes, it had been easy for them to capture vast expanses of Russia in 1941, while we now had to fight for each small hill to take it back!

The fifth assault would have also failed. But luckily, my battery had just received air-burst rounds. These rounds were designed to drive the enemy out of trenches: a deafening explosion above the ground and a deadly hail of steel splinters from above - and there was no refuge in a trench. When these shells started to explode above the German trench, they panicked and abandoned the trench, heading for the village. With the same rounds I forced them to leave the village as well. At that point our men rose to their feet, staggered up to the trench and dropped into it. I chose not to wait for them, had taken three guys ahead, and had flushed the German demolition team out from under the bridge that they had wired for demolition.

Now I was chasing after this German combat engineer. The distance between us dropped quickly. I'd been a good athlete from childhood, and I had exercised a lot at the Institute and in the reserve regiment. At first we had cursed the damn major who had forced us to run 10 kilometers each morning, but at the front we thought of him gratefully. So I was in a foot-race with this German. I don't know what he was thinking, because I could have shot him in the back at any moment. But all sorts of things happen in war, even outrunning your opponent and escaping. It happened with us and for the Germans alike.

When I had closed to within 5 meters, I felt like I had no strength left, my throat was burning, and my heart was pounding. 'That's it,' I thought, 'I just can't catch him.' The German was a long-legged athlete. I aimed my gun at him and prepared to fire ... and then an overwhelming desire to catch a *living* [author's emphasis] prey blotted out every other thought in my mind!

I surged forward yet another time until there were only two steps left between us. I could see steam rising from his undershirt. This was all happening in early spring; the snow had melted already, but there was frozen soil under a layer of slippery mud, and it was difficult to get traction. Korennoi and the two signalmen, loaded down as they were with field phones, cable and other equipment, had dropped out of the race long before. The main force of the Germans had long ago disappeared over a hill up ahead. This was a one-on-one race, and we were running across a slippery, open field. He was running from death, I was running in order to enjoy revenge. I had to capture him alive! Whatever one might say, the prospect of capturing a German was very exciting; not a surrendering and helpless one, but a resisting, struggling one! We didn't often see the enemy's face at close range. During an assault the distance could be dozens of meters, and you couldn't make out faces. In a hand-to-hand fight, there was no time to look the enemy in the face. Everything happened too quickly, mingling into a red morass.

We always sensed something mysterious, alien, dangerous and incomprehensible in the Germans. They were evil, cunning, agile, technically educated, tough and arrogant. It was not possible for us to imagine a peaceful coexistence with them. If you saw a German, even by mere chance, you had to shoot immediately, or you were dead! The Germans also despised us and were afraid of us. But in addition to hatred and disgust, we had some secret curiosity about the enemy. Although God spare you if you shared this interest with anyone else, even a close friend! This was a crime that was punished without mercy. The goal of our propaganda was natural – to inspire our men and to disparage the enemy. But the mocking depiction of Germans as cowards and idiots only made veteran soldiers laugh and created a false image of the enemy among the green soldiers. We learned the real strength of the Germans in battle at the front.

We wondered: Just who are these Germans? In whose name are they fighting so bravely and desperately? Why are they so well-equipped with everything – weapons, equipment and food? We always seemed to lack something. In battle, this lack often resulted in unimaginable suffering, expecting too much from our troops, and unnecessary losses. The Germans didn't care if we lacked something. In turn, we were very happy when we had plenty of food and ammo.

The Germans never seemed to spare ammunition; they seemed to have no limits. Sometimes they fired for so long that you would no longer be waiting for death, but for the end of the barrage. When we entered Germany, we were amazed by the amount of smoked meat we found in the attics. We'd been told that the Germans were dying from hunger. Everything German was polished, finely painted, tailored, foreseen, mechanically perfect ... However, German prosperity prompted not only well-concealed envy, but also additional wrath. So interest in the German as a human was a secondary concern. The main thing was the evil that they had brought and all that they had done. THIS German combat engineer, fleeing from me, was the embodiment of everything dangerous and disgusting about the Germans! It was *him* they had ordered to blow up the bridge. It was *this German* who was able to blow up bridges, might now catch up with his own troops, who would never surrender, and who might outrun me. He was the man who had just been in the trench, slaughtering our men from his submachine-gun. How many former collective farmers had *he* killed? How many orphans had *he* created during our five assaults? [author's emphasis].

This desire for vengeance kept me going. I somehow found the strength to make another surge and try to catch the German. He was so close! I raised my submachine-gun in order to shove him in the back and cause him to fall into the mud. But I couldn't quite do it – I lacked a couple of centimeters! The German heard my heavy breathing, glanced back at me, tossed away his gun and somehow accelerated again. I couldn't shoot the unarmed man any more. But I had to catch him! He would answer for everything! Awful pictures passed through my mind one after another. During the second or third assault on the trench, a bullet had struck an artery in my signalman's neck, and I saw fountains of blood spurting from the wound. I fell to the ground with him, and as he laid his head on my chest, blood gushing from his wound, I had tried to staunch the flow with my hand. I failed, and the blood poured through my fingers. This was my signalman Kolia Leonov! He was just a boy! So fast and daring! Even now he at first tried to be brave, but then suddenly something changed in him. He focused his unblinking, tear-filled eyes on me and shouted,

'Do you understand? I'm going to die now!' It is impossible to forget or express this heart-rending cry! Everything was in it – the despair, the prayer, the farewell to life, and the desire to communicate the tragedy of his situation to us...

The barrel of my submachine-gun was almost touching the undershirt of the German, but I couldn't stretch far enough to catch him. Would I let the Nazi go? This was not just another German! If he made it back to his lines, how much more misery he would inflict on us! This guy had not only been ordered to blow up the little bridge. In a village that we had captured a day before, we had pulled the bodies of three children out of a well. Their parents had also been shot by the Germans, and as their grandfather held the body of the younger grandson in his outstretched arms, he was bitterly asking, 'Why? Why?' The children were dead, we couldn't help them any more, but looking at the sufferings of this old man pushed us beyond our limits. The youngest signalman of our battery Volodia Shtansky (he was running behind me now) was so shocked by this scene that he had sworn: 'When I catch a living German, I'll cut him into pieces!' Probably, it was this very German who had been given the task to drown the children in the well, just before the Germans fled the village. In the same village we liberated seven Russian prisoners-of-war. They were lying on the bare ground in a locked barn, and were so emaciated that there was only skin and bones left. They couldn't even speak. Why did the Nazis have to torture people so much?!

All these memories flashing through my brain only strengthened my anger, but they didn't strengthen me physically, and I felt like I was reaching the end of my limits. But I sensed that the German was also on the brink of collapse; he was out of breath, his long legs were stumbling, he was so exhausted that he seemed almost to be asking me to end the chase and shove him in the back. Finally I stretched out and barely touched (not pushed!) the German on his back. The German stumbled, tried to catch himself with his extended hands, and then collapsed onto his stomach and ploughed through the muddy field with his face. I could barely stand myself, I was totally out of breath, but I ran up to his head and aimed my gun at it. The Nazi froze for a second, waiting to be struck with it or shot, and then quickly rolled over onto his back, drew his legs up to his stomach and covered his head with his hands. Flushed, deformed by fear and hate, his narrowed eyes were looking up at me from under his palms with distrust. He was still waiting to be struck or shot.

My joy had no limits! I had caught the villain! He was at my feet. I could do anything with him – shoot him, cut him into pieces, or just smash him in the face! The more desperate and bitter the German was, the calmer and happier I became. Now I could hold him responsible for everything that he had done! I guess the joy of the capture on my face was overshadowing the anger and resolve to settle scores. The German sensed this, the animal fear of death released him and he exposed his face. He was about thirty years old. He looked experienced, cunning and arrogant. He showed no intention to repent.

Just then my men ran up. The tall Korennoi with his long face and long nose who was the only forward observer still alive from the division's original group – we had suffered a lot of misery from the Germans together in the past two years of war. The other two were the young Shtansky with the boyish face, and the older, deliberate signalman Karpov.

'So, you got him, Comrade Senior Lieutenant?!' Korennoi shouted with satisfaction and a hint of admiration. 'Why are you just looking at him? Let me hit him!' And before I could say anything, he kicked the German in the side with all his might.

The Nazi groaned, jerked with pain and again hid his face behind his hands. Death was again near. Shtansky rushed to the German after Korennoi. Did he want to start cutting the German into pieces? But I threw my leg in his way and protected the German. It was hard for me to calm down my outraged men. The level-headed Karpov, who was three years older than us (he was about twenty-five years old) calmly proposed: 'Let's just shoot him, Comrade Lieutenant, and be done with it.'

'We can't do this, guys, he is a prisoner.' Then I said with emphasis: 'He will be tried according to military law. Korennoi, take him to the command post. Don't even think of trying something! I'll check!' This was now a strict order, not a discussion or explanation.

The German was following our conversation apprehensively, waiting for his fate. Korennoi lifted the SMG and angrily shouted: 'Komm!'

The German rose cautiously, and with hanging head, he set off in front of my scout. Just then Morozov walked up with the remnants of his battalion. The riflemen looked at the German with curiosity and anger. We joined up with the infantry to take the next village, where we would again together come under fire from Germans like this one.

We didn't lose our heads

It was now late March. Continuing our spring offensive, we encountered another German defense line in front of the Ingul (not Ingulets) River. We no longer had the strength to overcome it.

We had forced a crossing of a small tributary of the Ingul a couple of days earlier. The stream, swollen by the spring thaw, swallowed many of the rafts that were ferrying men and guns on that dark night. We rushed into a racing, icy current that was literally boiling from the explosions of mortar rounds and artillery shells. A storm of machine-gun fire hit us from all sides. Enemy illumination flares time after time cast their unnatural white light on a multitude of capsizing rafts and swimming men amidst geysers of water thrown up by explosions, before everything sank into darkness again. The survivors struggled against the current, frantically swimming or paddling their way across to the opposite bank. But even there our salvation was not waiting for us, but a savage battle with the enemy. As soon as we sensed something solid beneath our feet, we bounded out of the water and charged forward, firing on the move, in order to establish a bridgehead.

Establishing a perimeter on dry land did not come easily to us. Soon the remains of Abaev's rifle battalion, some fifty men, were lying in front of the German trenches, pinned down under the flailing fire of a machine gun. I was again next to battalion commander Abaev, supporting him with my battery.

'Something's fishy here with the Germans, they're firing only one machine gun,' I told Abaev, 'send some guys forward to see if they've pulled out.'

I could have sent my observers up to have a look, but there was no one left to send – all had been killed. There were only three men left at my observation post – Abaev, me and my last signalman.

Abaev's scouts reported that the trenches were empty. We decided to pull in the attacking line, bypass the firing machine gun on the right and head for Sidnevka – a small village on the bank of the Ingul. We wanted to reach it before the Germans consolidated their hold on the village.

'You – run back to the battery,' Abaev advised me. 'If there are no Germans in Sidnevka, I'll radio for you to move out, and you drive straight to the village with your guns.'

We had barely prepared our howitzers for movement, when the signal to move out came in over the radio from Abaev. That meant that the Germans had withdrawn across the Ingul and Abaev's battalion was already in Sidnevka. I took my place in the lead truck and the whole battery started rolling towards the village.

It was getting light. I checked the map: we had one more ravine to cross, and then there would be Sidnevka just beyond the next hill. All my attention was concentrated on the road in front of us. The truck, heavily loaded with equipment, and towing the limber and the howitzer, slowly climbed the hill. At the top, I could see fields gleaming far ahead in the distance, and closer, the glittering Ingush River and the huts of Sidnevka down below. As my heavy six-wheeled Studebaker just began to crest the narrow hilltop, I could see a couple of hundred meters ahead some outlying huts of the village, hedgerows, and the garden plots in front of some of the homes.

But what's this?! Right in front of us, Germans were walking around, digging trenches and setting up machine guns. We had bumped into the Germans! My insides started to churn. But hardened by years of war, I immediately stifled my fright. All sorts of solutions flashed through my mind. What should I do?! My brain was working furiously to find a way out of this jam. The main question was: how do I save the battery? We couldn't turn off the road – there were deep ditches on both sides of it. Reversing was useless, as there were three more Studebakers with guns behind us, and trucks carrying ammunition and the gun crews. My obliging memory immediately recalled the tragedy of the 7th Battery – in the midst of an offensive it had rushed into a German-held village and had been completely destroyed. My driver Nebylitsky also saw the Germans. Unaccustomed to combat situations, he took his hands off the steering wheel and lifted his foot from the gas pedal. The truck, counterbalanced by the 2.5-ton howitzer on the other side of the hilltop, came to an abrupt stop. The soldiers, who had been sitting in the back of the truck on ammunition boxes, pounded on the roof of the cab with their fists, as if to ask 'Where are we going?!' They'd seen the Germans too. I made the only correct decision in the twinkle of an eye: 'Forward!' I barked at the driver, while with my left foot I stomped on the boot of the driver to give the engine gas. The engine roared and the truck raced downhill at full speed, directly at the Germans.

Nebylitsky, frightened more by me than the Germans (he hadn't seen me like this before), grabbed the steering wheel again and began steering the truck. I waved my right hand from the cabin window to my men behind me. I wanted them to know that I was aware of the situation and had made a decision. Grabbing their submachine-guns, my batterymen opened fire over the roof of the cab as we roared into the German position. Among the enemy there was confusion and a lot of commotion, but then they also began to reach for their weapons. I watched as one German fumbled to set up his machine gun on its bipod, while another was frantically searching along the breastwork, unable to find his weapon. We sped past the German trenches and drove into the village; having quickly turned around, we turned off into a yard, so that the rear-facing gun would be pointing towards the Germans. Even before the truck stopped, I was leaping from the cabin and rushing for the gun, where I opened the breech. Even before I gave an order, someone shoved a round into the breech; the next man threw in the charge, I yanked the lanyard, and a shot thundered. The gun had not been set up for combat: the muzzle cover was still on, the trails hadn't been spread, the gun wasn't anchored – a gun shouldn't be fired like that under any conditions! But we desperately needed an immediate shot, and indeed we fired one! But this unaimed shot decided the matter. The Germans broke and fled along the streets to the river. They believed our mistake was part of a well-conceived plan to crack their defenses. I quickly ordered the deployment of the second gun next to the first one and ordered Lieutenant Oshchepkov to destroy the fleeing Nazis. Then I jumped onto the footboard of the third truck and led the second gun section by a side street towards the bridge over the Ingul.

I opened fire on the opposite bank in order to prevent the Germans from blowing up the bridge and bringing up reinforcements. Just then on our side of the river, the fleeing Germans appeared at the bridge at a run. I fired at them with canister, driving them into the river and killing them there. As we were consolidating our grip on the bridge, I radioed Gordienko about our success.

So, without losing a single man, we killed about 150 Germans, and, more importantly, we captured the bridge. A bridge is a crucial thing in a war!

But where were Abaev and his rifle battalion?! I couldn't hold the bridge without infantry! I sent three signalmen with a machine gun to the opposite bank and opened harassing fire from my guns.

Finally, around ten o'clock Abaev showed up with his battalion. It turned out that after bypassing the German machine gun, he had entered a different village 2 kilometers upstream from Sidnevka, mistook his location, and had radioed for me to move up my guns.

When Abaev's battalion arrived, the bridgehead on the other side of the Ingul was already being firmly held by the division's reconnaissance company. It had arrived on trucks not long after we had seized the bridge, rushed forward by the division commander as soon as he had learned from Gordienko about our accomplishment.

Crossing the Southern Bug

On 22 March 1944, forward units of the 52nd Rifle Division, consisting of Captain Abaev's 1st Rifle Battalion of the 439th Rifle Regiment and my battery reached the Southern Bug River in the area of Aleksandrovka. Using the element of surprise, Abaev and I decided to cross the river and capture a bridgehead on the opposite bank. During the day, we built rafts for the guns, mortars and heavy machine guns from the logs, boards, doors, gates and whatever other pieces of wood and timber we could scavenge from a nearby village. With the onset of darkness, we quietly brought all the rafts to a ravine about 100 meters from the riverbank. The enemy was not expecting us and remained quiet, only sending up a few illumination flares now and again. A gusty wind was blowing from the north-east, and rain was falling. The raging river was in flood and waves were loudly crashing against its banks. When we rolled two howitzers up to the bank and dragged up the rafts, the infantry was already waiting for the command to cross. Then at Abaev's signal, the soldiers, shivering from the cold, began slowly and reluctantly to enter the icy waters. We placed the rafts into the river, rolled the guns onto them, tied them down with ropes, loaded five boxes of shells onto each raft and shoved off. Standing by a gun, I was giving orders, while the crew began to row towards the opposite bank using large entrenching shovels. To the right and left, the heads of riflemen could be seen bobbing in the water; clinging with one arm onto a log or piece of wood, they paddled with the other and at varying speeds were making their way to the opposite bank.

Suddenly, the Germans fired a batch of illumination flares. The entire river was illuminated and it became as light as day. Machine guns opened up simultaneously, and artillery shells and mortar rounds rained down on us, their explosions creating huge fountains of water and whistling pieces of shrapnel. Logs, boards, and pieces of rafts flew into the air. Men, losing their supports, began to sink into the boiling rapids with terrible cries. The strong current carried our improvised, fragile rafts and both dead and living men downstream. A round went off beneath the corner of our raft, blowing it skywards, and a jumble of soggy boards, the gun, ammunition cases and men were thrown into the water. Some men managed to grab boards, but other gun crew members and I were instantly hurled far from the raft. I felt myself sinking. Working with my hands as hard as I could, I somehow struggled back to the surface. At just that moment, a beam struck me on the back of the head, and a large wave again completely inundated me. My saturated uniform, the submachine-gun on my back and the grenades in my pockets were dragging me down. I made it back to the surface with my last bit of strength and – what joy! – I saw a log next to me, bobbing in the waves. I grabbed it – and more importantly, didn't let go! The fear of drowning and being killed made me forget the hellish cold of the icy water that seemed to have frozen me to the bone.

With all my might, I paddled for the bank. The current carried me over 500 meters downstream. But then I felt the bottom under my feet and I struggled onto the bank. The ghastly white flash of illumination flares continued to rip away the darkness concealing the stark images of the deadly chaos in the river. When I struggled out of the river, water was pouring from my uniform and mud was squishing under my feet. But there was no time to dry out, as bursts of submachine-gun fire erupted from the enemy trench. Luckily, heavy machine guns on our side of the river immediately swept the German trench. The Germans ducked down into their trenches, giving us the chance to make a rush. There were some fifteen of us on this section of the bank, and judging from their fire, there were probably only five Germans in the trench ahead. Our machine guns ceased fire in order not to hit us, and the Germans immediately stuck their heads up, prompting an immediate burst from our submachine-guns. The Germans tossed hand grenades, but they flew over us and exploded well behind and below us. The Germans were now sending up fewer flares, and there were longer periods of darkness. We took advantage of one and rushed the German trench. But it was pitch-black! Dropping into the trench, I fired a burst to my right, because I knew I had a comrade on my left. When the next illumination flare lit the scene, I saw a dead Nazi next to me – I don't know whether I had killed him with my burst, or whether he had been killed earlier by the machine guns. But a hand-to-hand struggle was going on to my left; our man was wrestling with a German. Both were yelling, panting and floundering, but in the darkness I couldn't immediately distinguish which was our man and which the German. In the light of a flare, a German helmet flashed, and I fired a burst just below it. The Nazi collapsed. Our man could hardly catch his breath.

Just then, German mortar rounds rained down on the trench. This meant that there were no more Germans around. But the raft with our second gun had by now reached the bank. We quickly rolled the gun off the raft and offloaded the ammunition boxes.

'Start it rolling!' I ordered, and the gun slowly rolled away from the bank.

Meanwhile riflemen were firing from the trench into the darkness from time to time, to prevent the Germans from returning. We spent the rest of the night in the trench and became thoroughly frozen.

Reinforcements didn't arrive: the Germans had unleashed a storm of artillery fire on the opposite bank, and it wasn't possible for anyone even to approach the river here.

We defended the trench all day. With the fall of darkness indicating our second night in our tiny bridgehead, troops of the 492nd Rifle Regiment's 2nd Rifle Battalion broke through to us. They had crossed the river in the sector of our left-hand neighbor, the 58th Guards Rifle Division. That division had not only made a successful lodgement there, but it had also constructed a temporary bridge. The entire 52nd Rifle Division crossed over the Southern Bug using that bridge.

Captured guns

April arrived. We continued our offensive in the Kirovograd area. By now we had crossed the Ingul and the Southern Bug, and driven the Germans out of Veselyi Kut station. We were now pushing towards the Dnestr. The Germans had to abandon one defensive line after another. Even now, under our pressure the Germans were yielding a trench line ahead of us. We, the survivors, were so exhausted by the three previous assaults on this line that we weren't running, but slowly strolling towards the German trench under a bright spring sun. The sun was so hot by eleven o'clock that morning, that we were uncomfortable in our unbuttoned overcoats. The riflemen sat down on the edge of the German trench, dangling their legs into it, and lazily wiped their sweating faces with their side caps. To hell with the Germans; let them run away, no one had the strength to chase them again.

I was still with Abaev's battalion. Of my three signalmen, I had only one left alive. He was the 'untouchable' 17-year-old Volodia Shtansky. I had taken him into our battery the previous autumn at the insistence of his parents in a Ukrainian village, where we were staying over the night.

Volodia's parents had begged:

> Comrade Senior Lieutenant, please take our son with you, let him fight
> the war in your unit. He has already befriended some of your men and
> we like you. At least we'll know with whom he'll be fighting. When the
> Russians come, they'll set up a *voenkomat* and draft him, and we won't
> know where he'll wind up.

'Well,' I replied, 'but he's only seventeen; let him wait for one more year, then
he'll get drafted, receive basic training, and by then the war will be over. Our
unit is still fighting.'

Nevertheless, we took him into our battery as a signalman. When the sergeant
major dressed him in his uniform after breakfast and he said farewell to his
parents, his mother cried and told me, 'Do whatever you want with him,
Comrade Senior Lieutenant, but make sure he survives!'

Volodia was a good soldier who seemed to lead a charmed life. Several times,
death was hanging over him, but he survived. As it happened, I fulfilled his
mother's request, and he returned home after the war. But twice I personally
saved him from an imminent death.

On this particular day, Abaev had a little over thirty men left out of the fifty-
five with which he had started the day – but quite recently his battalion had
numbered almost 200 men. So, our infantry was taking a break, while I had no
connection to the battery, so I was unable to fire on the Germans, now over a
kilometer away, as they were running unpunished back to their next line of
defense. Shtansky ran off to find the line break, and I was impatiently holding
the receiver next to my ear – so if I heard a connection, I could still strike the
Germans. They were already sure they had gotten away! Then I heard the
familiar deep voice of Sergeant Mineev at the battery: '"Kolomna", can you
hear me?'

'I hear you well, pass on the command: sight setting six-zero, as a battery,
rapid fire!'

The 45-year-old Mineev from Penza was beyond joy that the line had been
fixed; he roared so loudly as he passed my orders to the gun crews that my
receiver started to crackle.

Some twenty seconds later, we could hear the rustle of our rounds passing
over our heads, and then dozens of powerful explosions covered the field
through which the Germans were running. Our riflemen immediately stirred
and craning their necks, they looked out across the steppe in front of them.
When the dust raised by the explosions dissipated, instead of the running
Germans we all saw scattered bodies here and there across the field. Some of
the bodies remained prone on the grayish-yellow field, but some of the

survivors among the fallen rose to their feet and started to run for their lives again. There weren't so many of them, and they clustered in small groups of three or four men. I saw glee on the faces of our riflemen; they were so excited that at first they couldn't say a word. Then they all started to cheer at once, looking back at me. Abaev was also happy. He grabbed me by the shoulders and shook me delightedly: 'Hit that group over there! Look how many of them there are!'

A command to the battery followed, and a shell swept away the fleeing Fritzes. The soldiers kicked up an even louder row, and now each man was trying to point out to me the group of fleeing Germans to shell next. The joy of revenge quickly restored their energy, freed them from the fear that they had experienced in the attacks, and softened their sorrow over the comrades they had lost in the fighting. Watching the enemy die in front of them was like balm for their rattled nerves.

So, the Germans had been destroyed and the riflemen had gotten a rest and had cheered up. Abaev ordered his battalion to move out, and we all set out in a rare crowd across the barren, unploughed field. Gradually the battalion's remnants shook out into an attacking line, with Abaev and me running on the left flank. Shtansky could barely keep pace, hampered by the roll of cable on his shoulders and the field phone dangling from his hand, which kept swinging and hitting him in the legs. I grabbed the phone so that it was easier for him to run. Crossing a hillcrest, we spotted a new German trench line in the distance. I thought to myself, 'How many more of these trenches would we have to take on our road to Berlin?'

The Germans spotted us and a machine-gun burst sprayed us, as if warming up for battle. Then a German howitzer battery, deployed in the open behind the trench, opened fire. We took cover. Shtansky had already connected the field phone to the cable and I called in fire on the German howitzers. They were not dug in; they must have just deployed to fire in a hurry. This made our job easier. Powerful explosions covered the entire battery. It immediately fell silent as the crews took cover next to their guns. Just in case, I fired another volley at the battery and then I shifted my fire to the German trench. My shells exploded along the whole length of the trench. The German infantry couldn't withstand it, clambered out of the trench and fled again. I gave them the chance to run away and then hit them again, to ensure they wouldn't try to return to the trench.

Then I again shifted my fire to the German battery to make sure it wouldn't resume firing. The fleeing German infantry reached the battery and the surviving artillerymen joined their flight. Abaev immediately ordered the battalion to charge, and we raced after the retreating enemy. When we reached the position of the German battery, I glanced to the left at the guns as we ran past them – they still seemed intact, and I wanted to give them a try!

When our battalion took cover for the last time, both Abaev and I understood that our offensive was over for the day. While his men started to dig in, I called my battery and ordered the battery's senior officer Lieutenant Oshchepkov:

> Leave two howitzers where they are. Bring up the other two and deploy next to the abandoned German battery. When they're ready to fire, move up the remaining two guns. Then immediately familiarize yourself with the German howitzers, see whether we can use them, and check to see that the sights and dials are OK. If the German guns are operational, pivot them 180 degrees.

Evening had already fallen. Oshchepkov split the gun crews into halves, and assigned his best men to the German howitzers. The German guns were intact; moreover four prime movers and around 1,000 shells were found nearby. The only thing missing were the firing tables. We did not know the value of the sight graduation and the panoramic sights were divided in 64 graduations, not 60 like in our guns (reflecting 6400 mils in the German circle and 6000 mils in the Russian circle). Another difference: when you increased the deflection, the barrel moved to the left, which was the opposite of our guns. I gave the command: 'Fire the German howitzers. Direction 16, sight setting seven-zero, number one gun, one round – fire!'

Abaev and I waited for the explosion of the German round. It slammed into the ground some 50 meters in front of us. I quickly placed my own shell down next to it and compared the sights. After some calculations, it turned out that the German sight setting of 70 corresponded to our sight setting of 44, which meant 2 kilometers 200 meters. Then with the help of firing from the German and our gun, we established corresponding sight settings for 3, 4, 5 and 6 kilometers.

That was it! The next morning we would give the Germans hell with their own guns!

This was exactly what happened. All the way to the Dnestr, I fired at the Nazis only from their own guns. Along the way we found tons of shells for them! There were whole trains loaded with ammunition at Veselyi Kut and Dolinskaia stations and no one else needed them, which meant no ammunition limits, authorizations, or reports. So I had two howitzer batteries, the Russian 122mm one and the captured 105mm one. Of course, my crews had more work to do as they now had eight howitzers to serve instead of four. But with the German howitzers, they could fire at the Germans as much as they pleased!

Students of the Physics and Mathematics faculty of Leningrad's Pedagogical Institute, December 1939. From left to right: Sergei Nazarov, Viktor Eroshnik and Petr Mikhin.

War is declared. Petr Mikhin, Ivan Zatsepin and Alexei Kovalev on their way to the military commissariat in June 1941. Only Petr will survive the war.

Lieutenant Petr Mikhin, December 1941.

Repairing the recuperator mechanism of a 122mm M-30 howitzer.

A 122mm A-19 howitzer in position.

A battery of 122mm M-30 howitzers.

A battery of 122mm M-30 howitzers on the march, 23rd Guards Rifle Division, 26th Army, 1943.

An artillery observation post.

Artillery division commander Captain Petr Mikhin, 1944.

Mikhin's artillery division staff. Top row, left to right: political deputy Karpov, Head of Staff Sovetov, Head of Signals Levin. Middle row: private Ryzhkov, Head of Staff deputy Medvedev, Head of divisional *Komsomol* organization Odintsov, former political deputy Zakharov. Bottom row: signaller Raikova, paramedic Matveev.

1028th Artillery Regiment officers. Standing, left to right: Head of Staff deputy Kochelaba, commanders of artillery divisions Mikhin, Vyskrebentsev, Yaryshkin. Seated: rifle division prosecutor, Head of Staff Shliamin, regimental commander Rogoza, political deputy Ustinov, head of regimental Communist Party organization Arzhatsky.

The commander of the 1028th Artillery Regiment S.F. Rogoza.

The squadron's Communist Party representative, Ivan Shevchenko, after the war.

Captain Petr Mikhin, Bulgaria, 1944.   Ivan Shevchenko and Petr Mikhin, May 1945.

May 1945, near Prague – the joy of victory. Petr Mikhin is on the left.

Scout Iasha Korennoi.

Veterinary Assistant Nikolaev and Sergeant Major Makukha standing on each side of Battery Commander Raskovalov, 1944. A month later Raskovalov was killed by a sniper.

Varvara Somova during her time as a student at the Ivanovo Medical University, 1940.

1944 photograph of Varvara Somova showing her as a medical officer of the 106th Field Hospital Medical Battalion.

V. Somova, Z. Ovsiannikova and E. Mishkina photographed in Prague in May 1945.

Back to university, December 1946. Petr Mikhin is on the left.

In 1942 bullets whizzed over these rails. Petr Mikhin, on the left, photographed near Rzhev in 1985.

CHAPTER TEN

Bridgehead on the Dnestr

The division reached the Dnestr River on 11 April some 5 or 6 kilometers north of Bendery. During the night of 11–12 April the enemy's main forces secretly abandoned their positions and crossed the Dnestr, leaving strong delaying detachments on the road behind them. On the order of division commander Miliaev, the 1st Rifle Battalion of the 429th Rifle Regiment, with which I was traveling with the captured German howitzer battery (we didn't dare risk my own battery on this mission!), bypassed the German blocking positions and slipped through to the Dnestr aboard trucks. The general had told me over the telephone to do just that:

> Take the captured howitzers and together with Morozov's battalion, strike for the Dnestr. If something goes wrong, abandon the guns, but make sure you disable them first. Mission: seize a bridgehead on the opposite bank of the Dnestr.

Now one hour before dawn, Morozov and I were lying in tall grass on the bank of the Dnestr. The river was quite wide and swollen with spring waters, while a cold wind was whipping tall waves that were crashing against the banks. Our rifle battalion was digging in a bit behind us, while the captured battery had deployed in concealed firing positions in a shallow ravine about a kilometer behind us and to our right.

Our left bank rose about 20 meters above the water, while on the lower German side, orchards stretched from the river's edge back to the Moldavian village of Gura-Bykuly. We had an excellent view all the way to the village, while the Germans could see us only from the bell-tower of the village church, the upper part of which was a bit higher than our bank.

The Germans were not expecting us. They didn't realize that we were already observing them, and they were strolling unconcernedly around the village, calmly but busily setting up their defenses and completing the masking of their forward trenches in the gardens. A few men were leisurely strolling through the bare orchards, which had not yet put on any foliage. It was a combat security garrison, the outposts of which were right on the riverbank.

'This is the first time I'm seeing the Germans at a river from above them,' noted battalion commander Morozov, 'normally, their bank has always been higher than ours.'

'Oh, you have a splendid view from here!' the soldiers admired as well, gazing out over the opposite bank.

In the meantime my men discovered that there was a tunnel leading from the village of Bychok, which lay about 500 meters behind us and to our left, to the river. In peacetime, the tunnel served to transport shell rock obtained from the river, and this tunnel exited at the riverbank right below us.

Morozov and I made the following decision: I would bring down my battery's fire on the Germans walking around the orchards and chase the survivors back to the village, and then prevent the Germans from returning to the riverbank. In the meantime, Morozov's battalion would slip into Bychok, quickly prepare rafts and locate any boats that were likely to be around in this river village, and then bring them to the river through the tunnel. At noon I would intensify my fire on the opposite bank and the village, while Morozov's battalion crossed the river and assaulted the village of Gura-Bykuly.

The explosions of the captured shells, fired from the German 105mm howitzers, struck the Nazis like thunder from a clear blue sky. They ran chaotically around the orchards and gardens, trying to find shelter in trenches, foxholes and rifle pits. I could see them from above, as if they were in the palm of my hand, and first I called fire down on any groups, before turning to hunt down individual survivors. It was important for me to intimidate them and drive them back into the village, in order to give Morozov a chance to cross the river without any opposition.

Regimental and divisional top brass suddenly arrived on the bank in the midst of the battle: artillery commander Major Gordienko, rifle regiment commander Lieutenant Colonel Azatian and the division's chief of operations, Major Nesterenko. General Miliaev had sent them to lead the operation to capture the bridgehead.

They had crawled up to my trench from the rear just when my shells were crashing down upon the Germans and they still hadn't managed to fire a single round in return. But now as Nesterenko and the regimental command officers arrived, the first spotting rounds began to explode on our bank.

I immediately realized that the Germans had an observer in the church bell-tower and decided to destroy it, but it was practically impossible to hit a bell-tower with indirect fire. While perhaps simple enough to hit with direct fire, with indirect fire even as the shell is flying on a plunging trajectory, the laws of dispersion alone hinder such pinpoint accuracy.

But my higher education in mathematics and vast experience in correcting fire were not in vain. Having prepared the fire mission data, I registered the square behind the church with a spotting round. Then having mentally charted the intersection of the round's trajectory with the exterior wall of the bell-tower, I corrected the next round to try to strike the target. To my glee and personal surprise, the next round appeared to fly right through the window in the bell-tower and exploded inside. Smoke and dust instantly shot through all the windows and the explosion collapsed the tower, destroying the enemy's observation post. The barrage on our bank ceased. All this happened before the eyes of the top brass and the multitude of other observers in their observation posts.

'He did the impossible!' Gordienko exclaimed. 'He hit the window! From a howitzer! A captured howitzer! With indirect fire!'

In the meantime, work was going on at a feverish pitch in Bychok. The men made improvised rafts, found some boats and brought all these items to the river through the tunnel. I couldn't restrain myself, left the commander of my command platoon in my place at the observation post, and went down to the river. The soldiers of Morozov's battalion loaded the rafts with weapons, and some started rowing them towards the other shore using whatever could serve as a paddle, while the remainder used boats.

Our plan worked. Without any losses, as if on a picnic outing, the battalion and then the rest of the regiment crossed the river, accompanied by the thunderous fire from the captured howitzers. By evening Morozov's rifle battalion together with other hastily brought up division units had completely captured the village of Gura-Bykuly.

We didn't then realize that Morozov's group was not the only one to force a crossing, and in fact the higher command considered our effort to be a secondary one – just in case other attempts failed. The main group of the 431st Rifle Regiment with the support of two battalions from the artillery regiment crossed the Dnestr almost simultaneously with our attempt, 2 kilometers upstream from us at Krasnaia Gorka village. But our neighbors were not as fortunate; almost all of them were sunk by German fire in the roiling river. Just a small group under the command of a Lieutenant Kulakov straggled across, where it hid among some bushes on the opposite bank until later relieved by a rifle company that crossed the Dnestr at our point.

Delighted with our success in seizing a bridgehead, the commander of the 429th Rifle Regiment Lieutenant Colonel Azatian promised to decorate me with the Order of Lenin. But somewhere along the line of command, this Order got stuck, and I never received it.

Ricochets helped us out

For the rest of April, bloody battles took place as we tried to expand the bridgehead. After a month of fighting, by mid-May, we had managed to expand the bridgehead on the Dnestr up to 3 kilometers in depth. But our neighbors on the left, beyond Byk Lake, were unable to take a small hill that the Germans had strongly fortified. The Germans on this hill were now in our rear, and fired not only at our attacking neighbors, but also shot at us from behind as we attacked the Germans facing us. The trump card of the Germans on this hill was the deep and very solid trenches they had dug into the dense clay soil. Our shells had little impact on such trenches. During a barrage, the Nazis would simply wait it out in the bottom of their trenches, but as soon as the barrage lifted and our infantry attacked, they would emerge, set up their machine guns, and start to riddle our attacking line.

On this particular day, the neighboring battalion had already launched two fruitless attacks against that ill-fated hill. No-man's-land in front of the hill was littered with the corpses of our fallen soldiers. From time to time I had observed the tragic fighting of our neighbors on the left, but I had no way of helping them, because we were busy fighting against 'our' Germans that entire day. I watched as the third attack of our neighbors withered under the German machine-gun fire, and I saw the slopes of the hill strewn with the fresh corpses of our men. I felt sorry for the neighbors and decided to help them, although they had not requested it. As soon as I had a few minutes of more or less free time from participating in the fighting of our own battalion, I turned back and inspected the hill through binoculars. Once again, the neighboring infantry was falling back towards their own trenches after an unsuccessful attack. Their supporting artillery could give them no help, because its shells were falling on one side of the German trench or the other, but not landing in the trench where the Germans were relaxing between attacks. I was pondering how I could pry these Germans out of their trenches, when the laws of dispersion would prevent me from scoring a direct hit on the trench. But then a thought struck me: What if I tried ricocheting fire? My battery was in a concealed position far behind me, but on about the same line with the German hill. My crews would have to pivot the guns almost 90 degrees to the left, and the range for them would only be a kilometer. It had to work!

So I issued the orders: 'Left fifteen zero, sight setting two zero, slow fuse, full charge, number one gun one round; fire!' My gun crews probably thought that I was crazy – the sight setting was for 1 kilometer, but I was ordering a full charge – for a range of 12 kilometers! I had also turned the guns 90 degrees to the left and set a slow fuse ... Oh Lord! – The gun barrel was almost horizontal; the shell would be flying on a flat trajectory right above the ground. We had never fired like that before! But an order is an order and my gun crews trusted me. They carried out my orders and the Number 1 gun fired. The signalman with the battery immediately transmitted to my observation post: 'Shot!'

Hearing this, I looked back at the hill even more carefully – at a slope of the hill covered by the bodies of our men that had fallen in previous attacks. Our howitzer round came in at high speed, struck the slope sharply, raising a small puff of red dust, ricocheted upwards towards the German trench and exploded in the air right over it! The thunderous clap of the air burst must have shocked the Germans in the trench, just before an avalanche of steel splinters poured down on them. I gave a new order: 'Battery, four rounds, rapid fire!'

Twenty seconds later, sixteen air bursts began to thunder over the fascists' heads. The explosions were so powerful and the hail of shrapnel so concentrated that most of the Germans were killed at the bottom of their trenches. The few survivors slipped out of the trenches and ran for their lives. I let them reach an open ground before wiping them out with regular firing techniques.

As I observed the explosions of my rounds and the Germans' reaction, I also didn't lose sight of our long-suffering neighboring infantry. Relaxing, they watched animatedly as the Germans rushed around in their trenches as my shells were bursting over their heads. Exhausted by their previous assaults, our neighbors were happy, jumping up and down and applauding my artillery fire like little children. Once the Germans had been dealt with, they clambered out of their trenches and slowly walked fully upright to the German trench. Once there, they took a seat on the breastwork and gazed down upon the German dead for a long time. Having seen enough, they wiped their sweating faces with their side caps and started looking to the right, towards my battery. They were so grateful! They kept looking and looking in the direction of my guns ... and I began to feel a bit offended, making me want to shout across the lake at them, 'Look along the lake in my direction, fellows – it was my idea to make their trench too hot for them with the help of ricochet fire!' But they were one and a half kilometers away from me, and couldn't hear my voice anyway.

General Miliaev's folly

During the war I had to carry out all sorts of the most dangerous combat missions: to go after a prisoner, when all the professional scouts had failed to catch one and had lost several groups in trying; to crawl on a rainy night across a minefield and barbed wire to penetrate the German lines; to get a rifle company to rise to an assault on an impregnable German pillbox; and to confront twenty German tanks with a single battery. I did all this together with my subordinates, who trusted me and relied upon my combat experience. They knew that the job had to be done, despite the mortal dangers.

But when one day in the bridgehead on the Dnestr I received an order from the commander of the artillery regiment to deploy one of my howitzer batteries for direct fire in broad daylight on open ground that the Germans had under fire from three sides, I was horrified! This meant putting my battery on a serving platter for the Germans! As soon as my four trucks, loaded with my gun crews and ammunition and towing the heavy howitzers appeared in the front line, the Germans would open fire with everything they had. My crews wouldn't even manage to unlimber the guns and fire a single shot under that hail of bullets and shells. And just what would they be firing at if they did manage to get the guns set up, without any knowledge of the terrain or the enemy's positions?

For the first time in my life I, now a young battalion commander, protested to my regiment commander on the advisability of this idea: 'Why should we waste our men and the guns?'

'When will you forget you are no longer a student?! This is the General's order; I'm only passing it on! Your job is to follow it!' Major Gordienko cursed me out and then threatened to have me shot for refusing to carry out an order.

A professional, pre-war officer, he felt that it was more convenient to follow a senseless order, regardless of the casualties, than to protest and fall out of the General's good graces. If the whole battery perished, well, that was war. He wouldn't personally have to lead the battery to its place of execution. Moreover, he'd just been promoted to command our 1028th Artillery Regiment – how could he dare object to his superiors!

If this move would have helped us in any way to expand the bridgehead, I would have accompanied the battery myself. But in this case the pointless destruction of the battery was unacceptable to me. I couldn't let the Germans wipe out the battery, even at the threat of execution. I'd been doomed for a long time anyway – they could go ahead and shoot me!

The newly-appointed regiment commander liked to earn personal glory through volunteering the lives of his subordinates. It was enough to recall the incident back at Rzhev, when as a battalion commander, just as I was now in 1944, he had volunteered his artillery observers for a mission, which they were not trained to do, in order to bring in a German prisoner, and then had sent us out to our certain deaths. We survived then only by a miracle. Now, two years later and knowing the ways of Major Gordienko, I had my doubts that this was the General's order. Could it be another of Gordienko's stupid ideas?

I decided to persist: 'In this case, I request your permission to address the General directly.' Oh, how Gordienko despised me for this!

'Go ahead, if you're brave enough.'

General Miliaev was a smart and fair man. I was sure that I could convince him that inserting a heavy howitzer battery into the front line wouldn't frighten the Germans, and that they had enough weapons to deal with it instantly. But I was wrong. Miliaev didn't even begin to listen to me. It was fully possible that Gordienko had managed to call the General to notify him of my insubordination before I arrived, or perhaps the corps commander, not knowing the situation, had ordered Miliaev to do this. Miliaev was short and tough, and grew even angrier than Gordienko in response to my request to cancel the order. Only my high reputation as a battle-seasoned officer rescued me from the General's wrath. Demanding that I follow the order unconditionally, he nevertheless respected my request to move the battery up not all at once, but by sections. I offered the following justification: while the first section would be moving into firing positions at the front, I would use the other section to destroy any enemy weapon emplacements that revealed themselves by firing. In reality, while I was planning to return fire at the Germans, I was counting even more on the common sense of the command: when they witnessed the destruction of the first two guns, they would necessarily cancel the order for the second section. So I was hoping to cut my losses in half. But obviously it would be a shame to lose even two guns with their crews without reason!

Of course, the General wanted by any means to expand the 6-kilometer wide bridgehead on the Dnestr. But we no longer had the resources or strength to accomplish this. That's why he even decided to try to frighten the Germans with the appearance of huge guns on the front line. He didn't know the real situation in the bridgehead, as his headquarters was located 6 kilometers in the rear, but Gordienko on the other hand saw everything from his observation post.

The situation was like this. For three months now we had been expanding the bridgehead by only a few dozen meters a day at the cost of enormous losses. When our spent forces bumped up against some high hills, in which the Germans had set up virtually impregnable defenses, we could go no further and dug into defensive positions. It was then the Germans' turn to attack us with every armor and the Luftwaffe, trying at whatever the cost to hurl us back into the river, while we clung to our positions by our fingernails. The lack of air support, armor and *Katiushas* (multiple rocket-launchers), and the constant losses and thinness of our ranks had exhausted us so physically and psychologically, that anyone who was still unharmed was on the verge of physical and mental collapse. I was burdened by the thought that the Germans only needed around 200 bombers to pound us into the dust – and that would be the end of the bridgehead. The survivors, if they managed to swim back across the river, would be executed by our own side as turncoats.

I was especially distressed by the upcoming senseless and certain death of my battery, and I was unmercifully tormented by my helplessness. By following orders, I would be placing my men under fire by my own hands. Of course, only one gun section would die first, but how would I choose which gun section to condemn to certain death? They were both equally dear to me. After all, it was my own former battery, which I had commanded for more than a year, and with it I had grown from a green lieutenant to a crack commander. In two years of deadly fighting I had become so close with the crew members that I knew the character and combat qualities of each man, and knew they had families waiting back home that were writing to them. I went through the list of gun crew members in my head: which two of the crews should be granted life, even if temporarily, and which two should I send to certain death? In order to keep my conscience clean, I decided to select the guns by the order of their number: the Number 1 and Number 2 guns.

I was given one hour to prepare the operation. I called the senior officer of the battery, the handsome young Oshchepkov. He was a tall, athletic, smart and diligent lieutenant. I briefed him on the situation and gave him some advice on what to do and how to do it. Only I didn't mention the fate that was awaiting his men. I also spoke with the gun commanders Sergeants Brailko and Bobylev. Both men were priceless to me. Their crews were so disciplined and well-trained – at any moment of the day or night, I could call in a fire mission, and an accurate shot would be on the way thirty or forty seconds later. I assigned the observer Drachev to the battery, for he knew where to go, where to set up the guns, and which targets to hit. He would guide the trucks. And he would die, too.

It was noon; a bright sunny day in June. Nothing was stirring or could be seen in our front line or the Germans': everyone was dug-in, and just the wind was stirring the dry grass. Not even any ground squirrels were visible. All of a sudden on our side, two large trucks with large howitzers in tow emerged from behind a hill. They sped across the field at full speed with the guns rocking on their carriage springs. I stuck my head above the trench and turned to watch them; I could see them clearly. The trucks drove right by my trench. The happy, smiling crew members spotted me and hailed me from the back of the trucks – me, their former battery commander and current battalion commander, who had just ordered them to speed to a senseless and imminent death, though they were not aware of that. The presence of a friend here, at the front line, encouraged them and relaxed them a bit. They were confident that just like before, I would never leave them in trouble, and I'd without fail bail them out. They were sure that they were on a dangerous but important mission. I greeted them in return, trying to smile, but tears were filling my eyes: I was seeing the guys for the last time. I was feeling tremendous inner turmoil. In principle, they only knew that they were going to the front, where everything would be visible and exposed to fire, and they'd be firing directly at targets in their sights. I knew what was waiting for them due to the General's whim, but there was nothing I could do. The refusal to carry out an order not only threatened me with the death of a traitor – the next commander would simply execute the same order, while the very fact of disobeying an order would only play into the enemy's hands.

These men, the gun crews, were accustomed to life around the guns, out of the enemy's line of sight. They never saw where their rounds landed, and learned about the results of their fire only indirectly, over the phone. That's not to say they didn't have a lot of hard work in the rear: they constantly had to dig emplacements for the guns, and to move the guns and shells into them. They were dexterous and precise in their movements at the howitzers, constantly passing 25kg shells from hand to hand. But as a rule they lived in dry and warm shelters. They could walk around without having to stoop. They were rarely hit by an artillery barrage or bombed, because I always deployed the battery in concealed positions and they were always well dug-in and camouflaged. When we visited them from the front line in order to wash up, dry out, warm up and walk upright, they welcomed us like brothers. They sympathized with us over our dangerous, dog's life at the front and always felt twinges of guilt around us: we were always under fire; we were more often killed or wounded; and we had to crawl through filth, hiding from enemy observation and bullets. They on the other hand lived and worked in relatively safe conditions, like collective farm workers working in the fields. But if now their fate was to move up to the front line, in order to fire over open sights, under enemy fire, they were doing it courageously. They were heading into an inferno, but they weren't flinching.

The trucks towing the howitzers stopped 200 meters in front of my observation post, in no-man's-land just as Miliaev had demanded. Before the crews even managed to leap from the trucks, they were hit from three sides by machine-gun fire. Then mortar rounds and artillery fire began to drop around them. But all the same under the destructive fire, as the trucks were being riddled by bullets and shell fragments and had become enveloped in smoke and dust, the batterymen managed to unload the ammunition cases from them and unhitch the howitzers. The wounded drivers somehow managed to turn the trucks around and drive back into our lines, while the crews dropped to the ground – some dead, some wounded, the living trying to find cover behind the steel trails and wheels of their precious howitzers.

The firestorm raged for thirty minutes until the Germans were satisfied that they had destroyed the menacing, but impotent in those circumstances, guns and their crews. Our guns were like large pike tossed up onto a bank. The Germans couldn't wish for a better target. That's how the two howitzers remained for the entire day on that empty field under enemy fire. The rubber wheels on the howitzers were smoking and the pulverized remains of their crews lay scattered around them.

In the first minutes I managed to spot two fiercely blazing machine guns and destroyed them with the assistance of the second gun section. The Germans' mortar and artillery batteries were delivering indirect fire from behind a hill and I couldn't bring my fire to bear on them. But on the left, just on the opposite shore of Byk Lake not far away, the barrel of a German anti-tank gun, having dropped its camouflage, was being raised. Its crew couldn't resist the temptation of the easy targets and decided to make a snack of them, even at the price of exposing their position. But it didn't manage to fire: a shell from our Number 3 gun exploded right in front of the gun. Having second thoughts, the German crew quickly lowered the barrel, and the gun, with its shield removed for easier concealment, again disappeared into the tall grass. But it couldn't hide from me any longer! Just then I heard the agitated voice of Gordienko over the phone; he was observing the operation from his post, and only now probably understood that I'd been right. He shouted: 'Petia [the diminutive form of Petr]! Do you see the gun?!'

'Look, the second round is already on the way,' I replied in a more subdued tone than usual, whenever 'Petia' with his skilled fire had saved the arrogant Major's bacon.

The second round exploded right between the trails of the dangerous gun. The gun somersaulted high into the air and landed upside down, and body parts of the crew lay scattered around the wrecked gun's position.

The happiness of everyone on the front line, who had witnessed the unfolding tragedy, knew no bounds: we had taken revenge! Gordienko also praised me. The destruction of the anti-tank gun with the second round by indirect fire impressed many. Even after the war some veterans recalled this episode with admiration and joy. But at the time I cared little for the praise: the wheels of the orphaned guns – the former menace to the Nazis – were smoking in the field; and the lifeless remains of men dear to me were lying around them. They had died completely in vain.

It was impossible to send scouts or medics forward to the guns to aid any possibly wounded survivors among the gun crews – no matter how they tried to remain concealed, the Germans would have cut them down immediately. My men reached the howitzers only at twilight. They brought back two heavily wounded men; both were unconscious. We sent them back to our medical battalion. We buried the eleven remaining men in the Moldavian village of Gura-Bykuly, which was behind us on the bank of the Dnestr River. During the night we even managed to recover the guns, which rather remarkably only needed new tires and sights.

But even now I cannot forgive my General for this insanity.

CHAPTER ELEVEN

Despair

Whatever one can say, the most horrible thing in a war is not breaking out of encirclement or a night-time hunt for a prisoner, nor is it raking fire from close range or hand-to-hand combat. The most terrible thing is when you have survived two years of slaughter, when in your early twenties all of your physical and inner strength has been spent, when your throat is always scratchy and burning, when you are ready to howl like a wolf and collapse into unconsciousness on the bottom of the trench, or to hurl yourself at the enemy in a suicidal assault, just to finish with everything. You are so tired of fighting that you simply can't take it any more. This only happened to a few men, as at the front you rarely lasted for very long without getting wounded or killed. On the offensive, a private on average lasted for a couple of assaults; a platoon leader lived for a day, a company commander for a week, a battalion commander for a month. If you keep a person constantly in the front lines for a year or two, he'll go insane. That is why the Germans offered leaves of absence to their soldiers at the front. We didn't have leaves. In fact, it wasn't really necessary – who would survive to see his leave day? There were rare exceptions, though. It was hard to call such people lucky; it was more of a curse. Besides, one couldn't survive the whole war on mere luck. A bullet or a piece of shrapnel always found a man sooner or later. This happened every day, every hour and every minute. The problem was that one never knew when it would happen – in an assault, under a barrage, while getting your grub, in one's sleep, or even at some more inconvenient moment. Of course, each man prayed and secretly hoped to survive, but with men constantly dying all around you, you knew your turn would come eventually.

Only one simple thought spared the long-term survivor at the front from additional stress: he no longer had any fear. You knew you were going to die; when it happened wasn't so important. Sure, it wasn't pleasant to ponder, but once a man grew accustomed to the notion of imminent death, he overcame a certain psychological barrier and lost a lot of his fears. At first, each deferment of death was a joy. But as time passed and thousands of deaths and horrible wounds happened to those around you, the grief and emotional toll eventually exhausted a man psychologically. But it was impossible to get accustomed to the deaths of your comrades, because each one of them was a man with his own life, family, dreams and fate.

But the rare survivor did develop a sense of invincibility, a feeling that the mercy of the Almighty had made you 'untouchable'. How could they kill me? Who would fight the war, who would lead the platoon or battery? Who would protect and look after his men? One simply had to move on, fight the war, and defeat the Germans.

Some prayed for a wound. But when you see a machine-gun burst rip open a man's guts or turn a face into a bloody mask, or watch as shell fragments rip off an arm or a leg, this desire to be wounded somehow fades.

At a crawl, with short rushes, standing and falling, leaving behind dead and wounded, under a storm of enemy fire we had advanced from the Ingulets to the Dnestr in just one month. But how many lives were we paying now to hold and expand the bridgehead across the Dnestr! For almost three months now, we'd been holding onto this bridgehead by the skin of our teeth. The Germans tried everything to drive us back into the river, but we held on.

One day we had just repulsed one of the most furious enemy tank attacks; eight tanks were still smoking in no-man's-land, while we were still recollecting ourselves after what had just occurred. A deadly barrage, a merciless air raid, attacking tanks, the snarling faces of assaulting Nazi infantry ... a cacophony of howls, thunder, shrieks, hysterical yelling, the screams of wounded men, enwrapped in clouds of smoke, fumes, dust and flying clods of dirt. The surviving Germans had just crawled back to their trenches; holes and pits still gaped in our bunkers and collapsed sections of our trenches needed repairing; writhing wounded men, waiting for medics, gave a peculiar motion to the quiet battlefield covered with the bodies of dead Russians and Germans. All my communication lines were down, and losses had still not been established. My mouth was full of dirt, I had lost my side cap somewhere, my ears were ringing and my head felt heavy. I was sitting on the bottom of a trench. I had not been wounded, but I was so exhausted. Iasha Korennoi crawled up to me, also safe and sound. His hair was disheveled and his face was covered with dirt. Iasha was a tall and always cheerful and kind man. He was smiling: 'Alive, Comrade Captain?!' he asked happily.

'We're both still among the living!' I replied.

We had been together since Rzhev. Korennoi had taken part in infantry assaults with me, had gone on the mission to snatch a prisoner with me, and like me he had been fighting non-stop at the front for two years. He was a survivor like me. We were the same age, we'd both managed to see our twenty-third birthday, and today we'd both been lucky again. Of course, a private in the observer platoon had less bothers and concerns than a battery or battalion commander, but we were friends and always together. The 2nd Battery had replaced its fifth commander by now, but our 1st Battery had been lucky – I was only its third commander, and remained such until I'd been promoted to battalion commander.

In the infantry, commanders changed more frequently than in the artillery. Only Morozov had stayed on; he'd been a rifle battalion commander now for almost a year. Whenever our 52nd Rifle Division had been decimated and its remnants consolidated into one battalion, Morozov would be appointed its commander. He was a friend of mine, and my battery had always supported his battalion. We'd been in so many battles together in the past year! And here on the Dnestr we had lost so many men while trying to hold and expand this bridgehead! Yet we were always lucky. Maybe experience played its role. Morozov and I were the 'invincible ones'. We had been together in so many tough spots. On that day we had repelled the German tank and infantry attack together.

Some three hours after the attack, when everything had returned to normal, only the sentries at the machine guns were left manning the trenches. Like after a hard workday, the men had returned exhausted to their dugouts, and were relaxing. I was also lying on some dry grass in my own 'kennel'. Suddenly the cape that covered the entrance was lifted with a rustle and Morozov ducked into my dugout. Ivan was older than me; he was a former agronomer who had been drafted from the reserves, and looked much more respectable than me. His face was weathered not only by war, but also by the hot winds during fieldwork before the war.

'What, you're still sleeping?' he asked happily.

He sat down on Iasha's bed and propped his head against the low, angled ceiling. I looked at him in the light of our little home-made lamp – although it was sunny outside, it was always twilight in the dugout – and spontaneously admired Morozov. He had just been in battle but looked as sharp as if he'd been in a parade! His belt and webbing were shining, the tunic was freshly pressed. He'd managed to change his uniform. His orderly knew his job well. Morozov was of noble origins; in the years of Soviet power, his family had hidden away somewhere in the Siberian back country, pretending to be exiled revolutionaries from the Czarist times. Possibly, they really were old revolutionaries, now hiding from the purges of the 1930s. But Morozov talked more about Leningrad; apparently, his ancestors had been living there before the revolution, and that's where he was born. I recall that it was from him that I first heard about Stradivarius violins. He respected me a lot. Not only because I had studied in Leningrad before the war and knew the city well, which gave us a lot to talk about. Having a higher mathematical education and extensive combat experience, I also handled my batteries well. Morozov and his men relied on my artillery battalion, just like it was some sort of magic wand – or like 'a solid wall', as Morozov put it. When my rounds exploded in the midst of the attacking Germans and their assault broke down, while I started to destroy the fleeing remnants of the German force, Morozov would be happy like a child, jumping up and down and shouting all sorts of things.

Morozov was already thirty. He was tall and slim. He was a serious guy; a smile only brightened his face a little and straightened out the deep wrinkles that ran from his nose to his tightly-clenched jaws. His dark eyes always seemed to express some concealed irony. I would have been extremely happy to exchange my ruddy baby-face for his tawny, determined masculine face. Morozov was especially inspiring once when he had to rally his men during an assault. He rushed down the line of pinned-down men, waving a pistol over his head, but the men wouldn't get up. Two or three men rose in response to Morozov's example, but were immediately cut down by enemy fire. But Morozov seemed charmed, as if nothing could hurt him. He grabbed one man and then another and then the whole line stood up and charged forward together with Morozov. My rounds were exploding above the German trench at the same time. The enemy buckled under the pressure and fled to the rear. I and my observers and signalmen, who were playing out the cable behind them, ran to catch up with the battalion, and then together we all surged ahead across the abandoned German trenches towards their next defense line. How many more such lines were there between us and Berlin! There seemed to be a new line of defense every 300 meters!

Now in my dugout, Morozov said: 'What were you thinking about? Let's take a walk, and go see what's left of your howitzers.'

'Never mind my guns. Have you yet counted your own remaining men?'

The battalion commander replied: 'I care for your howitzers more than you do. If not for your howitzers, we'd all have been dead by now! I am happy to see that even students have brains. You did a great job! It was as if you knew what was going to happen beforehand, and that's why you deployed your guns for direct fire the night before.'

Indeed, the night before I did have some feeling that something bad was about to happen. Going on intuition, during the night I had redeployed my guns for direct fire some 200 meters behind me. During the night, the gun crew members worked hard to dig the guns in and camouflage them thoroughly. The Germans didn't detect the appearance of my batteries at the front, and had boldly attacked our position with tanks. But this morning everything had gone wrong for them quickly. As soon as the tanks emerged from a hollow and headed for our trenches, my guns opened up on them. They knocked out all eight of them in two minutes. To be honest, we did have some trouble with the German infantry, even to the point of hand-to-hand fighting in our forward trenches. There were simply too many of them. If we had not destroyed the tanks, we would have been in a tough spot. Morozov was so happy. So now he wanted to pay a visit to my gun crews as quickly as possible: 'Let's go and drop in on your gunners; I want to thank them for helping us out.'

We exited the dugout into the brightly sunlit trench, and then headed together to the rear through a communication trench. The trench soon came to an end; we exited it and walked across an emerald green field towards my guns.

'Our field back home is also this beautiful, but we don't have poppies!' Morozov exclaimed. There were indeed bright red splashes of wild poppies in the field here and there. It was extremely beautiful! But also unusually quiet! No one was firing. Only the dark shell craters marred the landscape. All of a sudden I thought of my childhood, and how I had often walked barefoot with my father through a field just like this one. Where was my father now? Also fighting somewhere...

We had walked some 100 meters when we heard a high whistling sound from above. The whistling quickly changed to a low rumble and a shell exploded not far away. Soon another round exploded on the other side of us and we realized that the Germans had spotted us and were finding the range. Apparently a German forward observer didn't like the sight of our stroll. When I heard the sound of the next incoming round, I threw myself into the nearest old shell crater. The round exploded and splinters hummed past like angry hornets. I lifted my head to see where Morozov was and whether he was still alive. I couldn't believe my eyes: he was still standing where we'd been, grinning.

'What are you doing?!' I shouted in shock.

The next round pressed me down into the ground. I lifted my head again and he was still just standing there! A question flashed through my mind: 'Was he braver than me, or simply more careless?' I had never seen him like that.

I blurted out, 'Are you crazy?! Get down!'

'Oh no. I just wanted to see what you do to try to survive,' Morozov replied sarcastically, not budging from the spot.

The next batch of deadly rounds came in and exploded all around us. The Germans had opened fire for effect. The earth shook from a multitude of powerful and rapid explosions, billions of metal fragments sliced through the air around us with all sorts of sounds. My whole body shook, and by force of habit I wanted to duck for cover again. But an arrogant, judgmental glance from Ivan, who was still standing there, stopped me. Then my own wounded pride bubbled up. I also rose to my feet and asked carelessly: 'Shall we move on?'

'Yes, indeed,' Morozov calmly replied and together we slowly walked through the explosions towards my gun pits, putting on quite a display of foolish bravado. The German forward observer lost us in the dust and smoke. But when he saw us again still intact and unharmed, he became very angry and opened such a merciless fire that it seemed nothing and no one could survive.

I once called in fire on two fleeing German soldiers like this, but when the smoke cleared after the third shell, I saw the surviving German lift his wounded comrade to his shoulders and start to carry him. Then I ceased fire, amazed at the persistence of these two men and touched by this benevolent act of one soldier to an injured comrade.

We sensed the mood of this German forward observer when new volleys of rounds rained down on us. Grandstanding in front of each other, we walked onward through the barrage without increasing our pace. A blizzard of fragments flew all around us. It was surreal! Just like in a movie, when the main character cannot be killed because of the script, we sauntered through the fire totally unharmed. The German observer was not impressed with our bravery. He intensified the fire, activating all six guns of his battery! The rounds were exploding in front and behind, to the left and right, dust and smoke stung our eyes. Shell fragments howled, buzzed and whistled past our foolish heads and charmed bodies. We continued to walk at the same slow pace, silently, not looking at each other. My gun crews, craning their necks from the gun pits, were angrily and adamantly signaling to us to take cover, but we just continued to walk. When we finally jumped into a slit trench near the guns, the German observer lost sight of us and ceased fire.

Pale and sweating, we took off our side caps and started to wipe our faces with them. The top of Morozov's side cap had been torn by a shell splinter.

'Comrade Captains! You ought to be ashamed to expose yourselves to fire like that,' angrily buzzed the older soldiers in one voice.

'We're such fools, the two of us,' I said to Morozov with conviction.

Suddenly his face twisted into a grimace, large tears welled from his tightly-clenched eyes, and in front of the soldiers he covered his face with his large hands, burst into sobs and broke out in a loud, desperate wail: 'I can't take this any more! I can't! I caaaaan't!'

I had never seen him like this before and couldn't imagine that such a determined, brave man could reach such a state of complete nervous exhaustion. I was in the same condition, and only a thread was keeping me from a nervous breakdown as well. Likely, the presence of my own men also held me back. But I had already lost all common sense. Three months of uninterrupted fighting, assaults and barrages, panzers and bombers, and German attempts to drive us into the river – all this had taken its toll on us. We were at the point of complete nervous and physical collapse. Other men were getting wounded and killed, and this meant the end of their sufferings. Yet we were charmed!

Of course it was desperate madness, this desire to die. But what force was keeping us from death?

By evening, through both open and secret channels, the division commander already knew about our act of insanity. General Miliaev summoned us one by one and gave each of us a scolding, but understanding our condition, he nevertheless sent us both to an officers' sanatorium in Odessa. We weren't even aware such places existed, as they were primarily used by political, staff and supply officers, not combat officers. The General told us: 'I'm giving up the only two tickets we have to the seaside sanatorium to you; they're the first two tickets the division has received. I'm doing this only because I know both of you are irreplaceable combat officers.'

He would have court-martialed us, if we had not been his best officers in any battle. The NKVD would have been happy to see us, too.

Why didn't we receive leaves of absence from the front line as a policy? As I mentioned, the Germans gave their own soldiers leaves, even though their deficit in the ranks was by far greater than our own. I don't think that kindness or compassion pushed them to do this; it was more a matter of practicality. The German high command knew that a rested soldier fought three times better than an exhausted one, while our Supreme High Command never gave it any consideration. We fought on until we were wounded or killed, and one didn't have to wait long for this to happen. But what about those few of us who were spared by bullets? I know for myself that we were almost insane.

Ten days of vacation at the seaside, far from the front, completely erased all the stress and we returned to the front as shiny as new five-ruble coins. We were still hearing the sound of the blue waves in our ears, and still seeing the gleaming marble surfaces of the palace walls, when all of a sudden we were back in our trenches, the raw earth churned up by explosions right under our noses. We smelled the fresh black earth, something familiar, intimate ... and frightening.

Then we resumed the offensive, and encircled the Germans at Iasi and Kishinev...

CHAPTER TWELVE

My Heroic Crews!

We were almost too late, even though we had driven to the village of Karakui in Moldavia at top speed. I, a battalion commander, had received an urgent order from the regiment commander to pull together a gun battery within ten minutes and lead it to Karakui before the Germans arrived there. Some 20 kilometers from our position, a large German force from the enemy's encircled Iasi–Kishinev grouping had broken out of the pocket the previous night and was escaping westward along a wide, long ravine. We were ordered to intercept, delay and destroy the Germans. The 2nd Battery had all at once lost its commander and all three gun section leaders in previous fighting, so I chose this battery for the mission. We loaded 500 rounds of ammunition onto the trucks, picked up the crews and a combat medic, and moved out.

The sun was already up, the sky was clear, and a hot summer day was in the offing. But as is often the case in late summer, the dawn was chilly. As soon as we had arrived at the edge of the ravine and had unhitched our guns, the forward elements of the enemy's force emerged from behind a turn in the ravine about a kilometer away to our left.

They were moving quickly towards us in a dense mass that spanned the width of the ravine, but not in any formation. Each Nazi vehicle was trying to outrun the others, so the entire mass seemed to be seething and writhing. This monster's metallic spine flashed and glittered in the rays of the rising sun. Vehicles, wagons, half-tracks, mounted soldiers and men on foot were packed together, with hardly a gap between them.

My men, as they saw the enemy armada approaching, quaked in their boots, but no one openly expressed any fear or doubts. They just clenched their jaws and redoubled their efforts to prepare for the looming battle. We unloaded the ammunition and deployed the guns for firing in just three minutes. There was no time to dig in, so as soon as the guns' trails were anchored, I gave the order to fire. We had to hurry to try to halt the Germans as far from the battery as possible; if they managed to close in on us, they could easily outflank us and destroy us. My men realized the odds were strongly against us: four guns against such an armada! But we were determined to fight to the last man.

I decided to place the head of the German column under strong blocking fire to force them to stop. Then, after they turned back, I would destroy them. The rising sun was at our backs, so the Germans didn't spot us before we opened up; our fire was a complete surprise to them. The thunder of twenty powerful explosions and the geysers of dirt right in front of them threw the first ranks of the German column into confusion. Vehicles immediately stopped, horses reared in panic, and foot soldiers threw themselves down into the tall grass. But the rest of the column continued to surge forward, and the armada, rolling over the men lying on the ground and bypassing the explosions, just kept advancing at an even greater speed, as if nothing had happened.

I was lying with my binoculars on the very edge of the ravine, in some grass to the left of the left-most Number 4 gun. The other guns were lower and echeloned behind me to my right. Having stunned the enemy with the blocking fire, the crews froze at their guns, waiting for my next commands. Unexpectedly, the Germans set up some heavy machine guns to the right of the column, high on the ravine's slope. In just a matter of seconds, they swept our positions with concentrated fire. The half-tracks also opened up on us with machine guns. A hail of bullets struck the gun positions. The gun crew men were crouching behind the gun shields, but some bullets still found a mark and we had our first casualties.

'Number four gun,' I ordered, 'destroy the machine guns!'

In rapid order, the gun knocked out several of the German machine-gun positions.

'Battery! At the head of the column, rapid fire!'

At this point, the disorganized German column had advanced some 150 meters along the ravine and was continuing to approach us. Angered by the determination of the enemy and embittered by the first casualties, the crews redoubled their fire on the Germans, pouring shell after shell into the oncoming mass. I observed the explosions and the reaction of the enemy through binoculars. I had never before fired at such a packed target. Shells were exploding in the midst of the enemy mass. In the blink of an eye, soldiers running shoulder to shoulder, horse-drawn wagons, and vehicles squeezed in among this human mass were being blown apart and thrown in every direction. Gaps began to form in the onrushing mass, leaving behind growing piles of wreckage and the torn bodies of men and horses. The head of the column disintegrated in several seconds. But the determination of the German command and the desperate resolve of the troops didn't waver. They refused to turn back. The remaining body of the column, at least 500 meters long, split and started to climb both slopes in the effort to avoid the carnage and explosions in the bottom of the ravine, but stubbornly kept advancing. Leaping over the wreckage of wagons and the bodies of men and horses, falling and rising among the shell craters and explosions, the Germans were drawing ever nearer to us. They had no time to fire at us, but their commanders were somewhere behind them and kept on directing the hellish process, continuing to push the men, who hadn't yet been hit by our shells, or those who couldn't yet see the horror awaiting them because of the men in front of them, into the grim slaughter.

I was shocked by the determination of the enemy to break out of the encirclement; I spontaneously had the thought that they must have committed war crimes and didn't want to surrender to avoid retribution. But I had no time to psychoanalyze the enemy's behavior. My job was to fulfill the order to stop the enemy, whatever stubbornness he might display. I didn't stop to reflect on the price of executing this order either.

Just as I was about to shift the fire into the depth of the enemy column, I heard a familiar whistle of incoming mortar rounds. Several rounds landed in front and behind my battery. The Germans had us bracketed and were about to fire for effect. Dozens of mortar rounds were about to rain down on us; we couldn't prevent their fall, nor the terrible havoc they were about to make around the guns, killing everyone around with their shrapnel. We were doomed, as we had not had time to dig in and we were exposed. There was nowhere to hide, but we didn't have time for this anyway. We had to continue our rapid fire, disregarding our own fate. We couldn't see the enemy's mortars either and couldn't target them to try to destroy or suppress them. We could only continue firing as long as we could, while the German mortar crews ranged in on us.

'Battery, at the whole column, rapid fire!' I ordered, not stopping to think about other things.

The rapid shots of all our guns rang out all along the front of the battery – dozens of rounds that devastated the enemy's column. Fewer and fewer men were left standing. There were no longer thousands of them, but only hundreds that were still closing on us. We had to destroy them, before they broke into the battery's position and finished off anyone still alive after the coming mortar barrage.

Then here they were – the German mortar rounds! They dropped closer and closer to us, tightening into a cluster around our guns. It had become a monstrous competition to determine who would kill more before being killed!

Clouds of dust and smoke shrouded the entire battery. Seemingly millions of splinters were riddling the area. The crews, however, continued their frenzied work. One soldier fell dead, then a second. But a third one, obviously wounded and overcoming his pain, stretched out to the gun breech and loaded another shell. Dead and wounded strewed the ground between the guns' trails. But the survivors – on their knees, on all fours, on their back – were continuing to pass shells to the loaders, and the guns continued to fire. Decimated crews were down to just two or three wounded men who continued to operate the guns.

Suddenly a mortar round landed between me and the Number 4 gun, killing almost its entire crew. Only the loader remained standing at the gun. I took position at the sight and the two of us continued to fire as fast as we could. More shells exploded around us. One of them tore the legs off the loader, and a splinter penetrated the joint of my right knee. The pain was unimaginable, and blood began to fill my boot. Ignoring the pain but limping badly, I continued to load, aim and fire the gun. I took a glance: the Number 1 and Number 2 guns were out of action. The shouted casualty reports had stopped: 'Sidorov has been killed!' 'Nikolenko is wounded!'

There were more and more dead and wounded on the ground. The combat medic Gruzdev was working on casualties over by the Number 1 gun. He was bandaging the same men for the third or fourth time, or seeing that a man was now beyond saving, he was scrambling over to the next wounded man. Limber gunner Pokhomov, all in bandages, crawled up to the Number 1 gun. His legs were smashed. Pulling himself up on the breech, he loaded the gun and pressed the firing pedal. There was no one to take aim, nor was this even necessary. The round was bound to hit something or someone.

The only man who was still unscathed was the Number 3 gun commander, Sergeant Khokhlov. He was continuing to blast the Germans together with his limber gunner Kruglov. But then he ran out of shells! Crouching low, Khokhlov rushed to the next gun, fired it, grabbed a round and returned to his gun.

Mortar rounds kept plopping around the guns. Their deadly splinters killed those that had been wounded just seconds earlier. Medic Gruzdev died with a bandage in his hand. Just a second earlier, he had shouted that there were no wounded left. They had all died after receiving multiple wounds.

But the enemy had also suffered horrendous casualties. It was no longer a solid wall of soldiers, but small groups of survivors continuing to advance. Wildly neighing horses, mad with fear, intact and wounded, were darting around the field.

I took aim at the nearest group of charging Nazis. They fitted into my sight nicely. I placed the cross hairs on the center of the group, pressed the pedal, and watched my round blow the charging men to pieces.

In the meantime the mortar barrage on the battery subsided and then stopped completely. Apparently, the Germans were out of ammo. The explosions stopped, but the battery was already dead. Germans were now just 200 meters away from us. 'This was it,' I thought, 'there's only Khokhlov and me still alive, and we're almost out of ammunition.' The Germans were about to overrun us and finish us off.

I took aim at the next group of some twenty men, which for some reason had suddenly stopped in front of my gun. Just as I was about to press the pedal, I saw something white emerge among the men. With disbelieving eyes, I watched as one man placed a white undershirt onto the point of a bayonet, and began to wave the white flag from side to side. Were they surrendering? Indeed, they had raised the white flag!

'Cease fire,' I shouted to the battery, though only Khokhlov was still able to hear my command. Khokhlov rose up from behind the sight. He was also stunned, staring at the white flag and comprehending nothing.

I yelled over to him: 'Khokhlov! Get over there before they change their minds! Order them to drop their weapons! Order them into a column and lead them over to the other side of the ravine, so they can't see that the battery is gone!'

The long-legged Sergeant Khokhlov ran over to the Germans in long strides. I thought the Germans were going to cut him down. But Khohlov stopped 10 meters in front of them, raised his submachine-gun, and began gesturing to them. Apparently, there were officers among the group of Germans in front of Khokhlov. I heard them bark orders to the other groups of survivors and watched them give hand signals. Slowly, Germans began to walk towards the white flag from every direction. They threw their weapons down into a pile, and formed into a column of men eight to ten files wide. The senior German officer led the column away towards the other side of the ravine.

Khokhlov walked along the column with his gun ready. How many Germans were there: 500, a thousand? Then I woke up and started crawling from gun to gun, aiming them to the right at the German column. I wanted them to see that they were still in our sights, even though we had no one left to fire the guns and nothing left to fire. The men of the battery, twenty-four of them, were lying dead. Many had been disfigured beyond recognition by the explosions and multiple wounds. How had it been possible to survive in such a hell?!

I still firmly hold the opinion that there is no more effective and deadly weapon in close combat than an 82mm mortar. The rounds drop almost vertically, and the craters their explosions create are small, only about the size of a canteen. But when a shell explodes, it sends fragments flying just above the ground and in such numbers that they literally shave the grass, leaving only a blackened patch of earth about 5 meters in diameter. Any living thing inside this sinister black area ceases to exist, torn to pieces by the shrapnel.

Only Khokhlov and I survived out of the twenty-six men. As I moved from gun to gun in order to point them at the German prisoners, I also carefully examined the bodies around each gun, hoping that someone might still be breathing. But all were dead.

Time was still passing. The Germans were standing and waiting on the other side of the ravine, about 500 meters away, facing my guns and awaiting their fate. Khokhlov was with them, impatiently shifting from one foot to the other, also waiting. But I didn't know what Khokhlov was expecting me to do – he knew that I only had one functioning leg left! At the moment, I was feeling outrage at our truck drivers. After unlimbering our guns, I had sent the trucks away into a nearby ravine for cover. But they had to know that the battle was over; why were they still sitting there?! Perhaps they thought the battery had been destroyed, and they were afraid to show themselves? They were drivers, support troops that never were supposed to participate in battle. Would the regiment commander also show no concern about our fate? The Germans could strangle us with their bare hands. There were hundreds of them. That would be a tragic end to this battle!

As I was cutting my trousers with a pocket knife and bandaging my wound, no one on our side appeared on the horizon. I was becoming more frightened than I had been during the battle. I cut down a bush and made a walking stick – not very thick, but strong enough to support me. Then suddenly I caught the sound of engines! Had our drivers woken up? Trucks carrying soldiers appeared. It was the division's scout company. Captain Mikhailov, its commander, stepped out of the first truck. He knew me well from back when I'd been sent on that mission to snatch a prisoner near Rzhev.

'Take the prisoners,' I said, 'they're all standing over there.'

Mikhailov walked over to the prisoners. It turned out that there were more than 800 of them. He marched the prisoner column over to the village of Karakui, which was about 200 meters from our position, and ordered them to fall into a large yard. When I reached the yard, Mikhailov had just finished giving a speech and a German stepped out of the group. I stopped next to Mikhailov, leaning on my stick.

The German took out a yellow plastic jar from his pocket, twisted it open and showed us its contents. Then he told us in clear Russian: 'The Germans gave us so little butter! They gave more butter to their men! But we fight even better than the Germans! You could sense that for yourselves today. We were the ones firing the mortars at you.'

'Who is this?' I asked Mikhailov.

'He is one of Vlasov's men [a general term applied to any Russian found fighting on the German side; the reference is to former Red Army General Andrei Vlasov, commander of the Russian Liberation Army]. They are the majority of the 826 prisoners here.'

'What a bastard! He's boasting of destroying our battery!' Then addressing the prisoner, I asked: 'Where are you from?'

'I'm from Voronezh.'

'So, a compatriot!' I exclaimed and hobbled up to the traitor.

He was looking at me with perplexity. With all my remaining strength, I angrily struck the 'compatriot' on the head with my stick. He collapsed to the ground. I don't know what became of him. I wasn't interested. I returned to my position next to Mikhailov and asked in a loud voice, 'Any more of you from Voronezh?'

There was silence.

'You swine! You were killing your fellow countrymen and now you complain to us that the Germans gave you too little food!'

That was the end of my conversation with the prisoners. I wound up in the medical battalion with my wounded leg. No one in the command showed any interest in me, called me, or dropped by to express appreciation for what we had done in that ravine near the Moldavian village of Karakui.

After the war, I once visited our General. Miliaev asked me: 'Do you happen to know what became of the officer who stopped that avalanche of Germans in Moldavia, slaughtering thousands of them and taking about a thousand as prisoner? I walked that ravine after the battle. I think he survived.'

When I replied that I was the officer in question, he was amazed and asked, 'Why didn't we decorate you with the Hero of the Soviet Union's Gold Star?'

What could I say to the General?

PART THREE

Here it is, Eastern Europe!

CHAPTER THIRTEEN

Romania – Bulgaria – Yugoslavia

By the end of August 1944 we had finally destroyed the enemy's encircled Iasi –Kishinev grouping, and had finally expelled the German occupiers from our country. But they were still strong and we had to finish them off. We were to lose so many more men before we reached the ultimate victory! But we fought with much higher spirits: we were constantly on the attack. While we were struggling with the surrounded Germans, our forces had forced the Dunai [Danube] River, crossed the Romanian border and taken the port of Constanta.

Our division marched into Ismail – a town where Suvorov had covered himself with glory after successfully storming the Turk-occupied fortress there in 1790. Romania lay in front of us beyond the Dunai. We crossed the Dunai at Ismail on 31 August and headed south, towards the Bulgarian border.

The Romanians were hiding from us, especially the women, fearing that we would take revenge against them for the outrages committed by the Romanian soldiers in Russia. We, in turn, were shocked by the extreme poverty of the common people. Their huts were squalid and shabby. We entered one of them. Its floors were clay and there was virtually no furniture. Instead of beds, they had wood planking perched on trestles, covered by pieces of old homespun floor runners. There were no curtains, not even a single piece of fabric. The owners – a small, slim old lady and her husband, an unshaven old man – wore old and dirty clothing. When we sat down on the bench with our backs towards the table, the old lady asked us with gestures if we were hungry. Out of curiosity, we didn't refuse, and the woman pulled a pot from the stove holding some dark brown porridge with bits of corn in it. That was the only food they had. There was no bread or anything else. The dish was tasteless without butter or fat in it. In order not to offend the couple, we tried a couple of spoonfuls and thanked the owners. The sight was the same in the other huts we entered as well. We encountered cottages without chimneys or windows. The fields were divided into tiny plots of land. But the noblemen's mansions were surrounded with cherry orchards, and chestnut and poplar trees.

Then Russian village names began to appear on the maps: Babadag, Chernavoda, Khyrshovo. When we entered the villages, we were welcomed by Russians in holiday costumes. Russian speech and tasty food! On the grass near the barns, just like it was once in Voronezh oblast back in the 1920s, there were groups of women sitting in circles with their little children, eating, playing cards, laughing, and singing songs. The locals were celebrating: Russian soldiers had arrived! Apparently, these were villages inhabited by the descendants of Russian settlers who had arrived here in the time of Catherine the Great. They had preserved their language and the Russian way of life ever since the eighteenth century. They remembered and loved Russia.

We reached the Bulgarian border on 8 September 1944. The Soviet Union had declared war on Imperial Bulgaria, an Axis ally, on 5 September. We deployed for battle and were prepared to fight our way into Bulgaria. We sent our scouts ahead to the Bulgarian checkposts that were visible down the road. Soon the scouts gave us a signal: don't shoot, the Bulgarians are surrendering. It turned out that the young Bulgarian czar had fled the country with his regents, a popular uprising was under way, and the Fatherland Front had seized power. Men wearing white armbands with 'FF' on them were everywhere.

In the very first villages we entered, crowds of men greeted us with posters: 'Welcome, brothers!' They gave us wine, fruits, dinners, and recalled 1878 when the Russian soldiers had liberated Bulgaria from Turkish occupation. They asked us to stay and celebrate together with them. But we were marching according to a strict schedule; we had two weeks to cross Bulgaria on foot and horseback and make it to the Yugoslavian border.

We entered Yugoslavia in early October 1944. From the lowlands of the Danube in north-western Bulgaria, there was only one road leading through the mountainous areas of Yugoslavia to Belgrade, and it passed through the Yugoslavian border town of Zajecar.

The Germans had so strongly fortified Zajecar that to storm the city would have cost us half the division. This was just what the Germans were hoping: to give us a costly check here, where there were no other roads available. But we fooled the Germans. By that time we had learned how to fight and we didn't attempt to storm the city directly. With the assistance of Serbian partisans, we literally infiltrated Yugoslavia using mountain paths and forest trails. The lead regiments bypassed Zajecar and reached the main road to Belgrade beyond the town.

Leaving behind a strong blocking force in case the Germans attempted to break out of Zajecar and attack us from behind, we moved on to the west along the road to Belgrade. But the Germans had more troops in Zajecar than our generals believed. A tragedy happened: over thirty tanks, armored half-tracks and trucks with infantry sallied out of the town, brushed aside our rear guard, and linked up with friendly forces after smashing our division's rear. At this time, we had already advanced some 20 kilometers and had captured several villages in battle along the way. But we had pulled up in front of Bolevats, which seemed strongly defended and couldn't be bypassed because of the steep terrain and vertical cliffs that nearly surrounded the town. Rifle regiments were slowly moving up to storm the town.

Waiting for the division's main forces to arrive, together with a rifle battalion my artillery battalion deployed in temporary defensive positions on the edge of a grove. The highway ran through our positions, and then passed through a cornfield on its way down into Bolevats. My observation post was beside the road, while the riflemen were dug in on the left and right of the road. I set up a gun for direct fire on either side of the road in case of a German armor attack. The remaining ten guns of my battalion were positioned along the road behind us. Military units were virtually road-bound in this mountainous terrain.

Although we had tried to conceal our positions carefully on the edge of the woods, the Germans knew where we were and constantly harassed us with machine-gun and mortar fire. My Lieutenant Iurii Medvedev was wounded in the head by some tiny splinters from a mortar round. He needed surgery and I decided not to take any chances and sent him back for medical attention: 'Iurii, go back to the medical battalion. Although you say your head doesn't hurt, you should take care of it and get some rest. A 15-kilometer walk is a piece of cake for you.'

It was early morning. October in Yugoslavia was like late August in Russia; it was warm and the sun was bright, the trees were still green and flowers were still in bloom. Medvedev made himself a walking stick and slowly headed for the division's rear. Nature was at its finest all around him. It was extremely beautiful! Clean air, filled with the scents of trees, flowers and herbs, filled his lungs.

'The locals live in paradise,' Medvedev thought enviously.

After walking some 10 kilometers, the Lieutenant was passing through the village of Planinica, where our artillery regiment's headquarters were located. The road ahead was winding and hilly. About 5 kilometers away, through a gap in some bushes, the Lieutenant spotted tanks. He was happy – reinforcements were coming! But the tanks were advancing too carefully; they were prowling as if fearing an ambush ... The Lieutenant raised his binoculars to his eyes, took a close look ... and saw white crosses on them! They were German tanks! They'd broken out of Zajecar! Medvedev turned around and ran back to the regiment's headquarters in Planinica as fast as he could.

'German tanks are approaching from the rear!' he reported to the chief of staff. The latter called me: 'Mikhin, urgently deploy two howitzers for direct fire on the eastern side of Planinica! Tanks are coming!'

Less than fifteen minutes later, the guns had been set up in a garden and were ready to fire. The tanks were now just 700 meters away, advancing cautiously down the road.

Battery commander Oshchepkov issued the orders: 'Number one gun – target the lead tank, number two – target the tail-end tank! Fire!'

Both targeted tanks were knocked out; the rest had no room to maneuver on the hilly road. Three minutes later, all twelve tanks were in flames. Surviving tankers began to bail out through open hatches, and were shot down by our infantry that was emerging from the ravines. But this was only the head of the tank column. It turned out that the Germans had five times more troops in Zajecar than our command had supposed.

Fighting between our artillerymen and riflemen and the enemy column developed along the length of the highway. Just then, a report came in over the telephones that the Germans had overrun our rear guard and had destroyed our division's rear and the medical battalion, killing virtually all the wounded, nurses, doctors and medics. Unarmed and helpless, only a few managed to escape into a nearby forest. The whole division soon learned of this crime. Anger and hatred only made our men fight better and more bravely. The damn Fritzes – this was no longer 1941, when we panicked at any sign of the Germans in our rear! Everone wanted to kill and take revenge!

German infantry attacked the firing positions of our howitzer battery. They surrounded the guns and, firing on the move, charged out of the bushes towards the crews. They were too close to use the heavy guns, so the gun crews set up an all-round defense with machine guns and submachine-guns. The range was so close that hand grenades were employed. The bitter fighting ended with our victory. The Germans never got in among our guns; many were killed, six were captured, and the rest scattered. We also took casualties: two killed and three wounded.

Oshchepkov reported over the phone: 'We destroyed twelve tanks and many trucks with infantry. We captured two trucks intact and drivers are bringing them into the battalion's main position. Tell everyone over the phone not to fire at the captured trucks.'

The captured trucks turned off the main road into the battalion's area safe and sound. But for some reason there were two more tarpaulin-covered trucks following them, and they continued on towards the front line at top speed. Our units along the highway realized that the two last trucks were manned by Germans. They were either trying to use our captured trucks as cover, or else they had just joined up with them, believing they were still in German hands. When our captured trucks turned off the main road, the Germans realized their mistake and raced ahead.

Frantic firing at the two German trucks erupted along the wooded 3-kilometer stretch of winding and hilly road. Everyone shouted: 'Fire, they're Germans!' It seemed as if everyone was firing, but as if protected by a magic spell, the trucks roared through our positions. There must have been a lot of casualties in the back of the trucks from all the bullets that were striking it, but the drivers were obviously still alive. As they sped past our positions, the Germans also opened fire from the trucks and wounded several of my men. Almost before we knew it, both trucks had escaped the fusillade and were racing downhill through the cornfield towards their lines. The Germans were probably already celebrating that they were safe, as they had only 300 meters left to their own lines.

'Fire!' I shouted to Bobylev, the commander of the gun next to me. Bobylev fired his gun, but because the range was set for 700 meters and the targeted truck was only 100 meters away, the round flew just over the roof. But the sound of the passing round seemed to stun the Germans. The truck slowed, and two men bailed out of it into the cornfield. The driver recovered from the shock and accelerated, but Bobylev's second shot blew the truck to pieces. Body parts were seen dangling from the truck's wreckage. The gun on the other side of the road destroyed the second truck with its first round.

No German vehicle from Zajecar broke through our positions.

I sent scouts into the cornfield to track down the two Germans that had bailed out. After a brief exchange of fire, they caught the two Germans and brought them back to my position at the edge of the woods. When I walked over to them, my men had already searched the prisoners. One of the men, wearing an SS uniform, was carrying a photo that my men found and gave to me. The photo was small but I could see all the faces clearly: the SS prisoner was happily posing in the middle of a town street, his thumbs hooked in his belt. In the background there were gallows where the bodies of three men in civilian clothing, a woman, and a youth were hanging. Two small boys were standing to one side of the gallows, their hands clasped over their lips, looking fearfully and sadly at the hanging bodies. My men and the riflemen pressed around the owner of the photo: why had he executed the Serbs?! The SS soldier was scared and tried to convince us that he wasn't the one responsible for the execution. An infantryman, just wounded in the skirmish with the German trucks, ran up, started shouting something, and began shoving his submachine-gun into the German's face. Before I could intervene, he fired a burst and killed the prisoner.

'Don't shoot the prisoners!' I shouted, afraid they would also kill the second captive; I'd have to answer to the NKVD for them.

The second German had an edelweiss blossom on his field cap – he was a *Gebirgsjäger*, a specialist in mountain warfare. I led him away to the side and ordered a scout to take him to the battalion headquarters.

In the meantime, my crews were dealing with the prisoners at the positions of the 3rd Battery outside Planinica that had received the German attack. Outraged crew members had badly beaten the German prisoners, but the battery's Sergeant Major Makukha had somehow managed to take the prisoners away into a cornfield. He then started to bring them to regiment headquarters. As he marched the prisoners across the field, Makukha was full of hatred: they had killed such good men! Breech operator Nikolaev had two children, gunlayer Osetsky was single and didn't have any children, but he had many younger brothers and sisters and his father was also at the front. How could his mother take care of all the kids? If his father was also killed, it would be an awful thing for the family ... So Makukha impulsively decided to execute the damn Fritzes on the spot – after all, these were the most aggressive ones, and that is exactly why they had ended up as prisoners; their comrades had fled. The Sergeant Major decisively jerked back the bolt of his submachine-gun. But before he could pull the trigger, the wary Germans, hearing the loud metallic click and understanding what was about to happen, took off at a run in every direction. Makukha pulled the trigger, but the gun didn't fire. A cartridge jam! It happened with our submachine-guns sometimes. The Germans were gone!

I got the report. I summoned Makukha to the phone: 'Why don't you keep your weapon clean? It has been lying in your wagon for months, and it's probably completely rusted!'

Makukha tried to defend himself but I didn't listen, although I understood his mood very well. I continued, 'It's a pity that the Germans didn't come back and smash you over your stupid head with your own submachine-gun!'

The NKVD didn't bother me about the prisoners this time. I guess they understood the mood of the entire division after the Germans had slaughtered the wounded and the personnel of our medical battalion.

In Yugoslavia, for the first time we encountered the special conditions of combat in mountainous terrain, where all movement, maneuvers and combat takes place exclusively along roads. Enormous massifs, rapid rivers, abysses and gorges – and there was only a single, winding ribbon of road that connected the numerous villages. There was no front line as such, no neighboring units; the Germans would suddenly appear on our flanks or in our rear. We were fighting against troops that specialized in mountain warfare, and who knew the tactics to use in these conditions. The question asks itself: why didn't the analysts on the Soviet General Staff issue recommendations to us beforehand on combat tactics in mountainous terrain?

Rtanj Mountain

We captured Boljevac. There the road split. To the right, the road led north to Paracin; to the left, south towards Krusevac on the Belgrade–Saloniki highway and on the banks of the Great Morava River. My artillery battalion, supporting Abanshin's 431st Rifle Regiment, was to advance towards Paracin.

One could reach from Boljevac only through Lukovo, along a road squeezed between the highest mountain of Eastern Serbia, the Rtanj (1,565 meters) on one side, and a deep gorge with the Timok River at its bottom on the other. The road was 40 meters wide and was under fire from both flanks: from higher up the mountain on the right and from the other side of the gorge. The Germans had zeroed in on the road with machine guns, mortars and heavy guns firing over open sights. The pass was extensively mined, and explosives had been rigged above the road, in order to trigger powerful avalanches down on the attackers. In addition to all this, artillery shells and mortar rounds were constantly raining down on the pass from beyond the mountain, where the German artillery and heavy mortar batteries were positioned in a broad valley.

Well, how could I, an artillery battalion commander, help a rifle regiment break through the obstacle at Lukovo and penetrate to Paracin? I thought briefly about firing on the sheer rock wall to the right of the road, in an effort to create a screen of smoke and dust to allow the infantry and combat engineers to rush into the pass, but I knew this was also likely to just block the road with rubble. I also couldn't spot the German artillery beyond the mountain, in order to try to suppress its fire.

But I had help. Just like in Bulgaria, the local Serb population greeted us enthusiastically; the partisans and fighters of the People's Liberation Army particularly loved us. Not only were we fighting side by side to drive out the fascists, but I also often helped them out with the fire of my artillery.

I turned to the Serb partisans for assistance: 'Is there some other way to get over or around Rtanj, besides this road? Are there any paths up the mountain by which we could move our guns?'

It turned out that there were paths, but I could hardly move my guns along them: they were narrow, with sharp turns and a few extremely muddy locations due to recent rains. But I decided to leave my deputy, Captain Svintsov, at the command post and to take two guns each towed by ten horses, along with the crews and the ammunition caissons, and try to find an alternative route to the western side of Rtanj. It is hard now for me to describe our adventures, but by the end of the day we had reached a level area on the western side of the mountain beneath some large cider trees. At times we had been forced to haul the horses and guns out of mud bogs that were a meter deep, using nearby trees and sturdy ropes ... But it is equally difficult to describe our joy when we spotted the enemy's batteries from our location! They were the very batteries that were striking our troops in the pass with indirect fire!

We deployed under the cider trees and took aim at the German batteries. The guns opened fire on my command. The effect of our fire was devastating. Our rounds seemed to come out of nowhere and everywhere at once, as the echoes in the mountains made it difficult for the Germans to spot our location. Within minutes, we had destroyed four German artillery and mortar batteries totaling twenty-four guns and mortars and at least 100 German artillerymen.

The destruction of the German batteries behind Rtanj Mountain was a signal for our troops to storm the pass at Lukovo. For the Germans, it was a signal to retreat, as they had lost their supporting artillery. The 431st Rifle Regiment captured the pass in less than an hour with the support of my artillery battalion. The Germans yielded Lukovo without a fight.

I had three batteries in my artillery battalion, but as so often happens in war, one of them was particularly unlucky, having lost four commanders in the recent fighting. So about this time I received the fifth one.

'Senior Lieutenant Raskovalov,' he introduced himself upon presenting himself to me.

He was tall, slim, nice-looking and very modest, even shy. He was from the reserves, and had been a school principal in Siberia, where he had also taught mathematics. He was not yet used to wearing a military uniform and was always tugging at the bottom of his tunic. His thin, slightly long face always had an apologetic smile on it. He was about ten years older than me.

In order to acquaint him with the dangers at the front and to make sure he survived, I kept him for two weeks in a reserve battery. Then I brought him to my observation post, where I appointed him to command my on-call battery. I taught him what I knew and tried to keep him out of danger. He attentively watched my actions. He moved quickly at the front line, camouflaged himself well and was fearless. He directed his battery's fire missions well. He had mastered the rules of gunnery, and you could sense his background in mathematics. I knew he had three children. I just couldn't lose such a man.

We were temporarily on the defensive, anticipating a breakout attempt by German armor. I really needed to deploy Raskovalov's battery up at the front in direct fire positions, although I tried to postpone this for as long as I could. He asked for my assistance in selecting the firing positions for his guns. Early one October morning, as it was just getting light, after we had picked out places for his guns and crawled away from the dangerous location about 200 meters, we stood up and started walking along a ravine. All of a sudden the Senior Lieutenant stopped and said: 'Comrade Captain, if the tanks emerge over there from that branch of the ravine, we won't notice them right away from our selected location. Do you mind if I place my guns a bit higher?'

Praising him for his resourcefulness, I agreed, then added: 'Now quickly back to our trench, before the Germans spot us.'

But he persisted: 'Comrade Captain, take a look, from over there we'd have an excellent line of sight to the tanks. Let's go check it out.'

'No, it's already light, let's head back; the Germans might spot us.'

But Raskovalov detained me for a moment. I turned around and we both looked over at the German lines. All of a sudden there was the crack of a single rifle shot from the German side. We both dropped to the ground. I called over to him, but he was silent. I crawled over to where he was lying, and I saw a stream of blood shooting from his forehead like a fountain. I clasped my hand over the wound in an attempt to staunch the bleeding and immediately reached for a bandage in my pocket before it occurred to me that the battery commander was dead. Only a sniper could score such a precise hit from such a distance. It was a sniper that got him. But he couldn't do this! No! Not to this man! I was ready to cry out in a passionate protest to what had just happened. I lowered my head to my hand, which was still covering the wound, and the blood kept gushing out, flowing through my fingers. I could feel how warm it was ... I was overwhelmed by pity towards my friend and bitter hatred for the German that had killed him. I hated myself as well, for I had failed to keep the Senior Lieutenant alive. I imagined his wife receiving the death notice and his small children crying – and my heart sank, my sight darkened. I couldn't move, we were both nailed to the ground, but I was alive and he was dead.

When I regained my senses, I grabbed him by his shoulders and dragged him into the bushes. I caught my breath a bit, but I still had the German sniper on my mind: for days he'd been watching our lines from his concealed position, and finally in the dim light of early dawn, he spotted two men through his optical sight. But he only had time to kill one of us. Why had he selected Raskovalov as his target? Did the sniper manage to see our faces and notice that the Senior Lieutenant was older than me, and thus probably an officer of higher rank? Sitting by Raskovalov's body, I was so deeply shocked that I was not even happy that I was still alive. That the German sniper had not picked me, that this was already the fifth dead commander of the ill-fated battery, that I hadn't managed to keep Raskovalov alive – these thoughts kept hammering me in my head. Still pondering these sad questions, I rose to my feet, lifted the battery commander's body onto my shoulders and, making sure I was screened by bushes, walked back to my command post. Raskovalov was not all that heavy, but his feet were dragging on the ground as I walked and I recalled that Raskovalov had been a half-head taller than me. That's why the German sniper had selected him. He was taller and older, and these two factors sealed his fate: the German chose the taller and older man, thinking that he was the higher-ranking officer. Or was it just a random choice? But my Lord, how badly it hurt!

I still have a photo of Raskovalov, posing together with the sergeant major of his battery and a veterinarian, when he was still with the battery and getting used to life at the front. As if still alive, he is looking at me out of the photo with that shy smile. Likely, he had sent the same photo to his wife, and she with her children still often look at the dear features of her husband's face. Each time I see the photo, I think with pity: how perverse is fate! This man's own death spared me.

Trstenik. The frenzy of victory

The 52nd Rifle Division captured both Paracin and Krusevac from the march. The fighting for both towns was brief, but very intense. The division was then redirected westwards along the Western Morava River with the mission to capture Kraljevo, a town on the highway from Belgrade to Greece.

Cooperating with the units of the 2nd Proletarian Division of the People's Liberation Army of Yugoslavia, we advanced along the left or northern bank of the Western Morava from Velika Drenova towards Kraljevo. Still the commander of the 1st Artillery Battalion of the 1028th Artillery Regiment, my three batteries were continuing to support the 52nd Rifle Division's 431st Rifle Regiment. The other units of the division with the remaining artillery-mortar regiments were advancing along the opposite bank of the Western Morava towards Trstenik. This small town in eastern Serbia was defended by Germans and the local fascists – *chetniks* of Draze Mihailovic.

My battalion and the 431st Rifle Regiment assaulted the village of Bogdanje, which was situated on the high left bank of the Western Morava directly across from Trstenik. A railroad bridge spanned the powerful, rapid river here. Its intricate steel structure rose high above the boiling waters of the Morava. During our attack we somehow quickly advanced beyond the bridge and left it some 500 meters in our rear.

I was located in the combat formations of battalion commander Ivan Morozov's rifle battalion. When I was still a battery commander, I had always supported his battalion, and then due to the death of the commander of the 2nd Battery, Morozov asked me to assist him in the battle for the village of Bogdanje. Behind the line of attacking soldiers, Ivan and I were crawling towards the outlying houses of the village through some garden plots. I had no signal connection to the battery and I couldn't at that moment call fire in on the Germans – I had spotted German armor on the other side of the village and had sent back for a gun battery, planning to deploy it next to me for direct fire. The battery was still on its way, and the German machine-gun fire was so heavy that we and the infantry were pinned down, and were rarely able even to raise our heads.

Suddenly, as I looked back to see if the battery was coming up, I noticed a man in civilian clothes quickly crawling through a garden towards me from behind me and to my right. He was paying no attention to the intense machine-gun fire. A small man in his forties, he crawled up to my position, and in order to make himself heard over the din of the battle, he shouted at the top of his lungs almost directly into my ear: 'Friend Captain, I was told that you are the chief artilleryman here?!'

'Yes,' I replied as I curtly waved him off; I had no intentions of starting a conversation.

'Friend Captain, help us take our city!' He was now beside me and looking at me with beseeching eyes, raising his head above the crops.

A hail of machine-gun fire, clipping the twigs and stems of the vegetation around us, tore through our position. I pressed his head down. The fact that he wasn't afraid of bullets impressed me, so I decided to listen to his request, asking automatically: 'What town?'

'There, Trstenik on the opposite bank.'

I thought he was crazy. Even a civilian knew that one needed a whole army and river-crossing equipment to capture a town on the other side of a wide river. But the man in the dirty suit was in a hurry and was sure that I would assist him. I didn't want to offend the Serb partisan as we had supported them often with artillery fire, so I asked: 'How many men do you have in your unit?'

'Twenty!' he replied proudly. Then he continued without hesitation: 'The town is right across from you! You must fire on it! You'll be moving on soon, and then you won't be able to help us!'

'I have no time, I must capture this village; don't you see I am in a battle?' I replied.

'Friend Captain,' said the man in a sad and begging voice, with tears in his eyes, 'just take a look at the opposite bank!'

With that he grabbed my shoulder and tugged with such force that I almost fell on my back. From where did this little man get such power? He was so desperate for me to see the opposite bank that I decided to respect his wishes and follow him to the river. Two minutes later we were at a wattle fencing that separated the garden plots from a high precipice overlooking the river, and peering through its openings. What a view! Down in the valley far below on the southern bank of the roily waters of the Western Morava, a small, tidy city stood, cozily nestled at the foot of mountains rising from the far side of the river. Its multi-colored walls, roofs, cobblestone streets and green parks were gleaming festively in the rays of the sun. A church rose in the middle of the town. I could clearly see the school and the trusswork of the railway bridge. Garden plots descended to the riverbank. Right on the bank itself, dug into some bankside shrubs and vegetation, was a deep, 1 kilometer-long trench, dotted with machine-gun nests. Light-caliber artillery pieces and heavy machine guns were set along the bank at regular intervals for direct fire. Here and there among them, tents were visible. None of this was camouflaged at all! It was as if the Germans were putting on an exhibition! Gun crews were lounging in the shade of the bushes. I could see underwear and foot rags drying on stakes next to the tents. I was so indignant at the audacity of the fascists – how dare they set up their weapons like that! – that I decided on the spot to honor the partisan's request.

'What can we do without artillery?' the partisan sighed sadly, continuing to plead with me. 'Friend Captain, please hit these machine guns with your guns. I ask for nothing more.'

'Why haven't they camouflaged their guns and machine guns?' I asked my guest.

'They do it on purpose, to intimidate us. They know we have no artillery.'

'We'll put a scare into them now!' I said sharply.

Just then, the Dodge trucks towing my guns pulled into the garden plot behind me. I ordered the men to roll the guns into some wooden sheds overlooking the river. We punched holes into their walls and stuck the gun barrels through them. I counted about forty light guns and machine guns on the opposite bank. I ordered the battery's senior officer Lieutenant Konshin to distribute targets between the guns. Already tasting the joy of destroying the enemy, the gun crews were getting excited – it would be a simple matter to destroy targets by direct fire from a range of just 600 meters! At my command, the guns started pouring destructive fire down on the opposite bank.

The suddenness of our barrage shocked the fascists. Explosions walked up and down their line, smashing one weapon emplacement after another. While the Serb partisans watched the destruction unfold, they celebrated like little children, jumping, shouting and squealing with delight. The opposite bank became completely enveloped in the blue smoke of our explosions. Only blackened craters were left where the German machine guns and guns had been positioned.

Our barrage was enough for the Germans to raise the white flag. The first flag appeared on the roof of the school and then white flags began to flutter all over the town. The Nazis were surrendering. It was the first time we'd seen such a thing, and we couldn't believe that we had just captured the little city.

'Friend Captain, let's head into town across the bridge to take the garrison prisoners,' the partisan commander suggested.

The temptation was so strong that I agreed. I left Lieutenant Konshin with Morozov and walked back to the bridge together with the partisans, three scouts and Lieutenant Medvedev.

We walked to the middle of the bridge and saw two rows of barbed wire blocking our way. Nazis were approaching us from the other side of the river with a white flag held high. When they reached the barbed wire, they stopped and silently stared with amazement at our small band of twenty-five men. I became scared for the first time: what if they changed their minds? Our guns were demonstratively continuing to move their barrels, and would fire again if anything went wrong. But we were also most likely in the sights of any of their remaining machine guns. The bridge was metal, and it might be possible to take cover behind its beams and retreat, but the several seconds of silent gazing from the enemy scared me, or better put, horrified me: why hadn't I thought this over? But I made two decisive steps forward, pointed at the barbed wire and loudly demanded that the enemy's men throw them into the river to let us pass.

I heard a command, and the enemy's men threw themselves at the barbed wire and cleared the way. I walked up to the Nazis. They were all armed – they still had machine pistols and sidearms. I ordered them to drop the weapons at my feet. I relaxed a little only when the enemy's guns clattered on the bridge.

We followed the group with the white flag to the church. There were about two hundred *chetniks*, Yugoslavian fascists, lined up in formation on the square. We didn't see a single German. I pointed to a spot where they were to lay down their weapons. I suggested to the partisans to disarm the garrison, and then I started walking over to the mayor's office with Lieutenant Medvedev and the three scouts. We came upon another small group of about fifteen armed *chetniks*, who were preparing to surrender. I noticed a wide holster on the belt of an enemy officer. I immediately realized that he had a Browning with a clip for fourteen rounds; I'd been dreaming about this pistol for a long time. I stopped the officer and pointed at his pistol, ordering him to give me the gun. The officer silently complied and handed it over. I also demanded that he give me the holster. Happy with my prize, I walked on and then suddenly realized what would have happened if the officer had refused to obey the order and we had faced a fight. It finally struck me that we were in the midst of enemy soldiers, and probably would have found ourselves in deep trouble. I abruptly turned around and we quickly walked back to the bridge.

Our excursion took about an hour and a half. When I returned to Morozov's command post on the opposite bank, in order to resume the battle against 'our' Germans in Bogdanje, it turned out that they had already abandoned the village. Lieutenant Colonel Kozlov, the rifle regiment commander, arrived at the battalion command post. He was in his forties.

He told me: 'Great job, you captured the town! I've already notified the general over the radio. You made the correct decision to destroy the enemy's guns and machine guns, but if I were you, I never would have entered the town myself. You were taking a great risk.'

Half an hour later our division marched into Trstenik unopposed.

Whenever I recall those events, a shiver runs down my spine and I think that I would never have dared such a bold move now. I guess one could take such a foolhardy decision to capture an entire armed garrison with just four men and a handful of partisans only in the frenzy of victory. It must have been the Lord and not my threat to destroy them with artillery fire from the other bank that saved us from death then.

CHAPTER FOURTEEN

Command Problems

The Army Headquarters' Protégé

Raskovalov's death from the sniper bullet was a heavy blow, not only to the 2nd Battery but also to the infantrymen and my whole artillery battalion. He was a perfect officer: father to his men, friend to the infantry, and death to the Germans. He was always at the observation post, next to the rifle battalion commander and ready to support his infantry at any moment. What would the new commander be like...?

To my dismay, I received a demoted officer, Captain Shchegolkov, from army headquarters to replace the dead Raskovalov. Shchegolkov was an officer who had advanced rapidly during the purges of 1937, but had since become an alcoholic. He'd been demoted from lieutenant colonel down to captain, and sent to the front.

I remember when Shchegolkov first showed up in the battalion. Tall, slim, clean-shaven, in a brand new uniform with gleaming leather webbing, and wearing a polite smile on his pleasant face, he was the embodiment of a pre-war professional officer. There was not a single speck of dust on him. He stood in sharp contrast to us, who constantly had to crawl on our bellies under enemy fire. Looking at him, one could almost forget that there was a war going on. Somehow, from the pre-war army of 1940, he'd managed to flit straight into the terrible year of 1944. The place for such an officer was on the parquet flooring of some much higher headquarters. But I needed a brave field officer that could crawl, direct fire from any ditch and treat his men well.

Smiling cunningly, Shchegolkov gave a careless salute and reluctantly introduced himself: 'Captain Shchegolkov reporting to assume command of the 2nd Battery.'

'It's a pleasure, Captain,' I said, studying the new officer, 'take a seat!'

He sat down. Looking at me archly, from the height of his thirty-five years of age (I was then only twenty-three) he asked me breezily and with feigned courtesy, as if I were his subordinate: 'Excuse me ... How long have you been in the army, Comrade Captain?'

'Three years,' I replied dryly.

'Three years – and you're already a battalion commander?!' He was deeply shocked.

'There's nothing special here,' I objected, 'I've spent all three years at the front, leading troops, not at parades. We've now been in combat for five months straight.'

The Captain became lost in thought, though not because he was continuing to be amazed at my service successes. He was likely recalling his own dizzying upward trajectory in 1937. Not without pride, but also with some sadness and pity for himself, he spoke up in an instructive tone: 'I, brother, for over three years commanded only a battalion ... In 1937 I'd been promoted straight from gun section leader to battalion commander, and then in 1940 I was transferred to higher staff work...'

'So, you've never led a battery?' I asked worriedly. 'Do you know how to direct a fire mission?'

'Don't worry, Captain, I can handle a battery. You needn't inspect me; the battery is in reliable hands! I can make anyone knuckle under!'

'No,' I objected firmly, 'I will not hand over the battery to your full control; I will monitor you strictly!' Then I carefully asked: 'Why were you so sharply demoted in rank and post?'

'Just a conflict with superiors,' he replied vaguely.

I was not happy at all to have such a puzzling character in the battalion. I immediately sensed something bad and dangerous for our common cause in this man.

During the first week in his new position, after meeting his gun crews at their guns in the rear, Shchegolkov paid particular attention to the sergeant major and his business. He gave instructions to the cooks about when, where and how his meals should be prepared and delivered to him. He set up his command post at his battery's firing positions, posting his signalman at the entrance to his dugout – although Shchegolkov was supposed to be at the forward observation post together with the infantry. So, it appeared that the new battery commander was afraid to go to the front, because there was firing there.

In the territory of Yugoslavia, the combat was very mobile. Each of my three batteries was supporting a rifle battalion and rushing from one place to another along winding roads that snaked around high mountains. I kept in communication with the batteries over the radio and through infantry officers. I personally remained at the command post of the rifle regiment commander, Major Litvinenko. I was an experienced forward observer and when an urgent, difficult fire mission became necessary in case of a German breakthrough or when we encountered particularly stubborn resistance, I directed the fire mission of the on-call battery myself. I could not visit each battery personally and kept informed about the state of affairs in each one from the signalmen –

they were all friends and passed around all the regiment's scuttlebutt to each other. My batteries were providing critical support for the infantry, and the rifle regiment commander was happy with us.

But one day the Germans suddenly attacked the 2nd Rifle Battalion and the infantry fell into a very tight spot, because Shchegolkov's battery wasn't supporting them adequately. I found out that Shchegolkov was still at the guns some 3 kilometers behind the observation post, while the battery's fire was being directed over the telephone by an inexperienced young forward observer. I strongly rebuked Shchegolkov and ordered him to be at the forward observation post, and forbade him to leave it without my permission.

I had no time to fuss with Shchegolkov, because I was constantly changing the location of my observation post, trying to keep the enemy in my vision, and because during the action one or another of my batteries was being cut off by the Germans. I called my political officer Karpov and asked him to visit the 2nd Battery and spend a little time working together with Shchegolkov. The 2nd Battery was just 100 meters away from the political officer. But this representative of the Communist Party didn't move a muscle. He was used to being at the battalion headquarters, or in the rear at the field kitchen, and didn't do anything. When I asked him about Shchegolkov, he bluntly refused to visit the battery, even though both he and the battery were in the rear. He was not only afraid of a possible barrage, but also of a meeting with the dangerous officer. This was not my first conflict with Karpov, so I just waved off his refusal and decided to handle the matter myself.

Some three days later the Nazis sensed the lack of artillery support and again struck the 2nd Rifle Battalion. The Germans unleashed an artillery and mortar barrage on the battalion, and then attacked it with infantry. Our riflemen hoped that as the Germans approached our trench, our artillerymen would as usual blanket them with artillery fire. But the battery was silent. Having lost over twenty men killed, the 2nd Rifle Battalion had to fall back. Rifle regiment commander Litvinenko addressed me with a complaint: 'Why didn't your battery support the battalion?'

I called Shchegolkov over the phone, but he was again away from the observation post; completely drunk, he was sleeping at the 2nd Battery's firing positions in the rear.

It had become clear that the demoted Shchegolkov was still drinking in our artillery battalion as well. To make things worse, he had abandoned the observation post without orders and thus had left the infantry to face the Nazis alone. I was worried, but I couldn't leave the front line and walk the 3 kilometers back to the 2nd Battery where Shchegolkov was lounging, as the enemy was very active. I called Karpov again. This time I didn't ask him, I ordered him as my deputy to deal with the drunkard: 'You are superior to him both in rank and in age, and you can influence him. It is your direct responsibility to work with the personnel and I demand that you discuss Shchegolkov's conduct with him.'

A scandal ensued, but Karpov still didn't go to the battery. Outraged by the idleness and lack of responsibility of my political officer, I called the political officer of the regiment in order for him to influence Karpov. Major Ustinov recommended that I leave Karpov alone. I received the same answer from the division's political department. Realizing that Karpov would be of no use in this matter, I found a moment when the Germans were quiet and decided to deal with the matter personally. It was a hot summer day, but I made a quick run back to the battery. I ran up to the guns and asked, 'Where's the battery commander?'

The soldiers looked around timidly, and then whispered: 'Comrade Captain, the commander is sleeping in the trench and he ordered not to be disturbed. If you wake him up, he'll have you shot.'

'Do not disturb?' I thought. What a lord and master! Men were dying, the 2nd Battery was silent, and he was sleeping! I tore the canvas off the trench and found the sleeping Shchegolkov. I gave him a shake, and he didn't wake up, but just snored even more loudly. I ordered two buckets of cold water. The sergeant major refused to dump the water on his superior, so I had to do it myself. Shchegolkov woke up only after the second bucket – he jumped up and rushed at me with his fists. But after realizing that he was facing the battalion commander, he lowered his fists. There was no use in talking to an intoxicated man, so I ordered Shchegolkov to appear at my observation post three hours later. When he reported to me, Shchegolkov repented, made promises and swore. But I knew what the promises of an alcoholic were worth, so having given him a dressing down, I sent him to his observation post. My message was direct and clear: 'If you get drunk again, I'll come and shoot you myself! Don't you dare leave the observation post!'

However, within several days, just as I expected, there was another episode at the battery. Shchegolkov again left the front line and got drunk, and again the infantry suffered unjustifiable losses because of his battery's idleness.

Using the protection of the high command, Shchegolkov was not subordinate to anyone. The men in his battery also started drinking, especially the ones that were supplying him with alcohol. The battery was becoming non-combatworthy.

The ongoing combat was intense, and in the course of one week I was thrown from one rifle regiment to another three times; I had no time to deal with the troublemaker. I reported on the matter to artillery regiment commander Major Rogoza and demanded: 'Please remove Shchegolkov from my battalion.'

The answer was: 'We sent him to you for you to change his ways!'

'He is my father's age and he is a complete alcoholic! How many more men must die before he changes?'

'Don't touch him; let him fight. That's an order from above. Do you understand?' Rogoza threatened.

At the expense of my combat work, I wasted a whole week trying to change Shchegolkov's ways, but all was in vain. But two subsequent incidents totally exhausted my patience.

One morning Morozov spotted twenty German tanks preparing to attack his battalion and asked Shchegolkov to prevent the German attack by breaking up the German armor formation with fire. But Shchegolkov's rounds landed far from the tanks. Morozov was outraged – the tanks were about to level the trenches of his battalion together with his men. He asked for help from rifle regiment commander Litvinenko and the latter called me: 'Save your pal, run to his observation post; you'll be able to reach the Germans with fire from your other batteries.'

So I took off. Running, crouching, falling, crawling, ignoring machine-gun fire, in a matter of minutes I was with Morozov. The tanks were already rushing towards the battalion's positions. I blanketed the German tanks with rapid fire from my howitzers. Through the dust and smoke of the explosions, we could see two burning tanks. Blinded, the other tanks turned back. His face flushed, Morozov was excitedly pounding a birch tree with his walking stick. Then he fell on me and practically smothered me with a bear hug! Each man in the trench was also grabbing me by the shoulders and embracing me; the approaching tanks had thrown a scare into them! Indeed, I had literally saved them from being crushed under the tracks of the German tanks. But I had no time to celebrate with them, as I had to deal with Shchegolkov. Why couldn't he repel the tank attack without me, and why did I have to run to solve the crisis?

I jumped out of the trench and ran 200 meters to the rear, to Shchegolkov's OP which had been set up in a hut. A forward observer was sitting at the stereoscope in a shallow trench outside and shouting somewhere down below him: 'The round landed far to the left.'

'Where is Shchegolkov?' I asked.

'He's in the cellar,' the observer replied.

I quickly went down to the cellar and saw the Captain sitting on a stool beside a wine barrel with a cup in his hand, passing commands to the battery via the signalman: 'Right zero – fifteen!'

Outraged, I leaped over to Shchegolkov and knocked the cup from his hands. Confused, he rose to his feet. I spat out: 'So you're correcting the fire from here, from a basement, you bastard! March upstairs!'

The Captain quickly and guiltily ran up the stairs. I lashed into the coward:

'How can you direct the fire without seeing the target? How can it be that you're not pitying the infantry and not feeling shame when you're sitting in a cellar during a battle?'

I led Shchegolkov to battalion commander Morozov and ordered him to stay there. Clearly my 2nd Battery was no longer combat capable. I called the division commander directly, since my artillery regiment commander was of no use, and demanded the removal of Shchegolkov from my battalion.

'He is your subordinate,' Miliaev replied, 'you change his ways!' Again the same story!

In the second incident we needed urgently to shift the 2nd Battery to a sector in the line where German tanks were trying to break through. Every second was precious. I called the battery. They reported to me that two guns lacked a vehicle to tow them: Shchegolkov had sent one vehicle to pick up some wine, while Shchegolkov himself had driven off in the other one to search for liquor. My patience had run out! Again, I was forced to drop all my business and appear at the battery's firing positions. Two orphan guns were sitting there without tow vehicles. I took a Dodge and Iasha Korennoi with a light machine gun, and drove off in pursuit of Shchegolkov, for I could clearly see the tracks of his truck in the dust. I visited two villages through which he had passed. I finally caught up with Shchegolkov some 15 kilometers from the front. I gave the signal to stop, but the vehicle in front of us accelerated. I saw Shchegolkov putting a pistol against the driver's head – he was ready to shoot the driver if we caught him! I ordered Korennoi to fire a burst over their heads. This seemed to scare them and they slowed down. I drove around the Captain's vehicle and blocked the road with my Dodge. Shchegolkov stood up in the open vehicle and threatened me with a pistol: 'Well, come on then!'

It was insane to walk towards the pistol. I halted and started a conversation to distract him. Iasha Korennoi slipped out of the car, crept around behind the Captain and knocked the pistol out of his hand. I jumped up on the step of the Dodge, grabbed Shchegolkov by his shoulders and hurled him from the vehicle. I drove away, shouting: 'Don't come back to the battalion, or I'll kill you!'

I took Shchegolkov's place with the battery, led it to face the tanks, engaged them, and stopped their advance. In effect, by merely tossing the drunken Shchegolkov out of his Dodge, I had 'signed' an order for his dismissal from the battalion.

I reported to my artillery regiment commander: 'I threw Shchegolkov out of a Dodge that he took without authorization and I will not let him return to the battalion.'

'Calm down,' Major Rogoza replied, 'you are young and reckless.'

'I have no time to be careful; I have a war to fight!'

'Then have a talk with the General Miliaev.'

I called the General about Shchegolkov's misadventures and repeated: 'I will not let Shchegolkov back into the battalion!'

'So, I guess we'll have to court-martial him?' General Miliaev asked slowly.

'Do whatever you want, but I'm not going to let my battery die because of him!' The division commander hung up on me.

The top brass were angry with my behavior, but for the common cause they kept their mouths shut. Our 52nd Rifle Division pressed on to the west after capturing Trstenik. We drove the Germans back to Kraljevo, but failed to capture the place. The Germans were firmly holding that town located on the Belgrade–Saloniki road, as the other route from Belgrade to Greece had been cut when we captured Paracin and Krusevac. We were sent to Belgrade and we liberated the city on 20 October together with other Soviet and allied Yugoslavian troops.

After capturing Belgrade our division was pulled out of the line for rest and refitting in the town of Ruma. The exhausted division was replenished to a strength of 6,000 men.

The day 7 November 1944 arrived – our Revolution Day. We were in no mood to celebrate, as three days hence we were to march back to the front, which was just some 15–20 kilometers away. We could hear the distant echoes of heavy artillery fire. All three batteries were standing in firing positions on the northern edge of Ruma. I'd been sitting at a table in the summer kitchen of a nearby home since dawn. My place in battle was at the front, and it felt unusual to be at my headquarters in the division's rear. I had a topographical map in front of me on a long table that occupied almost the whole length of the kitchen opposite the entrance. I was studying the Danube valley region all the way to Vukovar, where we were about to engage the Germans. The battalion's chief of signals Senior Lieutenant Levin sat on my right at the same table facing the door, working on a field phone. We were of the same age, but he was from Riazan – with turned-up nose and pink cheeks, he had never taken part in a bayonet charge or a prisoner snatch mission, so he looked much younger than me.

Suddenly, the light door to the kitchen flew open with a bang and a tall officer appeared on the threshold. He had to stoop in order to step through the low entrance, and I couldn't see his face. 'Quite an impolite way to enter,' I thought with some irritation. The officer stood up with his head almost bumping the ceiling, and two angry, insolent eyes were brazenly staring at me from a drunken, alcoholic face. It was the former commander of my 2nd Artillery Battery, Captain Shchegolkov. He took a step forward, pulled his right hand out of the pocket of his trousers and pointed a pistol at me. The cocky face had an evil smile on it. He slowly cocked the gun with his finger, looked at me and spat out through his clenched teeth: 'So, boy, hold on. Your end has come. I've come to settle accounts. To take revenge!'

I had kicked him out of the battalion two weeks previously for drinking. In the ensuing fighting, I'd already forgotten about him. And now he was there to kill me for forcing him to serve conscientiously. He had believed that he would spend a couple of weeks in the rear of the battery, drink like hell, and then return to a comfortable spot at army headquarters with the laurels of an experienced, front-line soldier. His plan hadn't worked out, because I had stopped it.

The Captain had changed for the worse during the two weeks since I had seen him last, and he had become almost gaunt. His once-beautiful uniform was covered with dust and didn't present a striking appearance any more. The manners of a professional officer, the precision of movement and the self-confident look had also disappeared somewhere. His handsome, but hateful face was scary. It was a degraded alcoholic standing in front of me; he had just been rambling around the local villages looking for raki [a local distilled liquor]. Now the extreme hatred and alcohol were inflaming his eyes and keeping his bony carcass going. Apparently, he had drunk a bit to stiffen his resolve, and the alcohol hadn't depressed him but excited him. He still had the old dreams, hopes and plans revolving in his brain, and was recalling all the men who had ever offended him or delayed his career, which had begun so amazingly in 1937. Now I was in front of him – the young officer who had put an end to his career. The look of Shchegolkov – the hatred, the insulted arrogance, and the burning resolve showed that he had not just come to frighten me. Tortured by hatred and a will for revenge, he must have been nurturing his plans for a long time and had finally made his decision.

Levin lifted his head from the phone set. Although the gun was not pointed at him, he was more frightened than me. His hands started to shake and he didn't know what to do with them – raise them in the air or hide them under the table. I didn't expect any other reaction from the staff officer and sadly thought this man would be no help.

Shchegolkov's sudden appearance scared me too. Scared but didn't stun me. By that time I had seen so many tight places that no danger could dumbfound me. I immediately evaluated the situation, made a decision and carried it out with lightning speed. But in this case any movement would have been interrupted by an imminent shot. I had no time to grab for my pistol in the holster, which was hanging on my belt behind my back. I couldn't capsize the table onto Shchegolkov and knock him off his feet; he was standing too far away. Levin, scared to death, was completely paralyzed; he certainly wasn't Iasha Korennoi, who would have immediately found a way to distract the intruder's attention or do something else. The only thing I could do, however offensive it was to my pride, was to buy time and start an argument with my adversary, to engage him psychologically. I had an opportunity for this, as Shchegolkov was in no hurry to kill me. He wanted to torture and humiliate me first, to savor my agitation and only then kill me. To him, an old professional officer, as a former student I was merely a boy. Although I wasn't a coward and it was not part of my plan to survive the war, I really didn't want to die in vain, for nothing, at the hands of this degraded bastard.

Not lowering his pistol, Shchegolkov kept on glaring at me with rage, struggling to find the most insulting, merciless words to throw at me, but they kept slipping away from him. I remained seated, holding my head up high. I didn't have a single trace of fear on my face. My expression was sternly asking: 'What's the problem?' My opponent faltered, seemingly disheartened by my readiness to accept death. I was looking him straight in the eyes, trying to hypnotize and scare him with a steely look. I was trying to send him a clear message: 'Don't you dare! Don't you dare!' The Captain, not blinking, tried to stare me down. Our gazes locked, and a duel between two hateful pairs of eyes began. In its own way, it was a fight to the death, not much different from a hand-to-hand fight – only one could win. In this case it wasn't clear who would win: the arrogant Captain who had set his eyes on higher command for fifteen years or the young Captain who had been looking in the eyes of death for three years around the clock.

'Shoot! Why are you waiting?' I addressed my foe, suppressing my anxiety. No, this wasn't an invitation to finish off someone who had blinked first, who had become frightened and surrendered. I said the word 'Shoot' slowly, drawing out the ending, and it sounded not only like a challenge, but also a threat of imminent retribution. Not retribution from some distant and vague tribunal, but an immediate execution by my men.

Shchegolkov didn't reply, but he didn't fire either. Dissatisfaction and pain flashed in his eyes; somehow his fury had abated. He, who could have been my father in terms of age, hadn't expected such strong psychological resistance. My gaze kept on drilling into him: 'Don't dare! Wake up! Think of yourself!' My silent defiance probably had its effect, but his survival instinct was definitely frustrating his angry resolve: how would he save himself after shooting me? Was it worth aggravating his already large guilt before the law? It is one thing to be the cause of people's death in combat, but murder is something completely different. There were also my loyal subordinates outside the door, and in their wrath they would kill him immediately.

Shchegolkov silently kept his cocked pistol fixed on me. My life and death depended totally on whether or not he dared to pull the trigger. Which would prevail – evil or common sense? The alcohol in his blood was not on my side.

A map case, a must accessory for staff officers, was hanging from a thin belt across Shchegolkov's left shoulder. It would have only frustrated me in battle; the belt would have kept getting snagged as I crawled through bushes. With his free left hand, Shchegolkov quickly pulled a thin gray envelope from the map case. Apparently, it was part of his initial plan to play this decisive trump card against me, as the map case was open and I could see a corner of the envelope inside it.

'Here!' he angrily shook the once-sealed, but already opened envelope at me. 'It says that I am to be court-martialed! Read it!'

'I didn't send you to a tribunal, but I can't tolerate your presence in the battalion. Whatever happens next is not my decision,' I rapped out.

'Just read it!' he said, as he took a couple of steps forward and threw the envelope on the table. But before the envelope landed on the table, I grabbed the edge of the table, raised it violently and struck the pistol that was pointing at me. The long, light table didn't overturn, but it hid me from him for a moment. I dove beneath the table just before a shot rang out. Lunging forward, I tackled the Captain around the knees and knocked him on his back. As he was falling, he managed to fire two more shots before I grabbed the pistol. Levin finally woke up and came to my aid.

My men outside rushed into the kitchen immediately after they heard the shots. They quickly tied Shchegolkov up and passed the envelope to me. One soldier stayed to guard the disarmed Captain, while I moved to the battalion's communications center. First of all I inspected the envelope. The envelope had been carefully sealed, but it had been hastily torn open, as if with teeth. Indeed, the letter's preamble read: 'Captain Shchegolkov is to appear before a military tribunal.' But why had someone at army headquarters been told to give the envelope containing a letter with such a threatening introduction to the accused? I didn't get it. Did they rely on the fact that the envelope bore an official seal, or was the Captain just considered 'one of their own' at army headquarters? Of course Shchegolkov, being no fool, had opened the envelope. Having discovered his destiny, he had been in no hurry to meet it, and had decided to go on one last drinking binge, take revenge, and then either confess or defect to the Germans.

After I calmed down from the incident, I reported it over the phone to the division commander. General Miliaev patiently listened to me, remained silent for a long time, and then said in a strict voice, as if issuing an order: 'Give him back the envelope and his pistol and escort him out of the battalion. Let him go where he was sent!'

'What? He shot at me!' I was amazed and outraged.

The General hung up the phone.

All my men of the artillery battalion were outraged by Shchegolkov's behavior. Korennoi, the man I trusted the most, privately told me: 'Comrade

Captain, can I give Shchegolkov an informal escort into the forest?'

'No, Iasha,' I told Korennoi in a friendly voice, 'we can't do that.'

Who was Shchegolkov, whose son-in-law or nephew was he? Was he perhaps a friend of our young General? I don't know, and to this day I know nothing about his fate.

Right after we had dealt with Shchegolkov, we learned that the command was going to issue decorations on the occasion of the anniversary of the October Revolution. We were lined up and handed decorations. I received the rare Order of Alexander Nevsky.

The rest of the day and that entire night, we wildly celebrated the decorations. I was heartily congratulated, not only by the men of my artillery regiment, but also by infantry officers. All nine rifle battalion commanders from all the regiments of the 52nd Rifle Division paid me a visit. They were the most faithful combat friends that I had, and it was very pleasant to hear their kind words.

Battalion commander Morozov raised the first toast: 'When you are near, we're not afraid of the devil himself! Neither German infantry nor German tanks can scare us!'

The next battalion commander to speak asked, 'What makes Mikhin so good?' Then he answered his own question: 'First of all, he shoots like a god! He hits a target with his first round. Secondly, he isn't afraid of anything – be that tanks or infantry! He pounds the Germans under any amount of enemy fire!'

Then the other rifle battalion commanders chipped in: 'Do you know why he isn't afraid of the Germans or the top brass? He's untouchable! Tell me, which battery commander has outlived him?! He lasts forever!'

'No ill prophesies here! He survives because all the riflemen pray for him.'

'Do you remember when battalion commander Abaev rebelled? He refused to start an assault without Mikhin. He was so used to Mikhin's support.'

'Other artillerymen always have problems with ammunition or phone lines, but he has everything under control. Where does he get all his ammunition?'

'He once captured an entire 105mm battery with entire trainloads of ammunition; he can fire as much as he likes. God, let all artillerymen be like him!'

The battalion commanders were right in many respects. Due to my young age or my personality, but most likely due to my devotion to the cause and my sporting interest in destroying Nazis, or else to my vast experience and fantastic luck I was indeed always beside the rifle battalion commanders in battle and always survived. I directed fire on whatever target the rifle battalion commanders wanted. My presence among the infantry encouraged and cheered them up, gave them hope and assurance that I would help them out at the right moment. The feeling of being protected is a great matter! It removes stress and fear and gives you strength. Whenever I brought down devastating artillery fire on attacking German infantry, it would produce an amazing euphoria among our riflemen, as our rounds exploded in the midst of the German line!

That reminds me of a funny incident that happened with a green rifle battalion commander who had not yet gotten to know me. One day, the Senior Lieutenant demanded that I drop a round in front of his line. As he told me, 'Then I can be sure that if the Germans approach, you'll kill them all.'

'Won't you be scared of my round landing nearby?'

'What?!'

'Just what I said: are you sure you won't get scared if the round explodes where you want it?'

'Who do you think I am?!'

So I passed the order to the battery. When I heard over the phone 'Shot!' to let me know the round was on its way, I shouted to the nearby infantry, 'Take cover!'

Everyone flattened themselves on the ground – except for the new battalion commander, who remained proudly upright so he could see the explosion better. He probably didn't yet know that an incoming heavy howitzer round sounds like a modern jet passing just overhead. So as the round dropped, this horrible howl filled the air. The Senior Lieutenant wasn't expecting this and threw himself to the ground with fear. The powerful explosion sounded the next instant. After the splinters had whizzed over our heads, the battalion commander regained his senses: 'God damn it! You got me scared! I never thought that your round could be so terrifying!'

We partied all night long to celebrate my decoration. I'm not a heavy drinker, so all the toasts got me so drunk that I fell asleep sitting upright at the table in my uniform.

Taming the wild one

The new commander of the 2nd Battery that replaced Shchegolkov was a former gun section leader who did his job well under my supervision. Things seemed to return to normal, as the 2nd Battery began to support the infantry like usual. This calmed me down. But then one day I heard from the signalmen, who always seemed to know everything in the regiment, that there were troubles again in the 2nd Battery. Apparently, the forward observer Private Maidanov, a former criminal, had somehow taken control of the battery. Maidanov had been Shchegolkov's orderly and had served him diligently, obtaining alcohol for him and passing on orders to the cooks. Then he had started to run the battery himself in Shchegolkov's name. Seemingly, after Shchelgokov's departure, he had maintained his power in the battery through intimidation. It was not the headquarters platoon leader who decided who would go to the front and who would stay in the rear. It was Maidanov. Who on earth was this Maidanov, where did he come from, and how did he manage to seize power in the battery? I had to find out.

All three batteries of my battalion were fighting their own battles in support of rifle battalions to which they'd been assigned, and were somewhat separated in the mountainous terrain. It wasn't always possible to visit them personally, so I had to maintain contact with them over the phone or by radio. In recent days the Germans had launched frequent counter-attacks, so I was constantly sitting at my observation post in the front line, keeping an eye on the Germans, so that at any moment I could bail out a rifle battalion and battery in trouble with the fire of the other batteries. Thus I had no opportunity to leave the front line in order to visit the 2nd Battery, assess the situation, and personally get acquainted with Maidanov. From conversations over the telephone, primarily at night when the Germans were quiet, I learned that Maidanov was a former professional criminal over thirty years of age, who had wound up in a penal company straight from prison. He had been lightly wounded in a battle, and this was enough for him to receive a pardon: he had atoned for his guilt with his blood. This freed him from the penal company and he had been sent to my battalion as a replacement. Tall and massive, Maidanov clearly stood out from the young, thin replacements, and was thus assigned to the forward observers.

I recalled that he had once visited my observation post that summer with the 2nd Battery's headquarters platoon leader, Lieutenant Vorob'ev. I had immediately noticed something out of place: the young, slim Lieutenant had an enlisted man's belt and was carrying a submachine-gun, while his huge, boisterous observer was wearing an officer's belt and a pistol holster. When I asked why, the timid Lieutenant replied: 'The forward observer just wanted to have a pistol.'

I ordered them to exchange weapons and belts immediately and scolded the Lieutenant. I then immediately called my political officer Karpov and advised him to take a closer look at this private. But Karpov, as usual, did nothing and I had forgotten about Maidanov in the press of other business.

I suspected that Maidanov had started to dominate his immediate superiors in the battery from the summer onwards. Perhaps the constantly intoxicated Shchegolkov had also been dependent on his orderly Maidanov?

Everyone who saw Maidanov was struck first by the size of his enormous fists. They seemed out of proportion to his long, but strong arms. His head was big and round, and his thinning hair was close-cut and light. His face had a crooked nose and thin, bluish lips, which he always kept tightly compressed. His widely-spaced, round eyes were gray and looked evil and menacing. His whole appearance immediately made everyone around him uncomfortable;

some were clearly afraid of him, because he had a treacherous and violent reputation. He never talked about himself, where he was from or whether he had a family. He had no friends. But the men knew that Maidanov was a professional criminal who had been sentenced repeatedly. By the time he was swept into the penal company, he was serving forty years' worth of prison sentences.

Sometimes Maidanov deliberately told the men of the battery about his life in the gulag, where he had always been a boss among the prisoners. The men were particularly impressed about his story of escaping from Novaia Zemlia with two other men, who he said he killed and cannibalized for his own survival. He liked to end this story with the declaration that he now had a taste for fresh blood.

To kill a man in peacetime meant nothing to Maidanov. He just needed a reason. He had enough strength, cunning and treachery to do it. In the criminal underworld from which he had emerged, mercilessness and treachery were the equivalents to bravery and valor in our world; they prompted admiration among the criminals around him and fear in those who stood in his way.

After I learned about the situation in the 2nd Battery and realized the new threat to the unit, I knew I had to act immediately. But the situation at the front continued to prevent me from leaving my observation post. So I called the rear of my battalion, where my deputy for political affairs Captain Karpov always stayed, and asked him to go the 2nd Battery, which was located in the same village with him, meet with Maidanov, and restore order to the battery. This was exactly the job of a political officer. Karpov was older than Maidanov and had plenty of life experience. But Karpov bluntly refused to meet with Maidanov. From the conversation I realized that Karpov was not only afraid of a possible German barrage on the way to the battery, but also of facing the gangster. I couldn't order my political officer, because I was already in conflict with the artillery regiment's political officer, for trying to force the battalion's political staff to circulate among the batteries and meet the men. It was a pity that I couldn't solve the matter in this way and I was also offended: Karpov had only some 100 meters to walk to the 2nd Battery in the rear, while I would have to crawl on my belly under machine-gun fire to exit the front line, and then run 3 kilometers over steep terrain to reach the 2nd Battery. But there was little I could do – the political officer was the representative of the Communist Party, so I could only silently curse him for sitting around the headquarters doing nothing.

Having a moment when the Germans were quiet, I decided to make my trip to the 2nd Battery. It was ten o'clock in the morning and all was silent at the front. But as soon as I reached an open spot, an alert German immediately opened up on me with a machine gun. I tried to burrow myself into the ground and froze, waiting patiently for the German to tire of looking at me. Then I made a rush and dove behind some boulders. A late machine-gun burst angrily showered me with stone chips.

I found Maidanov at the 2nd Battery's field kitchen, which was nestled in a small mountain village and about 200 meters from the battery's firing positions. Kettles were steaming in a yard, while the cook and several men were preparing lunch. The battery's sergeant major, the small, quick Ukrainian Makukha, was struggling to finish off a calf with his pistol. The bullets kept ricocheting off the animal's forehead. I recommended that he shoot the calf in the ear, and the calf dropped dead. I heard that Maidanov was in the house and ordered the sergeant major to bring Maidanov out into the yard.

Makukha disappeared into the house, but quickly returned to report, 'He is resting, waiting for the calf's fresh liver and blood, and refuses to come out.'

'Did you tell him that he is being summoned by the battalion commander?'

'He knows, but he doesn't want to see you.'

This was unheard of! A private refusing to report to a battalion commander? But what could I do? I entered the house.

Three men were sitting on a low bench next to a wall, peeling potatoes. Maidanov was sitting on a wide bed with a large mattress, with a huge pillow under his ass. I recognized him right away from his round face and absent eyebrows. He had really put on weight since I had last seen him, and now he was disgustingly fat. As I walked in, the men peeling potatoes jumped up, stood at attention and greeted me. From the smiles on their faces I saw that they were happy to see their battalion commander visiting from the front, safe and sound.

Maidanov didn't even move. He imperturbably continued to sit high on his pillow, facing the entrance. A cigarette was dangling from his mouth. His crossed legs were hanging from the thick mattress, his feet not even reaching the floor. He was propped up on his left hand, which had sunk almost elbow-deep into the fluffy mattress, while the heavy fist of his right hand was lying calmly on his knee. In any other case I probably wouldn't have cared about his failture to come to attention. I didn't care much for routine discipline. But this wasn't just any other case. I was here on a special purpose from the front to deal with Maidanov. I had to notice his breaches of discipline. From the very first minute, I had to set the proper tone in my relations with the subordinate.

'Why didn't you salute the battalion commander?' I asked calmly but in a demanding manner.

From the army's point of view, to him I wasn't even a father; I was his great-grandfather. I was not a sergeant major or section commander, not even a battery commander or a staff officer. I was a battalion commander! But Maidanov, from the position of his forty years of prison sentences and his seat high upon the king-size bed, had his own view of this 23-year-old captain. He decided not only to dominate the battery, as he had once dominated his fellow prisoners, but also to refuse to obey the battalion commander. He was completely out of control! Looking at me with bemusement, Maidanov took an even more relaxed pose, shifted the cigarette into the other corner of his mouth, and said capriciously through clenched teeth: 'I don't greet just any asshole.'

I didn't expect this challenge. I was accustomed to the friendly attitudes of not only my subordinates but also the men from other battalions. Even the division's own arrogant scouts, who barely respected anyone else, greeted me politely. They trusted their lives to me, an artilleryman, whenever they crossed the front line. The infantrymen treated me like a god. If I was around, they felt protected and assured; they knew I could blanket the Germans with shells in any location. But this – what an offence! It was more than an offence - it was a challenge, a mutiny. The message was: what will you try to do to me? Such behavior had to be stopped immediately, or else it would be too late. But how? Turn around and leave in order to send in guards to arrest the bastard? No, escorts couldn't detain him; he'd murder one of them and show no regrets over his own likely death. Should I swallow my pride and lecture him about insubordination? He wasn't that type of guy. All these thoughts flashed through my mind in a couple of seconds, as I was wrathfully glaring at the bastard. The thought even crossed my mind: 'So, this is why the experienced Karpov didn't want to confront Maidanov.' So what should I do? I only had one choice: respond to his rudeness and cynicism with the same.

I had to stun him somehow. My main task was to dethrone and humiliate Maidanov in the eyes of the battery, to demonstrate that he was not all-powerful and to put an end to his domination in the battery. It was even a good thing that he had offended me, because it gave me a reason to attack him. We were also on even terms, in the best traditions of the underworld: let the strongest win. But how? He was physically stronger than me...

Then again I noticed his legs dangling in the air. The decision came instantly. I leaped forward and struck his left ear with my right fist with all the strength I could muster in that moment of deadly danger. I didn't think of my own safety until after I struck him, but I knew that I was faster than him and could evade his punches, and I was confident my men would come to my aid if necessary. The blow I delivered stunned Maidanov and knocked him off his perch on the bed. He only regained his senses when he was on all fours on the floor at my feet. He shook his huge head and looked up at me with his round eyes in shock, and then he looked over at the other men who were standing there silently. This pose and position were definitely something new to him.

I didn't wait for Maidanov to regain his senses completely. I shouted at him in an official tone: 'In one hour you will report to my observation post.' Then

I spun around and stalked out of the hut.

The triumphant news that the almighty Maidanov had been toppled quickly spread across the kitchen yard into the battery and then around the entire battalion. It was impossible for the humiliated Maidanov to linger in the battery, and he reported to my observation post one hour later.

As if nothing had happened, I appointed him to my headquarters platoon as an observer and ordered him to serve at my observation post. My other forward observers, who were now stuck in the same trench with a professional murderer, were quite unhappy about the new addition to our team. As I was their father-figure and their friend, they reacted to my experiment with sincere injury and rejection. Some men told me directly: 'What are you doing, Comrade Captain? He will shoot you at the first possible opportunity.'

'And what are you here for!' I countered and immediately advised: 'Treat him like nothing has happened, but keep an eye on him just in case.' My guys secretly warned Maidanov not to try anything against me.

I never even gave the appearance that something had occurred between Maidanov and me. I merely ordered him to move from the battery to my headquarters platoon, and that was all. My scouts and signalmen treated him well. Maidanov became part of our team at the front. He shared all our hardships with us – he spent time on sentry duty, spotted targets, built dugouts, constructed observation posts and stoically endured the German barrages. He didn't panic when our observation post was once surrounded by Nazis. When we charged, Maidanov ran beside me towards the German lines under the storm of fire. He was a brave, enduring and cunning soldier. With disregard for his life, he once under enemy fire rescued a wounded comrade from no-man's-land. As for any brave man, the feeling of deadly danger was like a drug to him. He used it not for crimes but for the common cause.

The friendly collective of forward observers and signalmen accepted Maidanov. He sensed this and became proud of it. In moments of rest Maidanov swapped jokes and opinions with the others. One day, when the time was right and we were both standing at the stereoscope in the trench, observing the German lines, he spoke to me sincerely: 'You know, Comrade Captain, you were the first man that ever dared to raise his hand against me, and your punch was a good one. That's why I respected you. Of course, your combat reputation as a front-line officer also played a huge role. I wouldn't have tolerated it from any other officer. But I'm proud to serve under you and I've forgotten the incident.'

I replied, 'I've also forgotten it. You're a good soldier, and that's why I'm glad you're here on my team.'

During our every attack, I worried for Maidanov. He made a large target for the Germans. Maidanov was often next to me in battles.

When Maidanov became our good friend in the unceasing fighting, he was transformed in our eyes – his face was no longer brutish and ugly, but instead he showed the regular, smiling face of a good man. Service and combat on our team changed him completely during the war. On the recommendation of some of my guys, he even started a correspondence with a girl from the Ukraine. They began a true love story, and when he was discharged from service after the war, he headed straight to Dnepropetrovsk to marry her. Our parting was touching. On his chest, the well-deserved decoration 'For Courage' was gleaming.

The Bulgarian officers

'Comrade Captain, the Bulgarians are coming!' my forward observer at the stereoscope announced loudly and happily, as if close relatives were approaching. I emerged from my dugout, brushed off some dust, and out of habit gave my tunic below my belt a tug to straighten it. I looked up the communication trench that led from our rear to the front line. About 100 meters away, I noticed side caps bobbing above the breastworks that were not our style or color. There were four of them. About a minute later, the Bulgarians emerged from around the nearest angle in the trench: they were two captains with orderlies. They were coming to my observation post to discuss the handover of our line to a Bulgarian unit.

This was all happening in December 1944 near the Croatian town of Vukovar. The Soviet forces had halted their offensive to the west up the course of the Danube, and were now being transferred across that river northwards towards Hungary. We were passing our positions to an allied Bulgarian army for it to defend. Our worn 52nd Rifle Division was being replaced by the full strength 11th Infantry Regiment of the 3rd Balkans Infantry Division. This regiment was to be supported, just as ours had been, by an artillery battalion.

The weather was cold with frequent rain. As usual during the quiet hours at the front, only random machine-gun bursts sounded from the German side. Individual German mortar rounds landed on our positions even more rarely. As if reluctant to explode, they would burst among our trenches with a nasty, temperamental snapping sound. Thousands of deadly pieces of shrapnel would spray the area around, before loudly falling to the ground, like apples shaken from a tree.

Catching sight of me and preparing to greet me, the Bulgarian officers smiled brightly and walked faster. They were the Bulgarian artillery battalion commander Captain Khristo Angelov and his chief of staff Captain Iordan Georgiev. They were both tall and strong, solidly-built men with dark hair and full mustaches, professional officers in their mid-forties. Their friendly faces were full of admiration and delight, in anticipation of a happy meeting with the representatives of a mighty, victorious and friendly army. An army that had twice liberated the Bulgarian people: in 1878 from the Turks and in 1944 from the German Nazis. Perhaps the guests, like I, for a moment recalled September 1944, when the streets and squares of Bulgarian villages were filled with colorfully dressed people, loud laughter and shouts of joy could be heard, and everything merged into lively conversations and embraces between the Bulgarian civilians and the Red Army soldiers. The meetings ended in great dinners and parties. Now another happy meeting between the Russian and Bulgarian brothers-in-arms awaited us. But this meeting was to happen not in sunny September but in rainy December, in trenches that were under enemy fire. We brought the Bulgarians freedom and liberation; they were bringing us the readiness to fight beside us against the German Nazis.

I saluted the officers and clicked my heels, then snappily introduced myself to our guests: 'Captain Mikhin, commander of the 1st Artillery Battalion, 1028th Artillery Regiment.' We shook hands with the Bulgarian battalion commander, greeted each other and gave each other a bear hug. When the hug was over, the Bulgarian gave me a fatherly look, and unable to restrain himself, affably and openly spilled out that which seemed to surprise him the most: 'You are so young! Yet you're commanding a battalion? How old are you?'

'I'm twenty-three,' I replied simply.

Despite the sincerity of his words and his kindness, I sensed he was expressing not a compliment, but a concern: Had the Germans indeed killed all the mature Russian officers, so that now we had boys leading battalions? In his view, only a personnel shortage could explain the fact that three artillery batteries were being entrusted to a young fellow in his early twenties. This had to reduce the troops' combat capabilities! The Germans, of course, had solid, mature officers directing the fire of their artillery battalions...

I immediately understood the concern of my colleague – the commander of a Bulgarian artillery battalion – and the delicacy of his position. First of all, he had come not to inspect me but to replace me, which meant that he was about to bear the full responsibility for this sector of the front and had to hold it as firmly as we had. Secondly, he had no moral or formal right to express even any doubts about the might of the victorious Red Army. After all, he was twice my age, but in essence, who was he in comparison to me? We had fought all the way from Moscow to this place, while they hadn't even tasted battle yet. I was a battle-hardened and experienced officer of a powerful army, while he was representing the armed forces of a rump government, whose czar had fawningly served Hitler. This was how I cheered myself up in my thoughts.

But Khristo continued to look down on me from the height of his age in a fatherly manner. He had no complaints personally about me. Possibly, he had a son of my age and he was viewing me in this light. But the question that tortured him the most was: Did I have tactical skills, and did I know how to handle my batteries?

I knew what I was worth and I was not offended by Khristo's doubts about my skills. But I also had mixed feelings towards my colleague. On the one hand, I respected his age, his self-confidence and life experience and knowledge. On the other hand, I was afraid that the inexperienced Bulgarians, despite their bravery and self-confidence, would find themselves in trouble in their first battle. The battlefield is not a classroom, not a drill square and not a firing range. I had to look after the Bulgarians if only for the first few hours of combat, to guide them, warn them, help them, and in case of extreme danger, even save them. No one had formally placed this wardship and responsibility on me, but I immediately realized that I had to do it, because my youth was leading the Bulgarians to be overconfident in their assessment of the situation: if such boys could hold the line, they could do it easily.

We slowly moved along the trench to the stereoscope, through which in concealment we kept the Germans under constant observation.

'How long have you been in the army?' my colleague asked again.

'Three years,' I sighed, as if I was speaking about fifty years.

'After three years of service you are already a battalion commander?' The Bulgarian captain was not delighted, but unpleasantly surprised.

'Three years at the front, in constant fighting. I also have a higher mathematical education,' I added to impress them.

But the Bulgarian officers weren't impressed at all. Their main criterium of experience was simply length of service.

'The commander and I are in our forties,' chief of staff Iordan Georgiev joined the conversation, 'we graduated from the academy and have been serving for over twenty years, and only recently were we appointed battalion commanders. By the way, could you introduce your chief of staff to us?' Iordan definitely hoped to see a mature, experienced officer who would balance the extremely young battalion commander.

Just then, Captain Sovetov, my chief of staff, walked up to us. He was a young man of my own age with a slim waist. Our guests were completely disappointed with us. At first they were silent, but then they started to ask all sorts of artillery questions, just to check our knowledge. They masked this by trying to find differences between Soviet and Bulgarian artillery practices. It sounded like an exam. I had to restrain myself and patiently reply to their questions, until I had convinced the Bulgarians that I knew artillery theory and praxis.

Moving along the trench, the guests were glancing into every nook, compartment and depression, and checking out all the bunkers and weapons emplacements. From time to time they stuck their heads above the breastwork to take a quick look in the direction of the enemy and to evaluate the location of our observation post: How much of our own lines and the German lines could we see from it? I felt that they were pleased with all that they saw.

We walked up to the stereoscope, the 'horns' of which rose above the trench, which allowed us to observe the enemy without exposing our heads. The secret exam continued.

'How many years did you study artillery theory?' Khristo asked.

'I had a three-month intensive course in a prestigious Leningrad artillery specialist school, with fourteen hours of classroom instruction every day.'

This amazing fact from my biography completely shocked the Bulgarians: they had studied artillery theory for eight years, even beyond their years in the military academy.

I offered to Khristo that he take a look at the enemy positions through the stereoscope, sweeping from left to right. I added, 'I will comment on what you've seen without looking.'

'I have good eyesight and enough knowledge to interpret what I see,' the offended Angelov replied.

'Don't neglect my information, you'll need it,' I answered imperatively and, despite the objections of the Bulgarian, started to comment on the enemy's positions.

'You seemingly took a stroll along the German positions, you know them so well,' Khristo praised me. 'I'd like to see an example of your gunnery; if you would, lob a few rounds at the Germans.'

'We've been ordered not to fire, so as not to disclose the rotation of forces.'

The Captain persisted: 'But you see, we've just been equipped with Soviet guns, and we haven't yet fired them even once. Please show us how you find the range. We've been given six rounds to accomplish this, and you?'

He clearly wanted to see if I knew how to correct the fire.

'OK,' I agreed with some irritation. 'Place the cross hairs of the stereoscope on the spot that you want me to hit.'

'Here, hit the area of this grove, please,' he said, as he turned over the stereoscope to me.

Both the Bulgarian officer and I knew full well how hard it was to give a precise command to a battery on the reverse slope of a hill that lay 3 kilometers behind you, in order to hit the right spot. But after three years of war, I had so much experience that his request was a piece of cake for me. I saw the familiar patch of woods through the stereoscope; I'd already fired on it, in fact. I gave a command through the field phone. A few seconds later, the battery reported, 'Shot!'

Khristo peered into the stereoscope to see where my round would land. Suddenly, he sprang back from it as if struck: 'This can't be! This can't be! You hit the bullseye! How can you do that with your first round?! I'm the best artillery officer in Bulgaria; in twenty years of service I fired 400 rounds, but I've never been that good. It's impossible!'

'In three years I have fired over a million shells at the Germans. You can see the result,' I replied dryly.

The cunning Bulgarian decided to try me again. He pivoted the stereoscope far to the left, and picked a target that lay a couple of kilometers behind the German front line. Then he asked sarcastically, 'Please hit this spot!'

I looked into the stereoscope. Again, I had previously called in fire on that location, and I had no problem shifting the fire to it. I gave the necessary commands. The Bulgarian was confident that my round wouldn't land anywhere near the chosen spot, but to his amazement, I once again hit the target.

Now it was my turn to be sarcastic: 'Do I have to expend more rounds to convince you that I know how to direct my guns?'

'That's enough,' Khristo said in a friendly voice. 'Speaking frankly, I didn't expect such phenomenal shooting. Let's go have dinner, our treat.'

After the dinner with wine the Bulgarians began to say their goodbyes. They were taking over the line and assuming full responsibility for its defense.

'Most of my guys are leaving, but I'm going to stay here overnight with my signalman,' I said to the surprise and dissatisfaction of the Bulgarians.

Khristo was perplexed: 'What for?'

I replied firmly: 'Just in case. Who knows what the Germans might think to try during the night? My on-call howitzer battery will also remain in its positions for the time being. We'll stay overnight together.'

Captain Khristo protested: 'Now you're offending us, dear Captain; we're the owners of this sector now and we can take care of ourselves.'

Anyway, I insisted and stayed overnight in my dugout, which the Bulgarians had already taken over. I slept next to Khristo. Upset with me, he didn't say another word. The Germans were also quiet and the night was peaceful.

At dawn, as soon as we emerged from the dugout to wash ourselves in the trench, the Germans struck our trenches with hundreds of artillery and mortar rounds. The barrage lasted about ten minutes. It didn't inflict many casualties, because all the Bulgarians were hunkered down in the trenches, but all our communication lines were down. We had no phone connection to our batteries.

Even as the final rounds of the barrage were falling, a dense line of German infantry rose from their trenches. Firing on the move, the Germans were quickly approaching. Heavy machine-gun fire from flanking positions prevented anyone from raising his head above the trench. But the Bulgarian infantry, crouching in the trenches, didn't waver and waited with fixed bayonets to meet the Germans in hand-to-hand combat. The shaken Khristo was running back and forth between stereoscope and the phones, but he didn't have a connection with a single battery. He couldn't fire. His signalmen sent out to repair the lines were being killed one by one. The Germans were now within 100 meters of our trenches. In another few seconds, they would be in our trenches and slaughtering the heavily outnumbered Bulgarians.

My signalman was shouting into the field phone, 'This is "Kolomna", NZO – A! NZO – A!' [*nepodvizhnyi zagraditel'nyi ogon'* – *A*; 'fixed barrier fire – A'] but no one could hear him at the battery. We needed a wall of impenetrable artillery fire urgently! Finally, the signalman found a solution and started to yell only a single letter into the phone: 'A, A, A...'

They picked up this transmission at the battery and guessed correctly that we were calling for the barrier fire pattern 'A'. These pre-registered fire settings had all been scribbled on the gunshields by the crews, and the howitzers opened a rapid fire immediately. As the Germans were about to reach our trenches, dozens of 25kg shells came raining down on them. Their line dissolved into thunderous explosions, smoke, dust and a storm of shell splinters!

When the firing stopped and the wind dispersed the dust and smoke, a horrible view lay in front of our trenches: the churned fields were littered with the corpses of Nazis; only a few survivors were trying to flee or crawl back to their trenches, but these were killed by well-aimed rifle fire of the Bulgarian infantry.

'Well, Captain, you saved us!' the once again calm Captain Khristo called to me as he walked up to me. Then he continued: 'Thank you for staying overnight. Without your intervention, our first battle against the Germans would have ended sadly. Tell me, just how did you get in touch with your battery? After all, all of your own lines had been cut.'

'The barbed wire saved us,' I replied.

'How's that, you say?!'

I told the Bulgarian about my experience using pieces of barbed wire as a phone line. It wasn't a simple matter. It was hard work to gather barbed wire from the battlefield, and even more difficult to link them together and wind the line onto spools. It was also no easy task to string the lines – they had to be isolated from the ground, and thus draped across bushes and branches. Audibility through them was poor. But the advantage of this type of phone line was its durability: it was almost impossible for a shell fragment to cut it. It had saved us today!

'That's what combat experience means!' Khristo said in full admiration. 'You can't read about this in any textbook!'

Having done our job, the signalman and I prepared to leave. But just then the Bulgarians were brought their breakfast, and they invited us to join them at the table. As was typical for them, we celebrated with a lot of raki, and afterward our allies confessed how they had taken us for boys, how they had tested us, and how we had saved them from destruction ... As we said our farewells, Captain Angelov touchingly gave me his wool-lined sheepskin coat as a parting gift, and told me, 'This is so you won't freeze in the winter and so you'll remember us.'

Later, I was very offended when I learned that while I was at the front, marauding members of a blocking detachment had stolen my sheepskin coat from our baggage train. They also took my brand-new uniform made from English wool, which had been a gift from the British monarch to the officers of the Red Army. These woolen khaki-colored dress uniforms had been sewn to fit and then distributed to the officers. I don't know if they were issued to every officer, or whether they were an award to individual officers, but I received one. Supply officers strutted around in them, but those of us at the front stored ours on the baggage train, as we didn't want to crawl around in the muck in such valuable uniforms. This action of the blocking detachment was outrageous: they had robbed our baggage, but they didn't touch the long, covered wagon of our medical battalion commander Rosenzweig. In 1945, when we were on our way to Mongolia to fight the Japanese, he had unloaded his wagon in Moscow and had the contents delivered to his father's summer residence. It turned out that he'd been transporting the contents of a whole German mansion: paintings, furniture, chandeliers, clothes, linen and kitchenware – even shoe brushes! Some were fighting during the war, while others were collecting!

After my belongings were stolen by the men from the blocking detachment, I stopped respecting these troops, although they were doing an important job in the rear, hunting down deserters. When I read a report from the chief of Don Front's Special Department to Beria in the book *Stalingradskaia epopeia* [Stalingrad saga], in which the *osobist* [a member of the Special Department] complained that the army commanders in critical moments were throwing even the blocking detachments into the battle as regular units, and that they had suffered casualties of over 65 per cent as a result – I didn't feel sorry for him. His men had to feel the difference between 'hunting down' and 'fighting a war'.

CHAPTER FIFTEEN

The Liberation of Hungary

We failed to capture Vukovar on the Danube River. Bulgarian troops replaced us on 19 December 1944, and we crossed the Danube at Bachka-Palanka and marched into Hungary on foot. In the city of Baja we crossed the Danube again and marched towards Szekszard. The citizens of Axis Hungary didn't come out to welcome us. Just like the Romanians, they feared retaliation for the atrocities committed by their soldiers in Russia. But women always and everywhere will be women. Hungarian women always found some opportunities and ways to have a bit of fun with our men. Once I unceremoniously kicked some of my soldiers out of a party, where I had found them singing and dancing with some Hungarian girls. Then in broken German I rebuked the Hungarian girls: 'What are you doing? Your husbands are fighting against us, spilling blood, and you are amusing yourselves with Russian soldiers!'

'Let them fight,' was the playful answer, 'but we want to have fun with your soldiers. They're so handsome ...'

On 25 December 1944, our 52nd Rifle Division, part of the 68th Rifle Corps of the 3rd Ukrainian Front's 57th Army, was transported by truck from Szekszard via Szekesfehervar to Csakvar, west of Budapest, where we took over a sector of the outer ring of encirclement around the Germans trapped in Budapest. Lake Balaton was not far away to our south. North of Csakvar, our division was attacked repeatedly by German armor that was trying to relieve their trapped forces in Budapest. The fighting was desperate, and our division lost three-fourths of its combat strength in those battles. Its remnants were withdrawn into some hills north of Csakvar, where we took up a defensive sector with a front of 15 kilometers! There were 500-meter gaps in our defenses. Only due to our maneuverability were we able to foil the German efforts to penetrate through these gaps. My batteries were constantly being shifted to block possible routes of advance for the German tanks.

The small Hungarian town of Pusztavam stood in a little valley just off the Vienna–Budapest highway. I don't know what it means in Hungarian, but in Russian the name didn't promise us anything good [this sounds like 'empty for you' in Russian]. The Germans were still trying to find some weakness in our lines around Budapest, and they also tried at Pusztavam. The town was

180

defended by Morozov's rifle battalion and my artillery battalion, as well as two anti-tank gun regiments and two mortar regiments – there were about 100 guns in all, including my eight guns, and the same number of heavy mortars. All the guns were dug in and well-camouflaged. The heavy mantle of snow masked them even better. Morozov and I felt confident that the town was well-protected. Just let Nazis try to break through here!

We celebrated New Year 1945 in peace. On the morning of 2 January, I climbed into an attic where I had set up my observation post. The town and its surroundings presented a beautiful and peaceful view. There was not the sound of a single shot. The bright white snow sparkled in the sunlight. The cold air was bracing and tickled the nostrils. So I felt like putting on some skis and doing a little downhill skiing in the nearby hills. But the war was still raging and I couldn't ski; instead I had to study the enemy's positions on those slopes. However, I spotted no changes in them from the evening before.

I passed the stereoscope to the on-duty forward observer and started to go down the stairs. At that moment, I heard the engines of prime movers and heavy trucks starting up in different parts of the town. What was going on?! I rushed up to the attic again, cautiously looked out of a small window and froze in horror! Hundreds of vehicles throughout the city were breaking camouflage and towing mortars and guns out of their emplacements, leaving behind dark brown patches of exposed earth on the clean, white snow. The town immediately resembled a disturbed anthill. Soldiers quickly mounted the vehicles loaded with ammunition and the stream of vehicles drove off into the hills behind us! Unfortunately, I wasn't the only one watching this – the Germans were also observing all this from other nearby hills! The density of the buildings in the town and the proximity of the ridge behind Pusztavam enabled the regiments to disappear from German sight in a matter of minutes. For some reason, the German artillery didn't fire a single round. This was the only thing that made me happy about what I was witnessing, and I thought with some pride that if the Germans had tried to do the same thing under my observation, I would have smashed them with my howitzers.

It took me a while to regain my composure after what I had seen – I was outraged! How could anyone do this? In broad daylight, dismantle prepared defenses, remove an armada of weapons from their positions and tow them out of the city, thereby leaving it practically defenseless – all in plain view of the enemy! It practically opened the highway into Budapest for the Germans. It also left those of us who remained in the town hanging out on a limb! Our eight howitzers and Morozov's several dozen riflemen could never compensate for the strength of the four regiments that had just left the town. Couldn't they have at least pulled out quietly during the night? This was nothing less than an invitation to the enemy: kill them, capture them, destroy them – they're exposed!

I contacted General Miliaev over the telephone and informed him that the regiments supporting us had just left, and in their haste they hadn't even bothered to inform us of their departure. I expressed my confusion and worries. The General didn't even start to explain things to me; he just strictly ordered me to reorganize the defense of the town with my own available resources.

Only some time later did we find out why the regiments had been withdrawn so hastily. It turned out that a powerful German armor grouping had broken through to the Danube to the south of us, and was driving north along the river towards Budapest. It was urgently necessary to stop the Germans.

It was easy for the General to tell me to defend the town with eight guns – all of which were positioned on its eastern outskirts, while the Germans would be coming from the north and west. I had to remove both of my batteries from their concealed positions and move them into open terrain. With my heart pounding, in plain view of the Germans I deployed one battery on the road leading into Pusztavam from the west, and the other on the road coming into the town from the north. Unfortunately, we couldn't use the trenches left behind by the departing regiments; their fields of fire were too restricted. While the batteries were executing my order to redeploy, from my observation post in the attic I was vigilantly watching the German positions and the approaches leading to them for any sign of movement. Then suddenly, just as I had expected, I spotted a German tank column! Of course, the Germans wouldn't overlook the departure of our troops. Although the tanks were moving in bounds from one covered location to another, I managed to count them. But I couldn't call in fire on them from my howitzer batteries; they were still relocating. I counted forty tanks – a fresh, full-strength panzer battalion! It had three panzer companies of thirteen tanks each and the battalion commander's command tank. I called in a report to General Miliaev. The round number of forty tanks made him sceptical, and just as I had anticipated, he didn't believe me. The General said nothing to me, other than to remind me: 'Your mission is to stop the German tanks from reaching Budapest, no matter how many of them there are.'

I was deeply offended that General Miliaev believed that I was exaggerating the number of German tanks! And all because many officers, especially the professional ones, often lied and exaggerated the enemy strength in order to obtain reinforcements, and then would boast of their own heroism after a successful battle. At one of the division's reunions after the war, I heard chiefs of staffs openly confess that they had lied in their reports and dispatches. They exaggerated our losses in order to get more replacements, and understated them whenever vodka was being distributed. I was brought up to be an honest man, and I was also a mathematician, so I always reported honest numbers, which caused me a lot of grief. After the war, signalmen of the 439th Rifle Regiment once gave me the transcript of their communications on 2 January 1945, and there they were: three groups of German panzers: 13-13-14 tanks. My eight howitzers were facing forty German tanks, moving on our front and flanks. On that day, however, General Miliaev believed that the Germans had no more than fifteen tanks.

Before my crews managed to entrench, or even to dig in the trail spades of the guns in order to fire, the Germans struck each battery with intense artillery and mortar fire. The explosions were cutting down the crews, because there was nowhere to hide from the shrapnel on the open, frozen terrain. German tanks attacked immediately. One panzer company attacked each of my batteries directly, while the third panzer company led by the battalion commander drove through our thin defenses, bypassed our positions, and then attacked the batteries from the rear. We had no time to hide – we had to fire! We couldn't let the tanks pass through Pusztavam!

I ran to the 2nd Battery, which was the nearest to my observation post. I gave the order to open fire. Only two or three men sprang up from the ground and rushed to each gun in the storm of shell explosions; the rest were lying dead on the snow. Both officers of the battery had also been killed. It was a good thing I had chosen to run to just this battery. Mortar rounds continued to explode among the guns, but the worst damage was being inflicted by the tank shells. The gun crews were dwindling, but now three of the German tanks were burning, and a fourth was spinning on a damaged track. The Number 1 and Number 2 guns were destroyed by direct hits from armor-piercing rounds. The gunlayer of the Number 4 gun, which was the closest to me, was killed by a fragment. I took over his post. I aimed at the lead tank and destroyed it. Yet another tank knocked out the Number 3 gun. I took aim at a tank that was in the process of advancing ahead of the others. Now it was in my cross hairs, the gun was loaded, and I pressed the trigger and immediately sprang back, so the ocular sight wouldn't smash my face with the gun's recoil. In the noise of the battle I hadn't heard the sound of German tanks, which were attacking us from the rear. It was the third panzer company. Nevertheless, as I dodged the gun's recoil, in the corner of my eye I caught the gleam of a quickly approaching tank track. I turned my head to the left and saw the tank just a half-meter away from me. The flashing teeth of the tracks immediately called to mind one of my childhood terrors, when I once glanced into the drum of a threshing machine and saw the whirling teeth. This terrifying flashback and a surge of adrenaline caused me instantly to throw my entire body into a somersault away from the passing tank track. So the coincidental combination of springing back to avoid the gun recoil and my somersault saved my life. If not for the recoil! I heard a loud metallic grating sound and the screeching-clangorous crunch of my gun being crushed by the heavy weight of the tank. I rose to my knees and for some reason realized I had lost my cap, so I grabbed the cap of the dead gunlayer and slithered away into some low bushes like a snake.

Meanwhile, the German tanks approaching from the front and rear had already met, and together they moved on to the southern outskirts of the town. All four guns of my battery had been crushed. Four surviving crew members crawled up to me, carrying the breech blocks in their hands. I was happy and praised the guys for remembering to disable the guns, and for bringing the proof that the Germans couldn't use them, even if they had captured them intact. Together, from our concealment we watched the German infantry arriving after the tanks finish off our wounded in the snow. Once this task was completed, they examined our destroyed guns with interest.

Through crawling, short rushes and ducking around houses, we headed back to my observation post. Captain Svintsov, my deputy, was already there with a handful of survivors from the 1st Battery. All the officers of both batteries had been killed in the fighting. I went down into the cellar where the rifle battalion commander had set up his command post, but I found only unplugged cables.

I decided to run from the town to the edge of the forest, tap into the phone line there that led to my 3rd Battery, and order it to halt any further German advance. I ran out into the street and almost directly into a crowd of firing and yelling German soldiers, intoxicated with their victory. I quickly ducked back into the yard through the gate. Choosing a different route through the yards instead of the streets, we bypassed the Germans and managed to reach the edge of the forest. Luckily, the signalman at the observation post had survived and was still carrying his field phone. I contacted the 3rd Battery, called in fire from its howitzers, and stopped the attacking Germans. Happily, battalion commander Morozov had also sought shelter in these woods, and some of his men were digging in on the forest's edge.

I sent Captain Svintsov to the remaining howitzer battery, so that he could pull it back to safety in case of a German breakthrough. Finally I could catch my breath and take a look around. With the assistance of the few survivors, I started setting up a new observation post. Only now was I suddenly struck by genuine fear over what had occurred. Two of my batteries had been destroyed, together with all the men and horses! We had given up the town, and I alone bore responsibility for it! I had lost the battle, even though the outcome was predetermined! I couldn't have been more depressed. What would happen next?! I wasn't even happy that I'd survived this battle. True, we had knocked out nine German tanks in return for the loss of the eight guns, but it was obvious that no one would remember this, or the fact that I'd been left alone to be slaughtered by the Germans. But I was sure that I would face a tribunal for losing two batteries and failing to hold the town.

Sure enough, at some point in the night, the deputy division commander Colonel Uriupin galloped up on horseback together with his female orderly. He was a veteran of the Russian Civil War, but also a dim-witted, rude and uneducated man. They didn't trust him with the command of a regiment or a division, so he went through the entire war as a deputy commander, no matter the level of command. It turned out that he had come for me, in order to interrogate me over what had happened.

'Where is your battalion?' the scowling Uriupin asked angrily and sharply.

I reported: 'One battery is deployed on a forest road in the Vertes Hills, prepared for indirect fire. My two other batteries have been destroyed in combat with German tanks. There were forty tanks against our eight guns, and we knocked out nine of them. The gun crews and horses were all wiped out in the fighting.'

'It would have been better if you had simply disappeared; we would have written you off together with your guns,' Uriupin said with complete sincerity. 'Now we'll have to put you in front of a tribunal.'

'Why?!' I burst out spontaneously.

'I'm sorry for you, but there's nothing we can do. The "Not one step back" order has not been canceled.' [This is a reference to Stalin's famous Order No. 227, issued in the summer of 1942, which introduced harsh penalties for unauthorized retreats or abandonment of the battlefield.]

Of course, no one recalled that I'd been left alone in Pusztavam after the hasty departure of the four regiments. Having cursed his orderly (who also happened to be his mistress) for losing his pipe, the Colonel rode off without saying another word.

I was in complete despair over the loss of my two gun batteries together with their crews. I was on the verge of tears. The Germans had pitilessly finished them off, but once again their bullets and shell fragments had missed me. But I couldn't do more than destroy nine tanks with my two batteries, even though I had tried my best, with no regard for my own life! It wasn't my fault that I had survived! My crews had fought skillfully and bravely – no one had abandoned their guns! They continued to fire until the end under a hail of bullets and shell fragments. But now I was still going to be tried as a coward and a traitor! I was facing execution or, even worse, a penal battalion. It was most horrible to contemplate being killed by your own side as a traitor.

I had no way to prove anything to anyone. There were no witnesses who could help me. Oh, how hard this was for me! I was only twenty-three years old, and because of my studies and the war, I had no real life experience. I knew only how to study and to fight. Sure, I'd been lucky at the front. But now there was no one to cheer me up, to give me advice, or to bail me out of this mess. The battery commanders were all dead; my deputy commander and chief of staff were of my own age, and had no more clout than I did. The only experienced officer in my battalion was my political officer Karpov. He was sixteen years older than me, smart, cunning, and knew his way around. He knew, of course, what had happened, but he just kept sitting around the field kitchen, kept his mouth shut, and completely isolated himself from me – fearing guilt by association, I suppose. He didn't even call me on the phone. He hadn't taken part in the battle and he hadn't lost the guns, so he wasn't guilty. The Party organizer Kaplatadze was of the same material. He spent all his time hanging around with the battalion's *Komsomol* organizer and Karpov at the field kitchen.

Only the new Party organizer, Ivan Akimovich Shevchenko, who had arrived to replace Kaplatadze, even bothered to call me from the field kitchen. He had only arrived in the battalion that day. He wasn't a professional political officer; he had been a regiment commander's adjutant. He was about thirty years old and had completed a postgraduate education before the war. Somehow he had displeased the regiment commander, or perhaps his commander was eyeing the same female staff worker – however it had happened, the regiment commander took care of the situation by sending him to the front as a Party organizer. Shevchenko knew my reputation as a combat officer, or else he thought he could give me some advice, so he promised to visit me at my observation post the next morning.

I couldn't calm down. Why had I not been struck down by a shell splinter? I was very unhappy to survive. I'd dodged that tank track by a mere coincidence: the tank had approached at the very moment of recoil after firing, or else I would have been squashed together with the gun.

But enough with the mourning: no one had canceled the war yet. The Germans were still firing and maneuvering, and might decide to resume the advance at any moment. Meanwhile I had only one battery left. I had to put everything else aside, pull myself together and assess the situation carefully. What was the rifle battalion commander doing? He was also a fine fellow! He had fled with his soldiers and had settled down here in the forest, yet no one was troubling him. He hadn't lost gun batteries.

The General called me in the morning:

> I know what happened. I believe that you did all you could. But all the same they're going to court-martial you. Be ready. However, I know you as a resourceful officer. Try to get your guns back from the Germans. Prove to the prosecutor that they had been destroyed and couldn't fire. That might lighten your sentence. I still haven't reported what happened to the Army headquarters. I'll give you forty-eight hours. Try to bring off those guns.

I replied:

> Comrade General! I fought honorably. You know that those four
> regiments had been pulled out. Forty tanks came at us. We knocked out
> nine of them. It isn't my fault that I survived. How can I salvage the
> guns? The Germans are digging in on the near side of town. Their
> tanks are patrolling the front line. My smashed guns are lying on the
> other side of town. I have no men or horses.

The General said nothing more.

What could I do? Just then Ivan Akimovich, the battalion's new Party
organizer, showed up, and I sure was happy to see him! He sympathized with
my situation, and we took a seat and began to ponder what to do. After some
reflection, I proposed: 'Let's put on white snow suits and sneak along the
German line with some scouts. You head left and I'll go right. Perhaps we'll
find a gap in the German defenses. Then tonight we could slip through there
and retrieve our guns.'

Korennoi and I set out at a crawl along our front at the forest's edge to the
right through the snow. During the night, the Germans had dug a continuous
trench line along their own front. It was lying about 300 meters away from us.
The German trench was anchored on its left by the small Altal-er River that
flowed out of the hills into Pusztavam. I noticed that the thick brush that
bordered the river extended from our line to the Germans'. The river itself was
covered with thick ice. Although the Germans had camouflaged their freshly-
dug trench, I could still see the trace of its dirt breastwork against the snow.

We worked our way to the river and slithered through the thick brush down
to the frozen river. I looked across at the opposite bank and saw that it too was
covered with dense brush. Although the German line extended beyond the
river, the happy thought flashed through my mind that the brush along both
banks blocked the view of the river from either bank. It offered us a perfect
route into the German rear!

Ivan Akimovich and I returned from our separate scouting forays by dinner.
Ivan didn't find anything useful when he scouted the German right. We decided
to use the route I had discovered to sneak into the German rear that evening. I
called the commanders of the 2nd and 3rd Artillery Battalions and asked to
borrow a couple of limbers with teams of captured German horses from each.
My colleagues, who sincerely sympathized with my misfortune, didn't refuse
me and promised to send drivers with the limbers to our forest by sunset.

One hour before sunset three of us, Korennoi, forward observer Kopylov and
I, taking along a captured German light machine gun, set off at a crawl along
the bankside brush towards the Germans. We moved along the riverbank

unnoticed from either bank and safely penetrated the German front line. We continued to creep another 400 meters or so, then clambered up the high left bank and dug into the snow. From our position, I could see the remains of my former 2nd Battery. The flattened guns were lying motionless in the snow. My heart ached: the Germans had turned my combat battery into heaps of scrap metal. I didn't see any bodies of my men; the Germans had taken them away with the assistance of locals. I sent Kopylov back to the forest where the limbers and teams were supposed to be, with orders to bring them here through the darkness. Korennoi and I took a look around.

'Comrade Captain,' Korennoi nudged me in the side, 'there are some people over there.'

Indeed, about ten Germans were walking smartly down a path out of the hills in single file, and were now heading towards our guns. They had submachine-guns slung around their necks, and each man was carrying a small case. They walked up to the guns and started to place the cases on the breeches of our guns. I immediately guessed that they were preparing to blow up our guns, so it would be easier to transport them to their rear as scrap metal. I ordered Korennoi: 'Cut them all down, Iasha!'

Firing short bursts, Iasha killed the entire demolition team. There was no enemy reaction to our fire. The Germans weren't paying any attention to the sound of a German machine gun firing in their rear. It was a good thing we hadn't brought along a Russian machine gun!

We waited impatiently for the gun limbers. It was now dark. Had my fellow commanders let me down? No, they were coming. Four limbers quietly arrived, led by Kopylov. There were now seven of us. We found an exit and drove the limbers to the wrecks of the guns. Fortunately, the drivers had thought to bring along some flexible steel cable, which we used to tie the wrecked guns to the limbers before hauling them down to the ice. We hadn't been able to close the gun trails, so the horses had to drag the wrecks with the trails spread. Although the trails kept digging into the thick ice, the powerful Belgian horses did their job and safely brought the four wrecked guns back into our lines.

Korennoi and I stayed put, waiting for the teams to return in order to try for the western side of town to pick up the remains of the 1st Battery. It was getting colder. The moon rose in the sky. It only made our job more difficult, as visibility improved. Thank God we had managed to bring off one of the batteries; half the job was done. We waited for the limbers to return. They were taking a long time. I grew worried: had the Germans spotted them and stopped them, or...? But there was no firing. I tried to calm down – surely they would come. Then there they were! But they were moving so slowly, it was as if they were heading in from field work on a collective farm, not driving through the German rear!

I took the horses around the town to the 1st Battery's final position. I could see for miles in the bright moonlight. The town was silent and dark; I didn't spot anyone on its outskirts or in the town itself. We quietly drove up to the scene of the 1st Battery's last stand. The view here was the same – flattened, smashed guns lying on the frozen ground. Six men started to work, while I climbed about 50 meters up the slope of a hill in order to get a better view of the surrounding terrain. The road leading into the town, which we had tried to block to the Germans, was still silent and empty. The closest houses were about 200 meters from where we were working. I glanced back and observed the quick work of the drivers and my men, who were tying the guns to the limbers.

While I was watching their activity, I suddenly heard the sound of many human voices over by the houses. I saw a disorderly crowd of men spilling out onto the street. They had submachine-guns slung behind their backs or dangling from their necks. It was a group of German soldiers. Most likely, they were heading to their dugouts to sleep, after celebrating their victory. The Germans were talking loudly, laughing and they were all in a party spirit. Judging by the way they were behaving and from the few words that I caught that I understood, it seemed that they had no officers with them. There were about twenty of them. Their sudden appearance caught me off guard, and of course they noticed the solitary figure standing on the slope.

I quickly ran through my limited options. If I ran to my men or dropped to the ground, they would suspect something and run over to investigate. I was sure they also saw the horses in the moonlight behind me. If I stayed where I was, they might well just walk by me. But they could also approach me and they'd immediately detect that I wasn't a German. I was in no position to engage them – they were clearly experienced combat troops, while I only had my two observers and the four older drivers. They also had numerical superiority. It wouldn't be much of a fight, and I most feared the prospects of being wounded and taken prisoner. The worst part was that we would fail in our mission.

No, they wouldn't just walk by us. They were drunk; men in such condition would surely start a conversation or pick a fight for no reason. On the other hand, they might be embarrassed by walking around in their condition in front of an officer and just hope to pass without getting his notice. It was obvious that I looked like an officer: I was standing there doing nothing while I watched my men working. While I stood there, more thoughts flashed through my mind. I wasn't in fear of my own life. I had already lived nine lives in this war! And just how long can someone remain untouchable? No, I was afraid of failing my mission. But then a larger fear suddenly bubbled up: what would our troops think if we didn't return? Did we go missing in action? Did we surrender ourselves to the Germans? I could be labeled as a traitor. That was horrible.

They would definitely say that I had defected to the Germans to avoid my court martial. No, I had to make it back to our lines. These thoughts flashed through my head in an instant, like lightning. I decided to stand still. Let it be anything, but not captivity! I was holding my pistol pressed tightly against my leg. I would have time to fire several shots, but I had to make sure to leave one round for myself.

Meanwhile, the Germans were approaching. When they reached the foot of the hill downslope from me, they stopped. Most of them were gazing with interest at the horses and the activity around the wrecked guns and limbers. They saw Belgian horses, which was a familiar view for them. They definitely thought the horses were German. My own men were so distracted by their work that likely they had not yet even noticed the Germans. Besides, they trusted that the Captain knew what he was doing.

The intoxicated Germans watched my men work for a minute or two, but it seemed like an eternity. Then several men shouted something up to me simultaneously. The others laughed. In all that noise I only recognized a few words: '*Russiche... Kanonen... fahren...*' I figured they were asking questions like: 'Why do you need these destroyed Russian guns? Where will you take them?' As the Germans were shouting all at once, I became convinced that there was no officer among them. They must have mistaken me for a German supply officer. Most likely, just like in the Red Army, their front-line troops looked upon a supply officer as a superior, but they also despised him. Yet their mood was amicably patronizing, and they wanted to get moving, or else they might not get sleep!

In order to stop this dangerous and unpredictable contact with the drunken Germans, I shouted a loud command: '*Genug!*' – which means 'Enough!' At this word I sharply dropped my raised hand with irritation and turned away from them, giving them a sign that I was tired of this nonsense.

With my back now to them, I wasn't sure if I had said that one word without an accent. My heart was pounding: had they detected that I was a Russian? But as I was pretending to be a German officer, I couldn't remain silent in that situation – they would have suspected something. Luckily, the Germans shut up and moved on.

We safely hauled the wrecked guns to the river. Then we took them over the ice through the German line and back into our lines in the forest.

So the small frozen Altal-er River helped me out when I was in trouble. The Lord was merciful and had sent me this salvation.

I sent the drivers and teams back to their respective batteries and stood among the heaps of scrap metal with my forward observers and the new Party organizer Shevchenko. So, I could write off my guns, they really were wrecked, but what would I have to fire? I would only get new guns much later, after the military prosecutor's office and the NKVD completed the investigation and wrote, to their regret, an exculpatory report. But the Germans wouldn't wait for the paperwork to be completed, and would likely attack again the next day...

In the morning I gathered the supply men and the remains of the crews led by a master armorer, and ordered them: 'Within forty-eight hours, I want four battle-ready cannons to be assembled from these pieces!'

The work began! We got assistance from the other artillery battalions and from the regiment's rear. Indeed, within forty-eight hours – in the middle of a forest, not a factory – we managed to assemble three complete guns, while the fourth was only lacking one detail: the barrel. One of the soldiers, who apparently had his own information network among the local residents, spoke up: 'There's a spare barrel in a village over there. It is being guarded by men from one of the departed regiments.'

'What if we borrow it from them, Comrade Captain?' another man offered.

'I have no objections,' I said, 'we have more need of it than they do.'

So I had four cannons! I managed to obtain two more guns from the other battalions, thereby giving me two batteries with three guns each. Hurrah! I reported to General Miliaev. He didn't believe that I had not only managed to evacuate the damaged guns, but also to repair some of them! The General told me: 'I knew your guns had been destroyed in the fighting, but we had to have proof of it for the prosecutor. You did a great job! You should get a decoration for this, but instead just thank me that you won't be court-martialed.'

I have always remembered this battle with the tanks and the subsequent adventure with the guns. There were forty tanks; I had counted them as they approached the village. We knocked out nine of them, which I reported to the regiment staff. Then, many years later, I learned from an official account of the action that the Germans supposedly had only fifteen tanks and that the combat supposedly all took place at night. There wasn't a single word about the tanks we knocked out. I was offended, naturally! We fought the war and they issued reports.

The division commander lets us bathe!!

Gant is a small village nestled in the hills west of Budapest. About twenty buildings are pressed up against a bluff of the Vertes Ridge. In February 1945 we were defending Gant and the ridge from the Germans, while they were attacking out of a small valley, trying to relieve their surrounded troops in Budapest.

Tiny Gant was marked on all the strategic maps of Russian and German high command, because it lay on the boundary between the 2nd and the 3rd Ukrainian Fronts. My observation post was perched on the bluff above Gant. I was the senior artillery officer in the regiment's sector of defense, and I was responsible for the boundary between the two fronts. Senior officers, worried by the defense of the junction, were visiting me all the time. I had to pass all sorts of interrogations! A colonel from Moscow especially scrutinized me. I had to open fire from my batteries at any spot within several seconds for him. He pressed me on what I would do if all the lines were down and the radio set destroyed. I demonstrated all the different means and ways of cooperation with the neighbor on our left, the 3rd Ukrainian Front, but the colonel didn't stop: 'What other connection do you have with them?'

'My Lieutenant is having an affair with a female radio operator from the 3rd Ukrainian Front,' I replied.

'What else?' the colonel asked.

'We share our vodka with them when we have it and their shipments have been delayed.'

Finally, the colonel laughed and stopped his exam.

The enemy had been bothering us even more than the inspectors with constant artillery barrages and attacks. We had very little infantry left, so we repelled the attacks mostly with artillery fire. For that reason I couldn't leave the front, not even to wash myself.

Only once, when it was quiet, did the division commander give me a two-hour leave to go wash in a *bania*.

Holding back my joy, I raced out of the dark dugout and ran towards a nearby gorge in order to make it to the other side of the ridge. A machine-gun burst made me dive for cover, reminding me that I had to be careful. I reached the top of the ridge, crawled over the crest, and ran downhill as fast as I could towards the rear units of my battalion. I was no longer a battalion commander anxious over the defense of a boundary between two fronts. I was a 23-year-old fellow, happy to see the winter sun, the shining white snow and a deer that he spotted in the distance.

Thirty minutes later I was at the foot of the ridge, where a sled was waiting for me. Two white Arabian horses took me and the driver Didenko to Csakvar in six minutes. The rear units and the batteries of my battalion were stationed there. I saw the mill on the edge of town, and the firing positions of my three batteries around it. The guns were dug in and well-camouflaged, which I was happy to see. I headed over to my dear 3rd Battery, which I had commanded for over a year.

The battery's senior officer, Lieutenant Oshchepkov, shifting a map case around to his back, quickly ran up to me, smartly snapped to attention and reported the situation at the battery in a clear voice. I always admired the sharp appearance of this smart professional officer. He had entered the service before the war, but had become stuck in the firing positions of a battery. Perhaps because he figured it was a little safer here. Any promotion would have inevitably swept him into the front line. Neatly dressed in tailored uniforms, Oshchepkov also performed all the regulation movements and routines sharply, and he was liked not only by the other servicemen around him, also the local girls. His swarthy and cleanly-shaven face with large black eyes was crowned by thick black hair. This handsome Siberian man's face had some Asian features. The typical expression he wore on his face made him look brave and decisive, which he was. Oshchepkov's battery was highly disciplined, and his crews operated quickly and with precision. He respected me, although I was younger than him and had only spent three years in the army. He appreciated my fire direction skills and ability to handle the battalion. I decided to have a bit of fun at his expense.

'What are these "forks" sticking out of each howitzer's trench?' I asked strictly, pointing at the quad anti-aircraft machine guns.

'The female gunners asked to set up near us, Comrade Captain, so they wouldn't have to dig emplacements in the frozen ground.'

I was outraged: 'They didn't set up next to you; they're in your trenches! They are bait for an air strike! As soon as they open fire, they – and you – will be blanketed with bombs. Where are the owners of these machine guns?'

'They're warming up inside our guys' huts, Comrade Captain.'

I walked over to the nearest quad gun and jerked back the bolt.

'What are you doing?! You can't shoot!' Oshchepkov grew scared.

I pulled the trigger in response. The four barrels emitted a terrible roar. A girl in military uniform ran out of the nearest hut, an overcoat hastily thrown around her shoulders. Her head was uncovered, and her hair was waving in the wind. She yelled at me in a demanding voice: 'On whose orders?!'

'Where is your sentry?!' I replied. 'Why are these machine guns unguarded?!' Then I addressed Oshchepkov: 'You are quite the gentleman, Senior Lieutenant! You felt sorry for the girls and practically let them into your beds together with their machine guns! Remove them immediately!'

I washed in a cold field *bania*, which was the same hollow barrel above my head, with tent canvas wrapping three sides of the shower. Then I visited my battalion headquarters. My staff officers were in the foyer on the first floor of the mill owner's mansion. The owners occasionally walked through this room. The Germans wouldn't have tolerated this at all, but my guys weren't just being polite – they wanted to talk to civilians, even if they were foreigners. We always felt a longing to be around civilians. I remember that in January 1943, after six months of the unceasing fighting at Rzhev, where all villages around had been burnt to ashes by the Germans, we were redeployed to Stalingrad. We would spend hours standing at the open doors of our cattle cars, hoping to catch sight of a woman or a child, because we had missed them so much after six months.

We had a leisurely lunch in the home together with my political officer and chief of staff. We ate at a table covered with a tablecloth, off of plates, like at home before the war. It felt strange that I didn't have to balance my mess tin on my knees and I didn't have to be concerned with dirt falling into my food from the breastwork. As my officers were freely using the owners' kitchen and dining utensils, I understood that they were on good terms. I was smothered with special attention.

It was always like that, when we came back from the front lines wet, dirty and hungry, to the relatively cozy, dry and warm quarters of the rear officers. Their lives were completely different. All our days were just a monotonous blur of fighting. We didn't note holidays or even know which day of the week it was. On the contrary, the men in the rear were flirting with local girls, organizing parties and hosting dances.

It was the same at Gant. If the Germans granted us one or two hours of reprieve from their barrages, the only entertainment we had in the trenches was watching a wild Mouflon ram in the hills. This beautiful, powerful animal with large round horns always appeared suddenly out of nowhere, and would jump up to his favored spot – atop a large boulder on the top of the bluff, and it would stand there for hours. With his bearded head held high, it was like he was examining the German positions.

'It's as if he knows when there will be no barrage,' Korennoi wondered aloud.

'What is he looking at up there all the time?' the young Shtansky murmured, still pressing the receiver to his ear.

'Well, perhaps he has a girlfriend there, over on the German side?' Korennoi answered seriously.

The interesting thing was that no one ever shot at the ram, even for fun. There was no fire from our or the German side. They were probably also watching it. The ram would stand there for hours. Our men started to say with assurance, 'If the ram's there, there will be no barrage.' I was indeed envious of the rear troops: we had this wild ram and they had girls.

I had about thirty minutes to kill before I had to return to the front. I was alone in the room. I paced back and forth a bit just to stretch my legs. I noticed some newspapers lying on the seat of an armchair. I sat down in the soft armchair and picked up a paper: a copy of *Pravda*. I hadn't experienced such bliss in a long time: I was clean, my belly was full, and I was perusing a newspaper in an armchair!

Suddenly I heard a soft knocking on the door. An amazingly beautiful girl was standing in the doorway. Apparently, she was the miller's daughter. She bowed lightly in my direction, greeted me in German and then slowly walked into one of the mansion's interior rooms. I kept gazing at the newspaper, but I couldn't focus. I was so excited by the girl's appearance that I was just waiting for her to return, just so I could see her again. Maria (which I later learned was her name) entered the room several minutes later, again apologized in German and started dusting off the paintings and photos on the wall opposite me. She was wearing slippers and a light, brightly-colored dressing-gown. I was now no longer looking at the newspaper, but more covering myself with it, as I looked at the shapely backside of the young woman. We didn't dare try to start a conversation. Occasionally she stole a glance at me. Apparently, she had heard about the visit of a young officer, the commander of the Russians that were staying in her house, and she was interested in seeing me. I saw her stand on tiptoes in order to reach the tops of the frames, and her dressing-gown rose to her knees. I was accustomed to seeing only the filthy padded pants of combat soldiers, and now the sight of bare female calves seemed like a dream.

Maria crossed the room several times. I gradually got used to her presence and didn't want to stare, so I buried myself in the newspaper again. I was reading Mikhalkov's fable 'The Beaver and the Fox', and suddenly smiled about something I'd just read. Maria noticed this and immediately asked: 'Kapitan, warum Sie lachen?'

'It's amusing, that's why I'm smiling,' I replied in German. We only spoke German with the Hungarians and understood them better than the Germans.

'How can there be something funny in the paper? It's all just politics,' the Hungarian girl was puzzled.

'Sometimes they do have funny stories,' I replied, and I tried to tell her about the fable in German, but I didn't know the German word for 'beaver'.

She understood nothing from my attempt to tell her the fable, and instead asked: 'What did you say this was?'

'It is called *basnia* (fable) in Russian.'

Maria's beautiful hazel eyes suddenly widened; she gasped, rose from her chair, burst out laughing and fled the room without saying a word.

Puzzled, I watched her go. I didn't understand what had just happened. She didn't understand the story, but she was shocked by the word *basnia*. My mood was spoiled and I was sorry about the incident. Indeed, I had very little time remaining to spend with the girl.

Before I could start reading the paper again, Maria walked back into the room, accompanied by her friend, a girl of about her same age and beauty. Maria asked: 'Captain, what was the thing that you were just reading?'

I tried to retell the fable again.

'No!' Maria interrupted. 'What did you call it?'

'*Basnia*,' I said clearly, playing Maria's game.

That was all the girls needed. They laughed and ran out of the room. Moments later, the miller walked in. He had received an incapacitating wound on the Eastern Front while fighting against the Red Army. He spoke Russian well.

'Josif, what does *basnia* mean in Hungarian?'

'Quiet, quiet, don't shout!' Josif waved his hands, clearly agitated. Then he calmed down a little and said that it was a dirty word signifying a certain part of the female anatomy. To make himself clear, he pointed below his belt.

The girls came back several minutes later escorted by Captain Sovetov, my chief of staff. We laughed at the funny coincidence and the four of us started to chat about all sorts of topics. It was such fun that we had completely forgotten the war and all its worries.

Then, in the middle of our pleasant conversation, I heard the rumble of distant artillery fire. It was coming from our forward positions and was intensifying with every second. I became anxious, and the smile instantly left my face. My anxiety spread to the girls, who also stopped laughing. I could see that the girls were extremely disappointed that the artillery fire had stopped our good time together so abruptly and that they also felt very sorry for me. I was also very worried about them. Our common emotional reaction to the sudden end of this party was so similar that it seemed that there was no language or cultural barrier between us.

I apologized, quickly donned my overcoat and ran into the street. I jumped into the sled and the driver Didenko started the horses to take me back to Gant.

The cold wind howled in my ears as we drove, but it couldn't shake me from the great anxiety I was feeling. This was it, I thought, the Germans had detected the boundary line between the two fronts and were assaulting it. Here, in the rear and without any information I was more scared than in any battle. The worst thing was that I had no way of influencing the battle from my current position!

We were approaching the ridge. The roar of the barrage intensified and I could clearly see black smoke rising into the sky beyond the ridge. I calmed down and started to think of the fastest way to Gant. It would take me forty minutes to cross the ridge on foot, and the battle would be over by then! Of course, I could make it there in five minutes through the 'gate' – a gap in the ridge that I could already see to our right, and towards which our road would soon be turning. But it was a risk – beyond the gap, the road turned left and ran approximately 400 meters to my observation post. That stretch was entirely in the enemy's sight. I made a decision. I reasoned that it was getting dark, my horses were white and almost invisible against the snow, the Germans wouldn't spot us immediately and by the time they did, it would be too late. Otherwise, I would be late and that would be the end.

'Didenko! Stay on the road and drive to the right!' I ordered the driver.

The horses galloped through the gap and we emerged from the pass and turned to the left. Now we were moving at full speed along the front line. On our right were the trenches of our infantry, and some 500 meters away on the other side of the valley – the German lines. But when I looked to the left I received a nasty shock: the rock bluff was not covered with snow! It was bare! Our white horses stood out against it like sails, and could be seen for miles!

I looked over at the snow-covered German lines with my heart sinking, expecting them to open fire any second. Then there it was! A stream of fire darted towards us like a cobra. It covered the 500 meters in one second and reached our sled, then seemed to hang between the front and hind legs of the horses. The machine gun traversed, but the tracers continued to flash beneath the bellies of the horses. If the German machine-gunner had halted his traverse of the gun, or had accelerated it slightly, he would have cut off the horses' legs and capsized our sled. But luckily this did not happen.

'The German has a steady hand!' I thought, giving sincere praise to the machine-gunner.

Frozen, holding my breath, I kept looking towards the machine gun's position. The glowing stream of its fire disappeared for a second, and then reappeared between the tails of the horses and Didenko. The latter leaned back as far as he could, afraid of touching the deadly beauty. But the red stream didn't stay in this position long. Suddenly I heard loud snapping, and the coachman's seat exploded into pieces. It was a clear demonstration of the power of this beautiful red thread. The horses, shedding flakes of white foam, snorted and galloped even faster. Suddenly the stream of bullets shifted and zipped between the driver and me. I pressed myself into my seat and leaned back as far as the back of the sled allowed. As if in slow motion, I watched as the glowing stream slowly moved towards my head, as if drawn by a magnet. The bullets were now flying past my nose just a centimeter away. I could hear the bullets hissing loudly, like a thousand snakes! When the stream of tracers drew even closer to my eyes, I suddenly felt as if my eyes were being painfully torn from their sockets. I closed my eyes in terror and blacked out for a moment. I woke up from thunderous sounds next to me – the German gunner's next burst blew my bench into pieces, and I fell to the floor of the sled with my feet sticking up in the air. The next moment we rushed into the village and the houses on the right blocked the ace German machine-gunner's view of us. The machine-gun fire ceased. The burning village of Gant was our salvation!

Now, in 1984, even as I write these lines, my hands are shaking as I recall that wild ride from forty years ago. The whole incident lasted only thirty or forty seconds, not more! But these seconds seemed like an eternity to me!

Later, when analyzing the incident, I realized why the bullets hadn't hit us. The German likely couldn't see the front sight on his machine gun in the twilight, and was aiming by the path of the tracer rounds. Because of the range, the bullets followed an arcing trajectory. At the top of their trajectory, the glowing stream of rounds seemed to the German machine-gunner to be hitting the belly of our horses, but in fact the bullets were dipping underneath them. The Nazi had a steady hand and firmly kept the top of the trajectory on the bellies of the horses, but to his amazement, he didn't hit the target. Irritated with failure, the Nazi fired at us and missed again.

What was the benign force that helped us evade the bullets? Gravity and a strong wind that was blowing at our back along the foot of the ridge saved us. The bullets were being blown some 5 centimeters ahead of us and downward, away from our heads. The German hadn't accounted for the wind, and we survived. The German machine-gunner probably thought we were under a spell and couldn't be killed by bullets!

'Thank you for helping me out!'

On 12 February, the 88,000-strong German grouping in Budapest was liquidated. We were still on the defense. We now faced Hungarian troops, which on German orders were making feeble attacks on our position every day. Early each morning, they would deploy five heavy machine guns on the edge of the village, form into an attacking line, and then tentatively start moving towards our lines. I would quickly call in artillery fire, and they would immediately crawl back into the village. If they had ever reached our position on the edge of a forest, they would have walked right over us, because we had very few troops left. I had three signalmen in a forest ranger's hut, battalion commander Morozov had two men with him and there was one man with a light MG positioned in front of the hut. There were no more troops on our right or our left.

Having attempted several of these lazy and ineffective attacks, the Hungarians started to surrender to us in entire units: led by officers, they would march towards us in formation, with their weapons. We had no more men left to escort them, but they kept coming across no-man's-land almost daily.

On this particular morning, yet another Hungarian platoon was marching towards us. Morozov jumped out of the window and personally ran out to meet them. He rudely grabbed the officer's submachine-gun. Offended, the officer shouted an order and his men surrounded Morozov, disarmed him, and started to lead their captive back to their lines. I didn't lose my head and dropped four rounds between the Hungarians and the village. The powerful explosions forced them to hit the ground. They understood that there was no way back. So they stood back up, re-formed into a column, and now Morozov started to lead them into imprisonment.

Having disarmed and handed the prisoners over to his guard, Morozov, pale as a sheet of paper, jumped back into the window and collapsed on the sofa. When he regained his composure, he swore and said: 'Imagine – ending up as a prisoner at the end of the war! Thank you for helping me out!'

The girl with the wounded hand

Thus, the German offensive against the Soviet forces in the area of Lake Balaton had been stopped. On 16 March we went back onto the offensive west of Budapest. We seized the cities of Bokod, Dad, Kocs and Mocsa with fighting.

The tragedy that I want to reveal happened somewhere between Dad and Kocs, to the west of the Danube. It was March 1945. There was already spring-like warmth in the air, but a cold rain was falling. We were attacking along the main road to the north. There was a lone farmhouse with a few outbuildings to the left of the road. The Germans were retreating rapidly, so we doggedly pursued them at the same pace, constantly snapping at their heels. We hurried past this particular farmhouse as well. But some 2 kilometers to the north the Germans had settled into some prepared trenches and met us with fire. We were forced to stop and hug the ground. I ordered over the phone for all three batteries of my battalion to come up. One of the howitzer batteries stopped and deployed right around this farmhouse. My headquarters staff with the rear units and the field kitchen also stopped there. It was obvious to everyone that we weren't going to make a move until the next morning; we didn't have enough strength to drive the Germans out of their trenches.

My Sergeant Major Makukha called: 'Where should I set up the field kitchen?'

I recommended that he set up in the house out of the rain.

'It isn't possible,' the Sergeant Major replied, 'the halls and rooms are full of mutilated corpses.'

'Get them out of there and set up inside! Are you seeing the dead for the first time?'

'It's better if I set up the kitchen in the rain by the back wall; I'm not going to touch the corpses. You can't imagine what happened here.'

The situation at the front was clear: the Germans weren't planning to retreat during the night, so we had to dig in where we were. I decided to make a run to the rear, to see how bad it had to be for an experienced sergeant major to be afraid to touch the corpses. It had to be something unusual, but I also had to discipline the Sergeant Major.

Until this afternoon, the house had been located deep in the German rear, before we had driven them out of their previous positions that morning. The Nazis we were chasing hadn't had time even to glance into the farmhouse, so whatever had happened must have occurred the night before. It must have been German rear troops, likely Waffen SS, who had killed the civilians.

I left a battery commander at the observation post, and then made my way back to the ill-fated house. I walked up to it, and was greeted by the Sergeant Major. I could see smoke rising from the kitchen, which was out in the rain. Produce was lying around on the wet ground.

'Why are you getting soaked here out in the rain? Afraid of dead bodies, huh?' I asked the Sergeant Major in a demanding manner.

'Take a look for yourself,' Makukha was unyielding. A nimble collective farm brigade leader, he was ten years older than me. He had already seen a lot in his life and was an experienced soldier as well, so it was hard to shock him.

I stepped into a hallway. Four male bodies, stripped to the waist, were scattered around on the floor. The middle-aged and young men, wearing civilian trousers, had been totally disfigured by knife wounds, and the floor was completely covered with their blackened, already dried blood. There were five more bodies in the same condition in the rooms of the house. 'Of course,' I thought, 'no one would want to take care of this bloody mess.' We stepped back out into the yard, and I grabbed the handle on the door of an underground cellar.

'Can't you put the food in here so it doesn't get wet?' I continued my bossy talk, as I opened the door.

The light of day partially illuminated an even more horrifying scene down below. In the dim light, we saw the naked legs of a raped woman lying on her back. She had several bullet holes in her forehead and exposed breasts. I quickly started to close the door, trying to rid myself of this awful image as quickly as possible. But before the door had closed completely, I thought I saw something moving down below. I took a closer look inside, and found a small child trying to hide from me in a darkened corner. A girl of about two years of age was sitting to the left of her mother, her little arm extended towards the body with her palm turned up. Her palm appeared to be bloody. Speaking softly and tenderly, I tried to take the little girl into my arms. But as I moved towards her, she scuttled back as far as she could into the dark corner. When I finally pulled the little girl out of there, I saw that her hand had been shot through. Her eyes were opened wide in terror. So, the rapists had executed the woman and then thought to fire a snap burst at the small child beside her as they were leaving. Somehow, the girl had evaded most of the burst, but one bullet had passed through the palm of her little hand.

I lifted the little girl into my arms and held her. I didn't know what to do with her. Where would I send this orphan? There were no survivors in the house. There were no nearby villages. The town of Dad, where our regiment headquarters was located, was some 10 kilometers in the rear. A courier from the regiment headquarters walked up as I was bandaging the little girl's hand. I remember his last name – Kopeikin. I handed the girl to Kopeikin and told him: 'Take this girl to Dad and give her to some local resident.'

'What if they refuse?'

'Put her on a chair in some rich person's house and leave. Let them take care of her, she's a Magyar after all. We can't take her with us, you know.'

The next day we drove the Germans out of their trench and resumed the advance. A little ways down the road, we found a house quite similar to the house of horrors we'd left behind. Two elderly women were living there. In my poor German, I still managed to find out that a local farmer had been living there with his wife and daughter. There had been several Russian prisoners-of-war living with them, but the old women didn't know how they had wound up there. But the farmer fed the Russians and they worked for him.

This awful tragedy remained a mystery to us. We found only the bodies of the mercilessly slain men and women, and a little girl with the bullet wound through her hand.

A matter of an instant

We took the city of Komarom on the Danube from the march, or better said, on the run. We literally ran into the streets of the town in hot pursuit of the fleeing Germans. We were exchanging fire on the move, but as they had to turn around to fire, and we didn't, we had the upper hand. When the Germans reached the river and threw themselves into the water, we continued to fire at them. Only a handful of Germans reached the opposite bank, the Czech town of Komarno.

We easily forced the river and took Komarno, then raced on towards Vienna. But we ran into the Hungarian town of Gyor that the Germans had thoroughly fortified and had resolved to defend at all costs. They had deep trenches, machine guns and guns deployed for direct fire, all well-camouflaged. Our situation was as usual: the remnants of a rifle regiment, consolidated into a composite battalion under the leadership of the 'invincible' Morozov, and my artillery battalion of three batteries. We had no armor or supporting artillery.

In the early morning of 30 March, thirty minutes before the attack, Morozov spoke to me: 'Thank you for helping us to take Komarom with your guns. Now, please, help me with this town; we can't win without you.'

Ivan had become accustomed to having a skilled artilleryman at his side. Well, what wouldn't I do for this old friend? I was ready to run into fire with him.

So, Morozov's battalion, supported by my guns, was ready for the attack. I, just like in the good old days, was right beside the battalion commander, but now I had three artillery batteries at my disposal instead of one. I had already pounded the German weapons emplacements. The next barrage was on the German trenches. Once I had finished my work, Morozov's infantry rose and charged ahead. The battalion commander and I were jogging along in the center of the attacking line. An intact German machine gun suddenly opened up. A short order to the signalman, who was at my side, and a few incoming rounds destroyed the machine gun. There were about 200 meters left to the German trench, so I shifted my fire to the outskirts of the town. The Germans lost their nerve and the survivors abandoned the trench, and started fleeing into the town. They were cut down by flanking fire from our heavy machine guns and the fire of our charging infantry.

At times, Morozov and I would move out about 40 meters in front of the attacking line, so that the men could see us and follow us. Forward observer Karpov and signalman Shtansky followed me on my heels. Cable was rolling off the shoulder of the signalman and I was ready to call in fire from my batteries at any second. We closed the distance to the fleeing Germans to just 100 meters, and now it had become dangerous to call in artillery fire – shell fragments might hit our own men.

Meanwhile, the German infantry were passing some mounds of soil. It turned out to be the position of a dug-in German anti-aircraft battery. There were six guns set up at intervals of 30 meters. Only the thin gun barrels rose above the breastworks. We didn't notice them at first and didn't realize that these piles of dirt were holding anti-aircraft guns. But they opened up on our attacking line at point-blank range. The powerful and rapid rattle of the automatic guns scared us at first. But the frenzy of the assault was so overwhelming that we continued the charge. The rounds of these guns were small, the size of a small carrot, and while they were very effective against low-flying aircraft, they weren't as good against dispersed infantry. Their rapid fire cut down only two or three men. I couldn't strike the anti-aircraft guns with my batteries, because of the risk of hitting our own men. So we raced towards the guns into the teeth of their fire. When we were within 40 meters, the crews panicked, abandoned their guns and fled together with their infantry.

We wanted to fire on the former owners of the guns with their own weapons! The fastest men in the line – Morozov, my forward observer Karpov, a young infantryman and I were the first ones to reach the abandoned guns. All four of us jumped into the gunners' seats almost simultaneously. I quickly pivoted the gun barrels 180 degrees and grabbed the handles – and I couldn't find the trigger! There was no trigger on the handles at all! Then I looked under my feet and saw a pedal near my right foot that had its factory paint worn off by the frequent contact of a German boot. I was delighted! I took aim at the backs of the fleeing crews, and just when I was ready to press the pedal, a deafening explosion sounded to my right, and the anti-aircraft gun there disappeared in dense black smoke. It was as if it had been struck by lightning – and in an instant I realized that these guns were booby-trapped. My foot, poised above the pedal, jerked back and froze. I was gripped with mortal fear, sweat began to bead on my forehead, and I began gulping air. I raised my eyes to have a look at the nearby gun and there was nothing left of it. The next moment I noticed an opened metallic box beside the gun shield – the tip of a stick of dynamite was sticking out of it. Here it was, the death prepared for me, too! I cried out a warning to the others.

The fear of my narrow escape from death wouldn't let me go, and I couldn't calm down. Although all these events lasted only a few seconds and the fleeing German crews were still visible in front of me, it seemed to me that they lasted for an eternity. Only now did I realize that I owed my life to the fast young rifleman, who had pressed the trigger pedal just a fraction of a second before me. He was now dead, blown into the sky together with the booby-trapped gun, while I was still alive. I looked with bitterness again at the empty space where the gun had been standing, with the young infantryman in the gunner's seat. Eternal honor to that guy. I would never, ever forget him. Although I was not guilty of his death, it just so happened that with his death he saved three of us, the ones who had been just a bit too slow.

We captured Gyor. We were amazed: how could it be that just beyond the final immaculate street of that town there was a tidy field of winter wheat – and no garbage at all on the edge of the town! But there was no time to waste and we raced on, following the fleeing Germans, towards Vienna.

CHAPTER SIXTEEN

Austria and Czechoslovakia

We crossed the border from Hungary into Austria on 1 April and had already captured Schwechat, on the southern outskirts of Vienna, by 5 April. It was hard to drive the Germans out of the cemetery of the Austrian capital. The beautiful tombstones of marble and granite were being shattered in the fighting. Eventually, we simply bypassed the cemetery through some nearby streets.

Urban combat is the worst type of fighting. It was impossible to dig in, and stone chips and slivers became as dangerous as the metal fragments. A deadly shot could come from any window. Once, I warily climbed into a window, my pistol at the ready. While I was still straddling the windowsill, the door to the room was suddenly kicked open, and I saw two Germans begin to enter the room. Silhouetted against the window, I was a perfect target. But they weren't expecting me there and I got the drop on them. Before they could raise their submachine-guns, I rapidly fired several times, and killed them with shots to the head. If I had started to climb into the room just a second later, or if I hadn't had my pistol raised, or if I had missed – I would have received a burst of submachine-gun fire from a range of 4 meters. It must have been the merciful Lord granting me this one second!

Our losses were very high. The tankers really helped us out. They were very worried about panzerfausts, so they tried to stay out of the streets, just like our riflemen did. If a house looked sufficiently flimsy, they would just drive their tanks right into it. It must have been quite unexpected for the dwellers to have a wall suddenly collapsing and a Soviet tank, all covered with dust and rubble, drive into their kitchen or bedroom! But typically, the heavy guns would simply blast holes into the sides of the buildings, allowing our riflemen to enter them more safely.

But we never reached the center of the Austrian capital. Vienna fell without us on 13 April 1945. Our 52nd Rifle Division had been pulled out of Vienna on 7 April, and sent to liberate the Czech city of Brno.

Just as in the other Slavic countries, the Czechs and Slovaks greeted us joyfully. Colorfully-dressed crowds of people stood along the road and waved to us as we passed by, or tried to touch us and hug us, and offered us all sorts of treats and fruit. The Czech civilians kept us informed about the movements of German troops and assisted us in our reconnaissance missions. They hated the German occupiers for their arrogance and negligence, and for their indiscriminate looting and violence. One German unit, trying to break through to the American lines, executed 120 Czechs in Velke Mezerici – for supposed violations of the occupation regime. By 21 April, we had fought our way to a point just outside Brno.

It was an early sunny morning on 22 April 1945. Brno was in front of us. We were all ready for the attack. I was supporting a rifle regiment with my artillery battalion. The regiment commander and I were at our joint observation post in a clay open pit on the slope of a hill just outside the town. The small observation post, 3 meters by 4 meters, was well-camouflaged, with only the lenses of the stereoscopes rising above the edge of the pit. With excitement, I was studying the German positions once again. Soon they would disappear in smoke and dust from our barrage and the infantry would charge.

Suddenly an infantry signalman ran up to our observation post with a bunch of phone cables in his hand. He was about thirty years old, experienced and self-assured. With his cap tilted rakishly to one side and his padded jacket unbuttoned, he looked like a collective farm's horse groom, not a soldier. Standing at full height on the edge of the pit, he started to uravel the cables.

'Get down; don't give away our position!' I yelled.

'I see you're artillerymen, always afraid of something,' mumbled the infantryman with a grin. The rifle regiment commander intervened, barked at the loafer and ordered him to get down into the pit immediately. Before the signalman could react to the order a German mortar round landed in front of us. A second round exploded behind us, and then we could hear the incoming whistle of the third shell. The Germans had obviously seen the cables in the hands of the signalman and realized that a Russian command post was in front of them, so now they were finding the range. Everyone in the observation post scrambled for the deep niche that had been carved out of the forward wall of the pit as a shelter. I also took a step towards the niche, but saw that it was already jammed with men. I was just about to drop into a crouch, so I could squeeze myself up against the exposed back of someone already in the niche, when the interloping signalman frustrated me. Frightened by the barrage, he leaped into the pit in front of me, but slipped and fell when he hit the bottom. Scrambling wildly, he was in the process of rising to his hands and knees when the third mortar round exploded just a meter or so behind me. It was a direct hit on the pit. Its lethal fragments might have killed me, but the greater portion of them flew low between my legs and riddled the backside of the signalman. However, the explosion's shock wave struck me in the back with terrific force. I fell unconscious.

My comrades clambered out of the shelter after the explosion and gathered around my breathless body. I was showing no signs of life and they decided I was dead. The man guilty of drawing the fire had been sprayed with shrapnel in both thighs and the ass. They lifted him from the trench and sent him away to the medical battalion. They were going to bury me on the spot, but changed their mind when someone proposed to bury me in Brno after we captured it.

Meanwhile, after some time I regained consciousness. My first thought was the realization that I was alive. But before I could even rejoice over that fact, another thought struck me like lightning: what if my head was still whole and thinking, but the rest of my body was in pieces? I opened my eyes and looked at my legs; they seemed to be intact. My chest and hands were also there. I tried to stand up, but I felt a terrible stab of pain below my right knee. I gingerly inspected it with my hand and my fingers came across a shell splinter that was sticking out of my boot by a centimeter or two. I decided to pull it out myself, but that was easier said than done. The splinter was embedded in the calf muscle and bone, and was as firmly lodged as a nail driven into oak wood.

The forward observers and signalmen were happy to see me alive. They cut open my boot and trousers and examined the wound. There was very little blood, as the splinter had sealed the wound. They also tried to remove it with their hands and failed. So then they bandaged the wound and helped me to my feet. The opening artillery barrage was about to begin. My artillery regiment commander Major Rogoza called. When he heard that I'd been wounded, he became mad and cursed me with the worst language: 'Who's going to direct the fire mission?!' he yelled.

I replied: 'I'm not leaving the command post. I'll be correcting the fire on one leg until the infantry break into the city. Only then will I go to the medical battalion.'

As soon as our assaulting troops disappeared into the city, my observers pulled me out of the command post and took me into the nearby bushes, where a Dodge WC 1/2-ton truck was already waiting for me. As soon as they threw me onto the back of the truck, it took off and raced towards our rear. Despite our assault on Brno, German artillerymen were still observing our lines. They spotted the truck and opened fire on it. Rounds were exploding all around the speeding Dodge. We crossed a railway bed, and the truck jumped so high that I felt as if I was thrown a meter into the air. I was afraid that I would be deposited on the rails of the track in the middle of the exploding shells.

We didn't reach the medical battalion until lunchtime. It had been set up inside a school in the village of Turany. There were many wounded inside. Men were sitting and lying around, groaning in pain or cursing; some were unconscious, some were asleep. We, the lightly wounded, were sitting on benches along a wide corridor, waiting our turn while they tended to the more seriously wounded first. Stretchers with the badly wounded men went by us in a constant stream. It was already evening when the last stretcher was brought in and placed at my feet. The wounded soldier was lying on his stomach with his head turned to the side and his eyes closed. Then he opened his eyes and looked up indifferently at the men on the bench. When he saw me, he addressed me with interest: 'Comrade Captain, we were both wounded by the same shell.'

'That can't be. I was the only man wounded in the pit; I was covering everyone else in the niche with my body.'

'You did a poor job of it. I jumped into the pit in front of you. I was the guy you were cursing for standing on the edge of it. The shrapnel flew low and tore my ass into pieces, so I can only lie on my belly. It hurts like hell. Please forgive me for drawing fire.'

'Don't ask for forgiveness; you've already paid a high price for your negligence.'

Then I thought: if the soldier hadn't jumped into the pit first, I would have been crouching there where he was when the round exploded. I shuddered to think of the consequences.

A surgeon in a white gown and rubber gloves peeped out from the doors of the surgery room and asked, 'Comrades, who can hold a portable lamp? It's already dark in there, and I can't see a thing.'

'I can,' I replied, 'I only have a wounded leg; I can sit and hold the lamp.'

When I hobbled to the surgery table, the man guilty of drawing the mortar fire on our command post was already lying on it, prepared for surgery. The surgeon took a scalpel and opened up the wounded man's buttock and upper thigh with one fast cut, all the way to the bone. A nurse quickly sponged the cut to absorb the blood flowing into it, and then clamped a large vein with tweezers. Her assistant quickly tied off the vessel with surgeon's thread. The surgeon started probing the opened thigh and buttock with his gloved fingers, and began very swiftly to locate and remove pieces of shrapnel. He then stitched up the first cut and made another cut next to it. This process was repeated over and over again. When the doctor was making the tenth cut on the other buttock and upper thigh, I could no longer stand to watch and turned away, shifting the lamp as I did so. The surgeon cursed and re-adjusted the light.

I said apologetically, 'I bandaged the most awful wounds at the front, but I can't watch you slice up a living man.'

'Now we'll take care of you. Show me what you've got,' the doctor said.

I placed my wounded leg on the table, the nurse quickly unwound the bandage, and the doctor grabbed a large pair of forceps.

'Are you going to yank it out with that?' I asked anxiously.

'Oh no, I'm just going to take a look at how badly the splinter is stuck,' the doctor casually replied.

I calmed down and curiously watched the hands of the surgeon. He spent a long time adjusting the forceps around the shell splinter sticking out of my leg, and then with a sudden violent jerk and a twist, he yanked the splinter from my calf. A terrible pain shot through my whole body, and my face twisted not just with the pain, but also the insult – the doctor had lied to me! A thick stream of blood gushed out of the widely-opened wound.

'What are you doing?' I shouted indignantly.

'Tourniquet!' the surgeon shouted to the nurse, ignoring my cry. The nurse quickly wrapped the tourniquet above my knee and the fountain of blood stopped.

Finally the doctor addressed me: 'You should thank me: the blood washed all the dirt out of the wound and there will be no sepsis. You only had to give one glassful of blood to wash your own wound!'

As they were working on my wound, I saw a plate holding a small pile of shrapnel, each about the size of a sunflower seed. They were from the buttocks and thighs of the man who had caught the attention of the German observer.

Two weeks later with my wound still not fully healed, I slipped away from the medical battalion without any discharge papers. Korennoi arrived in a car and took me away. On 5 May I returned to the battalion, using a stick for support. I was in a hurry to continue fighting. I thought the war couldn't end without me. But by now we were already fighting in the vicinity of Prague.

While I'd been recovering, a large German grouping had been surrounded by our troops south-east of Prague. But the most desperate group of Nazis, several thousand men under General Schörner [the remnants of Army Group Center], broke out of the encirclement and, destroying everything in their path, moved west past Brno towards the American lines. Our division had pursued the Nazis for over 150 kilometers, from Brno to Benesov near Prague. On the evening of 8 May we heard over the radio about Germany's unconditional surrender, but 'our' Germans under Schörner continued to fight.

The final remnants of Schörner's force were destroyed only by the evening of 12 May. Small groups of resisting Germans remained scattered in the forests around Benesov, and one rifle battalion of our division spent until 16 May ferreting them out. Some of our comrades were killed in those skirmishes after Victory Day. It was upsetting to lose so many men after peace had officially arrived!

Our 52nd Rifle Division celebrated the Victory Day at Benesov on 13 May. A week later, on 20 May 1945, the first official Soviet holiday was declared after four years of the war. On 5 June our 52nd Rifle Division was loaded onto ten trains in Benesov and started its journey to the Motherland, traveling through Prague, Ust, Dresden, Warsaw, Poznan, Minsk and finally Moscow.

I don't have many memories of that journey from Prague to Moscow. Dresden was lying in ashes. A young German woman was hiding in the ruins of the train station there, offering herself for chunks of bread. Then there was the broad Elbe River, in which we bathed before swimming across it. In Warsaw, the train station was so covered by human waste that one couldn't take a step. Belorussia had been burnt to ashes by the Nazis.

Our train arrived in Moscow on the day of the Victory Parade, 24 June 1945. The entire capital was rejoicing. We didn't know it at the time, but twenty-five men from our division had been selected back in May and sent to Moscow to participate in the parade. We only learned about this many years later, from conversations with the parade participants.

The trains carrying us only paused in Moscow, before continuing on to the east. After days of travel, we took a branch line from Chita towards Mongolia, and we realized we were going to war with Japan.

After a grueling and difficult march through Mongolia and the Gobi desert (where we almost died from thirst) into China, we never actually caught up with the retreating Japanese. Still, this campaign had great significance for me: I met my future wife.

When we had stopped briefly in Moscow on our way east, a captain in the 106th Medical Battalion of our 52nd Rifle Division, Varvara Aleksandrovna Somova met me with an order from the division commander to place her on my staff. I assigned her to the rail car carrying our artillery battalion's medical unit. Along the long route to Mongolia, we became good friends. We often met in Mongolia and China. After the war, when the division returned to Mongolia to disband, we decided to get married. We registered our marriage in the Soviet consulate in Choibalsan, and had a big wedding there in the sand dunes with over 200 guests in attendance.

It was only after the wedding that my wife and I recalled that we had met previously in Czechoslovakia. When I was recovering from my wound in the medical battalion, I had little to do and often spent my time hobbling around all the hospital offices. I was welcomed everywhere, and the young and cheerful nurses all seemed very happy to chat with me. Only one strict, serious and beautiful Captain of the Medical Corps had sternly rebuked me: 'I can see that you're bored, but we have a lot of work to do here.'

Index

211

Stackpole Military History Series

Real battles. Real soldiers. Real stories.

Stackpole Military History Series

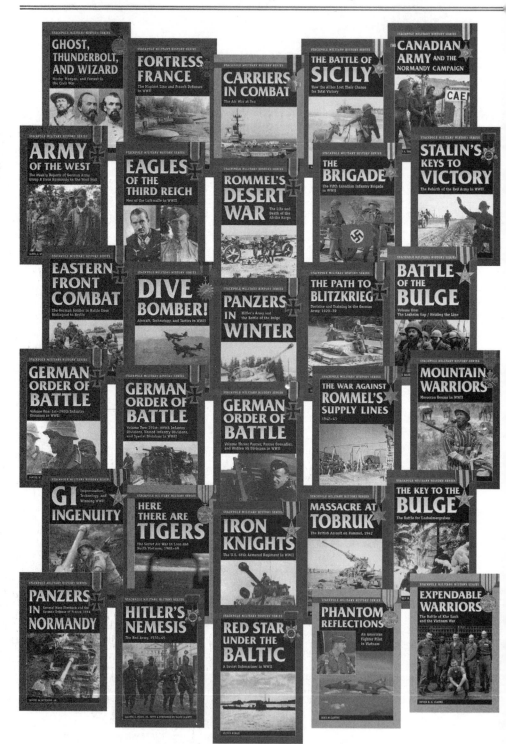

Real battles. Real soldiers. Real stories.

Stackpole Military History Series

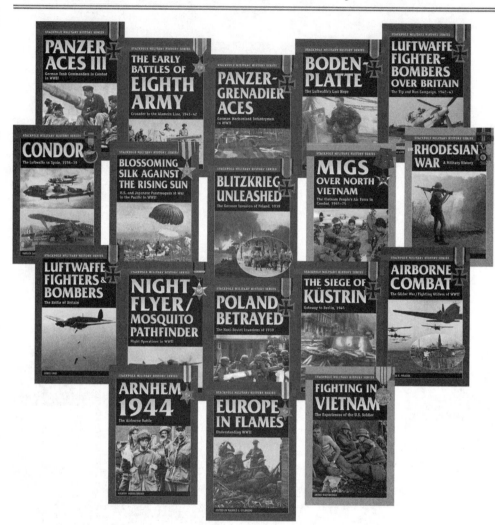

Real battles. Real soldiers. Real stories.

NEW for Fall 2011

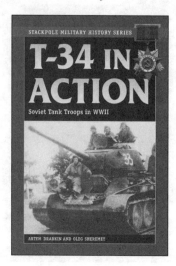

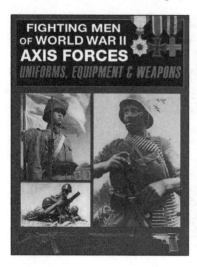
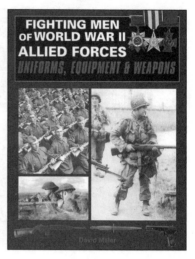